The Oldham College

039903

D0178684

A PRACTICAL GUIDE TO MENTORING

Developing initial teacher education and training in schools

Arthur Geen

OLDHAM COLLEGE

039903

ACC No........................

CLASS No...370:71 GRE

DATE....SEPTEMBER 2003

© Geen 2002

ISBN 1-902724-55-0
Published by UWIC Press
UWIC, Cyncoed Road, Cardiff CF23 6XD
cgrove@uwic.ac.uk

Designed by Andy Dark
Printed by Delta Colourprint

Contents

Introduction

This book has been compiled to meet the needs of mentors in schools committed to initial teacher education and training (ITET). It is based upon materials used by the author within the MA(Ed) course at the University of Wales Institute, Cardiff (UWIC), together with some of the findings of research which have been conducted at the university since 1996. In many chapters the perceptions of students and mentors who participated in these research projects are quoted, and suggestions are offered for ways of improving the quality of ITET in schools.

It is hoped that mentors and others with an interest in teacher education and training will find this volume easy to read. Throughout, I have made use of numbered headings, bullet points and checklists. At the end of each chapter are 'issues for consideration' intended to help readers check their understanding of the main points, reflect critically upon current mentoring practices and, where appropriate, contemplate change. Reference is made to the new professional standards for the award of qualified teacher status in England and to the current standards in Wales.

I should like to thank Phil Bassett, formerly Head of Partnership in the School of Education at UWIC and now Head of the School of Education at the North East Wales Institute of Higher Education, and Lesley Douglas, formerly Partnership Administrative Officer, with whom I collaborated in the research studies into mentoring over the period 1996 – 1998. I am also grateful to my colleague Charlie Harris, MA(Ed) Course Director at UWIC, with whom I have undertaken the surveys of students' perceptions of partnership over the period 2000-2002. Thanks are also due to the mentors who advised UWIC on the construction of the original module within the MA(Ed) course: Robert Hutt, Modern Languages Subject Mentor, Y Pant Comprehensive School, Pontyclun; Margaret Simpkins, Senior Mentor, Olchfa Comprehensive School, Swansea; and Robin Smallwood, Deputy Headteacher, St Cenydd Comprehensive School, Caerphilly. Finally, I should like to express my gratitude to Cathy Grove and Neil Jones of the UWIC Press for their invariably helpful advice and encouragement.

ARTHUR GEEN,
March 2002

Mentoring
and mentoring roles

I: Legal requirements in intial teacher education and training

(a) **School-Based and School-Centred Initial Teacher Education and Training:** Initial teacher education and training (ITET), more frequently designated by government as 'initial teacher training' (ITT), must by law be organised in accordance with the regulations issued by the Department for Education and Skills (DFES) in England and the National Assembly for Wales (NAW) in the Principality. The regulations which came into force in September 2002 in England are set out in the publication *Qualifying to Teach: Professional Standards for Qualified Teacher Status and Requirements for Initial Teacher Training* (DFES and Teacher Training Agency [DFES-TTA], 2002). In Wales, the current regulations are contained in Welsh Office Circular 13/98 (Welsh Office, 1998). These will be revised in September 2004.?

Under the **Education Act 1994** and sections 177 and 294 of the consolidating **1996 Education Act** there are two basic approaches to ITET:

(i) *school-based* initial teacher education and training, where schools work in partnership with higher education institutions (HEIs). These are sometimes known as higher education administered partnerships (HEAPs). The basic requirements for such schemes are that:

- There must be a clear-cut division of roles and duties, schools must be fully involved in planning and delivering ITET as well as in the selection and final assessment of trainees, and funds must be transferred from HEIs to schools to assist them in the training of student teachers. Providers must make clear how resources are divided and allocated between the partners.

- HEIs must establish selection criteria for partnership schools which take account of such indicators as inspection reports, test and examination results, exclusion rates, etc. and procedures for the de-selection of schools which no longer meet these criteria.

(ii) *school-centred* initial teacher training (SCITT), where schools - either individually or in groups - may organise their own teacher training courses and buy in whatever services (if any) they require from HEIs. Examples of schemes in operation in 2002 are Lindisfarne SCITT, Bexley Primary SCITT, Cornwall SCITT, and the Devon Primary SCITT.

The 1994 Act also established the Teacher Training Agency (TTA), a quango consisting of people appointed by the Secretary of State for Education and Skills to accredit ITET institutions and to fund ITET courses in England. Its remit did not officially extend to Wales, where accreditation and funding have been under the aegis of the Higher Education and Funding Council for Wales (HEFCW), which is responsible to the National Assembly for Wales.

(b) **Routes into Teaching:** Currently, there are several routes for people wishing to enter the teaching profession. The most important are:

(i) *undergraduate routes* in which subject and professional studies are combined. Most of these schemes are of three or four years' duration. Some five-year part-time programmes are available, while students who have completed at least one year's full-time higher education can apply for a two year course. These undergraduate routes are usually designated as BEd, BA/BSc(Ed) or BA/BSc(QTS).

The following amounts of time must be devoted to school experience, though it is recognised that a student's former experience of working with pupils may count towards these totals:

- thirty-two weeks for all four year programmes;

- twenty-four weeks for all two and three year programmes.

(ii) *the post-graduate certificate in education (PGCE):* For most students, this is a thirty-six week course with twenty-four weeks of school-based training for those planning to teach in secondary schools and eighteen weeks of school-based training for those aiming to work in the primary sector.

(iii) *employment-based routes:* These routes were created by the Labour government and have been available since January 1998. They consist of:

- THE GRADUATE TEACHER PROGRAMME, whereby trainees follow a postgraduate training programme while working as a teacher in a school. Usually the scheme is of one year's duration, but it may be less, depending upon the qualifications and previous experience of the trainee. The minimum period is three months but students would need to have considerable teaching experience to achieve qualified teacher status (QTS) in this time.

- THE REGISTERED TEACHER PROGRAMME, in which mature non-graduates undertake classroom-based training, usually over two years. They must have completed at least two years' higher education before they can embark upon the scheme. Successful students receive a degree as well as QTS.

Applications for trainees to join either programme are made to a 'recommending body', for example, a school, local education authority [LEA] or HEI, which then has responsibility for devising and delivering a personal training programme for the applicant. Students have to be aged at least twenty-four, unless they have already qualified as a teacher overseas and the length of the course depends upon their previous experience. They are employed within their school and receive a salary, currently £13,000 *per annum* (TTA, 2001).

In discussion papers issued by the former Department for Education and Employment (DFEE, 1998a, DFEE, 2000a, DFEE, 2001b), the DFES (2001a), the former Welsh Office (1999) and the National Assembly for Wales (2001) further changes to the routes into the teaching profession have been proposed:

- the creation of a scheme whereby undergraduates can integrate ITET modules into their first degree work and gain credits towards QTS. The 2001 Green Paper (DFEE, 2001b) suggested three such modules within an eighteen-module course. It was argued that "training could then be completed in a reduced period of time in school, through arrangements similar to the Graduate Teacher Programme or other flexible routes, so that the new teacher earns a salary after three years". Students working in the classroom under this scheme would be known as 'teaching associates' and would be paid for this work at the same rate as teaching assistants. Such an arrangement, it was argued, would provide extra adult support in the classroom and would help students decide whether they wanted a career in teaching. The Green Paper announced that pilot schemes would be introduced in England and, that, subject to their success, this new approach would become a major route into teaching (p. 67). The White Paper *School Achieving Success* stated that the first pilots would be launched in September 2002 (DFES, 2001a, p. 54).

- the creation of a network of 'training' or 'mentoring' schools with expanded computer facilities to support the further development of SCITT. This announcement was made despite the fact that OFSTED had failed a number of SCITT schemes. For example, the Douay Martyrs Consortium in Middlesex was closed after reinspection in October 1998.

- the encouragement of more employment-based routes into teaching along the lines of the graduate and registered teachers programmes.

(c) **Competence-based ITET: the 'Standards':** Whichever route students choose, they must be assessed in relation to a set of 'standards' set by the DFES and National Assembly for Wales. QTS cannot be awarded to any person unless he/she demonstrates mastery of all these standards. This system of competence-based assessment was first introduced by the then Department for Education (DFE) in Circular 9/92 and the then Welsh Office in Circular 35/92 (DFE, 1992; Welsh Office, 1992). The competences were subsequently revised, and since 1998 they have been known as 'standards', the first set of which were announced in DFEE Circular 4/98 and Welsh Office Circular 13/98 (DFEE, 1998b, Welsh Office, 1998). The current standards defined by the DFES and TTA (2002) for England and by the Welsh Office (1998) for the Principality are set out in the Appendices to this chapter.

(d) **Mentor and Mentoring:** In both school-based and school-centred schemes it is the normal procedure to appoint members of staff who act as *mentors* to student teachers. In the next sections of this chapter it is proposed to consider the concept of 'mentoring', key functions of the school mentor and issues pertinent to the role.

II: The concept of mentoring

(a) **Origins of the Word:** The origin of the word is Homeric Greek; Mentor was the friend, adviser and protector of Telemachus, the son of Odysseus, in Homer's *Odyssey*. He is depicted as a reliable adviser who is endowed with wisdom. In books II, XII and XXIV of Homer's *Odyssey*, Athene, goddess of wisdom, appears in the guise of Mentor.

(b) **Current Meanings:** Several writers have pointed to the absence of any agreed definition of a 'mentor' (Bova and Phillips, 1984; Dodgson, 1986; Blank, 1988). These are some of the many descriptions which have been offered:

(i) "Information provider, role model and door opener" (Schmidt and Wolfe, 1980).

(ii) "Someone committed to good teaching and professional development" (Her Majesty's Inspectorate [HMI], 1987).

(iii) A person "with expertise in the specialist subject of the intending secondary teacher" (Department of Education and Science [DES], 1989b).

(iv) Mentoring is "the process of helping another learn and enhancing their professional role" (Watkins and Whalley, 1993).

(v) Someone "who guides and teaches" (as opposed to a supervisor who oversees) (Wilkin, 1990).

(vi) "A person who oversees the career and development of another person, usually a junior, through teaching, counselling, providing psychological support, protecting, and at times promoting and sponsoring" (Zey, 1984).

(vii) "The role of the mentor towards the student teacher in schools is an example of a good teacher, coach, supervisor and assessor. Part of that role will be to work with students, helping them to reflect on their own practice and form their own mental framework to encapsulate their work" (Fidler and Lock, 1994).

(viii) A mentor is "an experienced adult who benefits and guides a less experienced adult" (Fagan and Walter, 1982)

(ix) Mentoring is "a dynamic, reciprocal relationship in a work environment between an advanced career incumbent (mentor) and a beginner (protégé), aimed at promoting the career development of both" (Healey and Welchert, 1990)

(x) "Mentoring is a complex, interactive process occurring between individuals of differing levels of experience and expertise which incorporates interpersonal or psycho-social development, career and/or educational development, and socialisation" (Carmin, 1988).

(xi) Mentoring is "a nurturing process in which a more skilled or more experienced person, serving as a role model, teaches, sponsors, encourages, counsels, and befriends a less skilled or less experienced person for the purpose of promoting the latter's professional and/or personal development. Mentoring functions are carried out within the context of an ongoing, caring relationship between the mentor and the protégé" (Anderson and Shannon, 1988 and 1995).

(xii) Mentors are people who "take the 'raw goods' that university sends them" and helps "fledgling teachers to develop and evolve into a finished product" (Abell, Dillon, Hopkins, McInerney and O'Brien, 1995).

(c) Criteria: Some writers, wishing to clarify the meaning of a term, utilise criteria rather than definitions. Criteria pick out the chief characteristics of a concept. Suggested criteria for 'mentoring' are:

(i) an *intentional* process;

(ii) a *nurturing* process which fosters the growth and development of the protégé towards full maturity;

(iii) an *insightful* process in which the wisdom of the mentor is acquired and applied by the protégé;

(iv) a process in which the mentor serves as a *role model* for the protégé;

(v) a *supportive and protective* process in which the mentor guards the interests and wellbeing of the protégé. Hence, key aspects of the relationship are encouraging, counselling and befriending.

(d) **Models:** Various models of the mentoring process have been devised. The three which are discussed in much of the literature on this subject are:

(i) *the APPRENTICESHIP model*, which assumes that the optimum way to learn to teach is to emulate someone with experience. Hence, the mentor's role is to provide a *model for imitation*. The philosophy is associated with such people as Anthony O'Hear (1988), Sheila Lawlor (1990) and the members of the Hillgate Group (1989). Lave and Wenger (1991) also conceive learning on the part of ITET students as a process of participation in 'communities of practice'; trainees learn to act within a particular world with its own customs and routines.

This approach clearly has value. As Donald McIntyre (1994) notes, 'modelling' on the part of mentors is essential as they can demonstrate to newcomers to the profession ways in which pupils can successfully learn. The model is, moreover, reflected in a number of important activities in which students engage in many schools, for example, observation of the mentor's teaching and collaborative teaching with experienced staff.

On the other hand, it has its limitations.

(1) As Val Brooks and Pat Sikes (1997) observe, apprenticeship is commonly used in industrial settings for training novices in skilled trades. It is, they feel, dubious whether a scheme of training used for the inculcation of lower-order craft skills can be relevant to intellectually demanding, higher-order professions such as teaching. They write that "the capacities which a skilful teacher exercises are the product of a complex synthesis of personal values and beliefs, professional preparation and training, a store of relevant experiences and detailed situational knowledge" (p. 18).

(2) Maynard and Furlong (1995) point out that student teachers need to interpret what they actually see in the classroom so that its significance is evident to them. "In the early stages of their training the purpose of that practical experience is to allow them to start to form concepts, schemas or scripts of the process of teaching. But in order to 'see', trainees need an interpreter" (p. 18). Without some rationale or explanation, the process of lesson planning, the acquisition of specific skills and the ability to evaluate lessons effectively are rendered much more difficult. Thus, it is argued that, important as activities such as observation may be, they need to be supplemented with more detailed exposition and discussion.

(3) This model pre-supposes that the teacher is an infallible expert and suggests that students should become 'clones' of the mentor. It does not make very provision for any

experimentation or original thought on the part of the learner.

(ii) *the COMPETENCY model.* This model is based upon the assumption that teaching involves the acquisition of a specific set of competencies (more commonly referred to by government as 'competences'). A competence has been defined as "what a person knows or can do under ideal circumstances" (Messick, 1984), and in this approach the mentor's role is fundamentally to act as a *coach* or *systematic trainer* who observes the student's teaching and who provides regular feedback upon the progress made with reference to pre-determined knowledge, understanding and skills. To a large extent this model has been imposed upon all programmes of ITET in England and Wales as the award of QTS is dependent upon mastery of the standards defined by central government.

This model has the advantage that the standards which students are required to reach are clear both to them and to their mentors. Nonetheless, critics of competence training in education have argued that teaching cannot easily be broken down into a series of tasks. Nor is it always possible to assess students in accordance with a list of competences. For example, a trainee teacher may be able to "establish a purposeful learning environment" (DFES-TTA, 2002, p. 11) with two class but fail with a third which even experienced staff find difficult to control. Can he/she be said to have mastered that standard?

Again, some commentators have drawn attention to the large number of standards required of students in English, mathematics, science, ICT and Welsh (Richards, 1999), while others have expressed the fear that professionalism will be displaced with 'performability'. Instead of considering important value-judgements relating to the content and methodology of teaching, ITET providers will be concerned only with specific outcomes determined in government circulars (MacGuire, Dillon and Quintrell, 1998).

(iii) *the REFLECTIVE PRACTITIONER model:* Some writers have argued that the two models described above are adequate within a system of initial teacher *training* (ITT), but are insufficient for a system of initial teacher *education* (ITE). Calderhead and Shorrock (1997) make reference to *teacher education* which involves "the all round education and development of teachers, emphasising teaching as a profession involving well-informed judgement", whereas *teacher training* relates "to a more mechanistic approach to teacher preparation, more akin to a craft apprenticeship involving the mastery of well-defined routines" (p. 192). Arthur, Davison and Moss. (1997) likewise argue that teaching involves *values* and *attitudes* which are largely ignored in the apprenticeship and competence models (p. 62).

It should, however, be noted that there is no one specific set of strategies constituting the 'reflective practitioner' approach, though key elements in certain of the models are:

- PLANNING a lesson with attention paid to aims and objectives, teaching strategies and criteria for evaluating the lesson;

- TEACHING the lesson;

- ANALYSING THE LESSON in terms of the achievement of the objectives and the criteria selected for evaluation;

- IDENTIFYING STRENGTHS AND AREAS FOR IMPROVEMENT in the lesson, devising an appropriate ACTION PLAN and ensuring that this action informs the planning of the next lesson.

One of the most influential writers on reflective practice is Donald Schon (1983; 1987). He refers to:

(1) *KNOWING-IN-ACTION*, which relates to the type of intuitive knowledge we all possess and reveal in everyday actions. "We reveal it by our spontaneous, skilful execution of the performance; and we are characteristically unable to make it verbally explicit" (Schon, 1987, p. 25).

(2) *REFLECTION-IN-ACTION*, when the teacher faces an unknown situation, brings aspects of her/his experience to the level of consciousness, reflects upon it, reshapes it and puts into practice a course of action based upon this deliberation. Very often this is intuitive; the teacher acts in a certain way without being able to explain the reasons underlying these actions.

(3) *REFLECTION-ON-ACTION* where the teacher endeavours to describe her/his actions and to put into language her/his thinking about the course of action taken.

He argues that the *verbal reconstruction* of events is a key to professional artistry. By moving from knowing-in-action to reflection-on-action teachers can develop their professional skills. In *Educating the Reflective Practitioner* (Schon, 1997) he offers three models for use in the school by which mentors can encourage their students to put into practice his precepts on reflection.

(1) *JOINT EXPERIMENTATION:* Here the student knows what he/she wants to accomplish and the mentor helps him/her to plan different approaches. The mentor's skill is to help the student to search for ways of operating ("working at creating and sustaining a process of collaborative enquiry", [Schon, 1987, p. 296]) without being overly prescriptive and telling the student precisely how to proceed.

(2) *THE FOLLOW ME APPROACH*, where the mentor demonstrates some strategy which the student attempts to imitate. This is followed by analysis of performance.

(3) *THE HALL OF MIRRORS APPROACH*, where "student and coach continually shift perspective" (p. 297). First, they focus on the student's practice, engage in dialogue about it and redesign it. Discussion then ensues about the approaches adopted by the mentor with emphasis upon alternative ways of working and the adoption of different strategies. Schon feels that, when student and mentor work in this fashion, they act as "on-line researchers, each inquiring more or less consciously into his (*sic*) own and other's changing understandings" (p. 298).

Other writers such as Van Manen (1990) and Fish (1995b) stress that the reflective practitioner should be concerned with fundamental attitudes and values as well as issues of pedagogy. Fish's 'strands of reflection' approach is described in chapter ten.

It has also been argued that by reflecting on practice students can derived personal theory from experience and may relate this to 'formal' theory which is acquired in reading and from other sources (Sixsmith and Simco, 1997). A similar mode of reflection has been urged by Arthur, Davison and Moss (1997), who distinguish 'pragmatic' and 'discursive' dialogue between mentor and trainee. The former restricts the conversation to events which took place in the lesson, while the latter requires the student to consider wider educational issues pertinent to that lesson.

Further reflective practices are described by LaBoskey (1993), Richards (1998), Loughran and Northfield (1998), Ghaye and Ghaye (1998) and Bolton (2001).

It can be seen that the term 'reflective practitioner' has been used in different ways. Arguments presented by advocates of this model of ITET include the following:

(1) It is important for students to analyse their teaching and to contemplate ways in which they can improve practice. In a survey conducted by Jones, Reid and Bevins (1997) mentors in partnership with the University of Manchester considered that reflection on the part of their students was vital if they were to learn from experience. McDiamid (1993), Richards and Lockhart (1994) and Hyatt and Beigy (1999) likewise contend that the process of reflection can change radically a teacher's beliefs and lead him/her to adopt different practices.

(2) Eraut (1994) considers that reflection is vitally important if student teachers are not to become narrow practitioners who unquestioningly follow practices which they have absorbed from experienced teachers. Without reflection, he writes, they will be "prisoners of their own school experience, perhaps the competent teacher of today, certainly the ossified teacher of tomorrow" (p. 83).

(3) As far back as 1834 James Bryce argued the need for newcomers to the profession to "study the general scientific principles" underpinning teaching to help them escape from a model of training which encouraged a "slavish following of others' performance" .

On the other hand, it is possible to draw attention to a number of criticisms which have been made of various models of reflective practice:

(1) The purposes of the process of reflection and the criteria which should be used for forming judgements are not always clear. It is not easy to define precisely what distinguishes acceptable and unacceptable practice. Some writers feel that Schon's notions of reflection-on-action do not really provide any clear framework for students to pursue. Terence McLaughlin, for example, believes that they do not offer criteria for judging the outcome of a course of action. The assumption is that self-evaluation is a good thing in its own right. Yet there is no guarantee that it will necessarily lead to improved practice. If reflection is to have any value, McLaughlin argues, it must be in the context of some agreed standards for assessing teaching (McLaughlin, 1994. See also Zeichner and Tabachnick, 2001).

(2) In practice, some students want mentors to offer their opinions on their teaching rather than to put questions which encourage reflection (Tann, 1994). Indeed, in a survey of eighty-one students at the University of Stirling, Drever and Cope (1999) found that the reflective practitioner approach was used by students to a far smaller extent than the other models.

(3) David Leat (1995), working with PGCE students at the University of Newcastle, attacks the assumption that reflection invariably leads to new ideas. Much, he feels, depends upon the student's character. "Some students are better problem solvers than others" (p. 168). Some, he reports from his experience, become 'stuck in a rut' and need an input of fresh ideas from outside. Other writers have also assailed the notion that, by requiring students to reflect, ITET providers in schools and HEIs are in some way automatically producing good teachers (Gore, 1987, Korthagen, 1993). Again, Ross (1992) argues that ITET courses which claim to accommodate the ideas of Schon and others have not been

transformed in any way.

(4) Sternberg and Hovarth (1995) suggest that reflection along the lines depicted by Schon encourages an intuitive or arts-based conception of teaching and so limits the view of teacher expertise.

(5) Edward Pultorak (1993) writes that reflecting on experience in the classroom environment can be a complex process and one which even some experienced teachers find difficult. It can be a challenging process for students whose knowledge and understanding of teaching is rudimentary. Gilroy (1993) and Newman (1996) share this judgement. In the view of Gilroy, notions of teacher education and professional development are far more complex than has been recognised by Schon.

(6) Demanding workloads militate against mentors' spending time with students in complex questioning calculated to stimulate reflection on experience. Indeed, Skrtic and Ware (1992) feel that requiring students and teachers to reflect in the depth needed in some of these models is unrealistic in the present climate.

(7) Andy Connery (2001) expresses the view that Schon's ideas on reflection are not very helpful in practice. Individuals, he feels, tend to focus upon immediate rather than underlying problems. Moreover, reflection of this type can lead to problems of motivation where students feel that all the difficulties they face are the result of their inadequacies. Consequently, Connery argues, reflection needs collaborative discussion in which a 'critical friend' can help the student to discern what is relevant. He writes that "reflective teaching requires an approach that is social and collaborative rather than individually introspective" (p. 140).

(8) Tricia Maynard and John Furong (1995) argue that "trainees are unlikely to be ready for this form of reflection on their own practice until they have gained some mastery of their teaching skills; they need to be ready to shift their focus from their own teaching to the pupils' learning and that cannot come until they have gained some confidence in their own teaching" (p. 21).

(e) **Functions of the Mentor:** The following analysis (Geen, Basset and Douglas, 1999b) focuses upon key aspects of the mentor's function. It is based upon the assumption that all three of the models described above – apprenticeship, competence and critical reflection upon practice - contribute something to an understanding of the essential nature of the mentoring process.

(i) *Providing a FRAMEWORK for students' school experience:* Mentors have to undertake many administrative duties such as inducting students into the school, providing them with a suitable teaching timetable and ensuring that they receive constructive feedback on their teaching. In many partnerships mentors are expected to maintain a progress file on each student, to monitor attendance, punctuality and attitude and to hold an hourly planning, review and guidance meeting each week, culminating in the setting of targets and the compilation of a final summative evaluation of trainees' performance.

(ii) *Serving as a ROLE MODEL:* The mentor is someone with experience whom students can observe teaching. They can also engage in collaborative teaching with this person and learn from her/his greater experience in planning, teaching and evaluating lessons.

This would correlate with the apprenticeship model described above. Observation and collaborative teaching are discussed in chapters three and four respectively.

(iii) *COACHING students in pre-determined standards:* Specific examples of the coaching function are:

- The mentor aids the student's lesson planning by contributing to her/his understanding of pedagogy. Tomlinson writes that "student-teachers need introducing to a systematic repertoire of teaching strategies, along with rationales concerning their strengths and difficulties, suitability for differing pupils and contexts and so on" (p. 39).

- The mentor provides direct assistance and support for specific teaching activities. This may include helping students plan lessons, offering advice and guidance on presentation and organisation, suggesting the use of specific teaching strategies and helping them acquire skills and competences. Frequently, mentors make use of *scaffolding*, where support is progressively withdrawn as the learner begins to master a competence (Drever and Cope, 1999, p. 102).

- The mentor offers feedback on lessons taught by the student, again with the aim of developing knowledge about teaching strategies. It is important that in fulfilling these coaching functions mentors pay attention to *all* relevant QTS standards. Research by Geen, Bassett and Douglas (2001) suggests that in debriefing many mentors focus upon the standards associated with planning, teaching and the management of classes at the expense of those relating to monitoring and assessment. In the case of the mentors involved in this survey, where assessment was discussed in lesson reviews, there was a tendency to concentrate upon the quality of students' responses to answers given in class or upon the use of recall questioning to ascertain the degree of understanding which had taken place. Little reference was made to the full range of standards, for example, ways by which the outcomes of assessment could be employed to plan future learning.

(iv) *Encouraging students to evaluate their performance as REFLECTIVE PRACTITIONERS:* This may take the form of feedback from the mentor on a specific lesson with questions designed to help students reflect critically upon their teaching. Tomlinson contends that students should be encouraged to engage in this practice from the very outset of their school experience by working with mentors who themselves analyse their own teaching. Each of these mentors then acts as a 'reflective coach'.

He feels that they should not merely review what happened in the lesson but also analyse the reasons underlying these events - exploring, interpreting and explaining. The results of this deliberation can then be utilised in planning future lessons. This process relates very closely to Schon's reflective practitioner philosophy, and Tomlinson hopes that such practice will become embedded in the student's approach to her/his work.

(v) *Taking account of SKILL ACQUISITION phases:* Several researchers in this field have shown the importance of the mentor's being aware of students' needs at different stages in their development. One of the best analyses is offered by Furlong and Maynard (1995):

● **BEGINNING TEACHING:**

Focus of student learning: rules, rituals and routines, establishing authority;

Mentoring role: model;

Key mentoring strategies: student observation and collaborative teaching focused on rules and routines.

● **SUPERVISED TEACHING:**

Focus of student learning: teaching competences;

Mentoring role: coach;

Key mentoring strategies: observation by the student; systematic observation and feedback on the student's performance.

● **FROM TEACHING TO LEARNING:**

Focus of student learning: understanding pupil learning; developing effective teaching;

Mentoring role: critical friend (i.e. trying to focus the student's thinking on the pupils' learning rather than her/his performance);

Key mentoring strategies: student observation; re-examining lesson planning.

● **AUTONOMOUS TEACHING:**

Focus of student learning: investigating the grounds for practice;

Mentoring role: co-enquirer, (i.e. the mentor and the student work in partnership in the planning, execution and analysis of lessons);

Key mentoring strategies: partnership teaching; partnership supervision.

(vi) *Practising appropriate INTERPERSONAL SKILLS*, for example, harnessing students' motivation and commitment, counselling, communicating clearly to enable students to be fully aware of their level of attainment, offering constructive criticisms without damaging their morale, building confidence and helping them manage their time and resolve everyday problems. Key mentoring skills are discussed in chapters seven and eight.

(vii) *Making provision for the student to develop knowledge of a wide range of PROFESSIONAL ISSUES*, for example, in areas outside the context of teaching lessons in the student's subject. Important elements include:

• WHOLE-SCHOOL POLICIES, for example, organisation of the curriculum, including personal, social and health education, citizenship, religious education, sex education and careers education; admissions policy; arrangements for the transition between primary and secondary schools; policy on assessment; target setting by the school; policy on special educational needs (SEN) in the light of the Code of Practice on the Identification and Assessment of SEN; policy on equal opportunities;

- SCHOOL ORGANISATION, for example, school development plans; the organisation of pupils, for example, streaming, banding and setting; the academic structure of the school; the internal financing of subject areas and other cost centres; charges for school activities; staff involvement in decision making; quality control systems;

- PASTORAL ISSUES, for example, reviewing pupils' progress across subjects; observing, exploring and coping with changes in patterns of attendance, achievement and behaviour; the teacher's role in offering guidance on educational, vocational or personal matters; supporting individual education plans; promoting the development of understanding and skills for adult life including employment; utilising/devising materials for use in work with a tutor group; understanding the role of the education service in protecting children from abuse;

- LEGAL AND CONTRACTUAL ISSUES, for example, the role of secondary school governors; induction arrangements for newly qualified teachers (NQTs); the Teachers' Pay and Conditions Act; performance management; school inspection; opportunities for staff development; teachers' legal liabilities; health and safety legislation; employment law;

- RELATIONS WITH PARENTS, for example, communicating effectively with parents through written reports, face to face meetings and parent consultations.

In school-based ITET it is important that the understanding students acquire at the HEI can be applied to their experience within schools. School and college components of a course need to be fully integrated. These issues are explored further in chapter six.

(f) **Influencing Factors:** Brooks and Sikes (1997) suggest that the ways in which a teacher mentors a student are most likely to be influenced by the following factors:

- the training received by the mentor;

- the model required by the partnership scheme. Thus, reflective coaching and progressive collaborative teaching are important emphases within the Leeds University Secondary School Partnership Scheme described by Tomlinson (1995);

- personal preference and the mentor's views on the role of a teacher;

- the personal qualities and interpersonal skills possessed by the mentor;

- the personal relationship between the mentor and mentee;

- the point reached by the student within the ITET course, for example, the four stages depicted by Furlong and Maynard;

- the desired learning outcomes associated with a particular activity. For example, observation may be the best technique to help a student acquire a specific competence.

III: The concept of role

In essence 'role' involves *position*, usually designated by some title such as 'principal' or 'subject leader', together with a *set of expectations* concerning what is appropriate behaviour for a person occupying that position.

It can be viewed in different ways, e.g.

(i) *the function performed by the role incumbent as seen by the role incumbent him/herself:* The incumbent's definition of a role is often referred to as *role conception*. There is sometimes the danger that people set themselves unrealistic expectations, which can lead to anxiety and increased levels of stress.

(ii) *the functions performed by the role incumbent as seen by other people:* On this interpretation of role there are role *demands* emanating from the role set consisting of the other people in the organisation. These demands seek to channel, guide, support, adjust and prescribe the behaviour associated with a certain position.

According to this interpretation a role does not exist in isolation but is a set of interactions with other people. Thus, a teacher with new responsibilities for mentoring may have to take into account the expectations which others have built up in the past. A newly appointed person who 'steps into someone else's shoes' can experience problems where he/she is unaware of previously defined expectations, for example, misunderstandings and 'treading on toes'. The process by which other people convey their expectations is known as *role-sending*.

(iii) *role in the sense of actual performance or the observed behaviours of the individual:* Role is seen as a set of behaviours which often results from the interaction of the role demands, the individual's role conception and the characteristics of her/his personality. This is known as *role performance*.

IV: Mentoring roles

Studies of mentoring in schools by Barker, Brooks, March. and Swatton (1994), Cross (1995), Tomlinson (1995), Watt (1995) and Moyles, Suschitzky and Chapman (1998) have identified a number of roles:

(a) **The ITET Co-ordinator.** This role incumbent is often known as the *school mentor*, the *professional mentor*, the *school organiser* or, in many secondary schools, the *senior mentor*. In addition, Rowie Shaw (1995) refers to the *phase mentor*. Throughout this book the term ITET co-ordinator will be used. The role is often - but not always - fulfilled by a senior member of the school staff, for example, a deputy headteacher, with whole-school responsibility for co-ordinating the experience of a group of students in that school. Fundamental responsibilities include:

(i) organising the framework of ITET within the partner school. Issues of organisation are discussed in the next chapter.

(ii) communicating information about the scheme to the whole school community - the headteacher, teachers, parents, governors and ancillary staff;

(iii) ensuring the appropriate induction of all teachers working with students;

(iv) co-ordinating and supporting the work of teachers in whose classes students are located;

(v) providing for the induction of students into the context of the school, for example, arranging a tour of the school, providing them with information about the school and key policy documents and allowing them to observe important aspects of the work of the school. The co-ordinator will also ensure that they are invited to relevant staff planning meetings.

(vi) operating regular tutorial classes for students in the wider professional aspects of the teacher's role, for example, school organisation, and the role of the school in the LEA and the national framework. Ideally, where students attend HEIs, these classes should relate very closely with the programme of educational or professional studies offered at those institutions.

(vii) moderating the students' progress in the classroom and organising additional support for those experiencing difficulties;

(viii) discussing students' progress with colleagues, college tutors and, where appropriate, external examiners;

(ix) co-ordinating the steps taken to profile students;

(x) monitoring the progress of the ITET scheme within the school;

(xi) liaising with the HEI, for example, attending meetings concerned with ITET, working with college tutors to evaluate the course and taking part in staff development activities;

(xii) operating a system of quality control to ensure that students' experience is of a consistently high standard and enables them to attain the QTS standards.

The research by Barker, Brooks, March. and Swatton (1994) focusing upon the University of Warwick partnership showed that ITET co-ordinators were rarely involved in:

• joint lesson planning with students;

• joint lesson delivery with students.

One such co- ordinator in this study commented: "My perception of the role is to have overall responsibility for their (students') progress and development during their year of initial teacher education. That involves really co-ordinating the work of the subject mentors, ensuring that the general programme is properly provided for and most of all, I think, being the person to whom any of the students can come if there is an issue in school, a personal issue or a group issue that they need to address" (p. 8).

(b) **The Subject Mentor:** This role is also known as the *teacher tutor* or the *teacher mentor*. This person is an established member of staff who takes agreed responsibility for students in her/his area of the curriculum. The term is most often used in secondary schools, where the role is frequently fulfilled by the head of department (Geen, 2001c).

Important duties include:

(i) the induction of students to the department, for example, providing them with such documentation relating to the organisation of the department as syllabuses, rules, procedures, and assessment policies;

(ii) contributing to the provision of a suitable programme of classroom experiences in the subject area in accordance with the scheme of ITET agreed with the HEI;

(iii) promoting students' expertise in the teaching of their specialist subject. This can involve serving as a role model, engaging in collaborative teaching with the student, helping with lesson planning and preparation, assisting the student to meet the QTS standards, observing teaching on the part of the student, offering constructive feedback, encouraging reflection on practice and checking that action plans are being implemented;

(iv) reviewing progress, counselling and target setting;

(v) assessing (in conjunction with the ITET co-ordinator, other teachers and HEI tutors) students' acquisition of the QTS standards. Issues of assessment are discussed in chapter ten;

(vi) contributing to the development of a student's profile. Issues relating to profiling are examined in chapter eleven;

(vii) liaising with other key personnel (e.g. staff from the HEI).

(c) **Class Teacher Mentors or Class Teacher Tutors:** In primary schools these are the teachers who assume responsibility for mentoring a student who is located in their class. In secondary schools they are members of a department which accommodates students other than the official subject mentor. Although they are not always accorded a *formal* title, they do work as mentors with students and have an important part to play. Their main role is to:

(i) act as role models and advisers;

(ii) plan lessons jointly with students;

(iii) observe lessons, provide feedback and help students to acquire the requisite skills and competences prescribed in the standards;

(iv) liaise with the subject mentor and ITET co-ordinator, especially in the task of assessing performance against the standards.

(d) **The HEI Subject Tutor:** This is a member of the HEI staff specialising within a defined subject area of the curriculum who provides students with access to models of teaching and learning in that subject area.
Responsibilities include:

(i) introducing students to ways of teaching their subject, for example, principles and practice in teaching the subject, catering for common learning difficulties, assessing and recording pupils' progress, applying learning to the world of work and taking into account safety issues The subject tutor also provides information relating to research, current pedagogic developments and professional support networks;

(ii) linking with and contextualising other course inputs, for example, programmes in educational and professional studies, and dealing with issues of learning and class management;

(iii) undertaking appropriate research into the teaching of the subject;

(iv) co-assessing the acquisition of competences by students;

(v) moderating the assessments reached by staff in schools within the partnership;

(vi) liaising with other key personnel.

(e) **The HEI Link Tutor:** This role incumbent is also known as the *college/university tutor*, the *college/university mentor* or the *general tutor*. In many HEAPs these tutors have responsibility for a group of students specialising in a variety of subjects. They conduct seminars with students in educational and professional studies and visit them in their schools. Usually, link tutors have responsibility for all the trainees in a specific number of schools. They liaise with ITET co-ordinators to help ensure that the students receive a coherent programme of training.

Specific duties include:

(i) maintaining regular links between the partner school and the HEI and ensuring that the necessary administrative functions are carried out;

(ii) ensuring, through liaison with the ITET co-ordinator, that non-subject-specific aspects of the teaching role are covered, for example, wider professional issues;

(iii) ensuring that students gain experience within the pastoral and welfare system of the school;

(iv) co-ordinating the assessment process, counselling, target setting and offering guidance in liaison with HEI subject tutors and appropriate school staff;

(v) monitoring in partnership with others the acquisition of competences by students;

(vi) moderating the work of schools within the partnership.

V: Issues in mentoring roles

Important issues pertinent to mentoring roles are:

(a) **the need for teamwork:** It is vital that schools and HEIs work as a closely integrated team (Alexander, 1990). However, Tomlinson (1995) and Watkins and Whalley (1993) note that in some cases this teamwork is not as effective as it could be. Examples would be:

(i) *the 'Get the College' syndrome* where the teacher may suggest to the student that the college is an ivory tower filled with staff who either cannot teach or have forgotten how to do so;

(ii) *the 'Get the School' syndrome* where a tutor may apologise to the student for putting her/him in that particular school;

(iii) *the 'Get the Student' syndrome* where the school and college staff 'gang up' on the student.

In order to try to obviate these problems Watkins and Whalley suggest that:

- people are clear about their precise role in the process of helping students reach the required standards and their different perspectives;

- they communicate openly and frequently and treat each other as adults (p. 32).

Tomlinson also stresses the importance of clear communication between schools and colleges. In the Leeds University Secondary School Partnership link tutors make at least one visit each week to schools where they conduct tutorials with their students. School staff work with them in partnership in the delivery of these tutorials.

(b) **the question of experience:** In many schools it is assumed that mentors should be people with considerable teaching experience, but writers like Corbett and Wright (1994), Tomlinson (1995) and Brooks and Sikes (1997) feel that younger teachers may also have a role to play, as they can more easily identify with the anxieties and aspirations of trainees. In many secondary school departments a combination of staff with different ages and experiences can be useful.

(c) **the use of role-labels:** Tomlinson refers to the issue of role-labels and raises the question: 'Who is to be regarded as a mentor?' In most secondary schools the title tends to be restricted to the co-ordinator and the subject mentors whose principal responsibilities have been described above. Yet, as is clear from the analysis of roles, other members of staff often play a significant part in providing students with valuable experiences, for example, special educational needs, assessment policy and pastoral care. Problems could arise if attempts were made to designate 'official' mentors in such a way as to create an 'us' and 'them' division. This, Tomlinson fears, may threaten not only the quality of ITET but also the broader ethos and effectiveness of the staff and school as a whole (p. 216).

VI: The use of role mapping

(a) **The Concept of 'Role Mapping':** From the above analyses it appears that mentors need to take into account their relationship with their role partners. In considering this issue it is often beneficial to make use of a 'role map' (Watkins and Whalley, 1993, pp. 28-29) or a simple diagram, where role incumbents enter the names of the partners with whom they must work in fulfilling their role. Thus, an ITET co-ordinator may use the role map to chart her/his relationship with mentors, college tutors and external examiners. The map has the advantage that it can highlight goals, problems and potential solutions.

ROLE PARTNER	MAIN GOALS OF CONTACT	INDICATORS OF SUCCESS	PROBLEMS	POTENTIAL SOLUTIONS
1				
2				
3 etc				

(b) **Specific Questions:** Questions can be put to help clarify thinking about role issues under the following headings:

(i) *role tension or ambiguity.* Role strain occurs where an ITET co-ordinator or mentor feels that he or she is at the centre of conflicting expectations. Examples of pertinent questions which can lead to identification of this problem are:

- Do you and your role partners agree on what it is you should be doing?

- Do you hold similar or different views on key areas of responsibility within the mentoring structure?

- Are there any overlaps of function in the mentoring system? Do any mentors try to fulfil the same functions as the ITET co-ordinator?

- Are there any general problems which arise in the mentoring procedures adopted by the school, for example, excessive demands upon your time or issues relating to resources?

- What systems of quality control can be identified within the role map? How effective are these judged to be?

- Have specific problems been identified at any point in the role map, for example, teachers who have expressed opposition to having a student teacher in their class?

(ii) *role overload.* This is where the demands upon the mentor are too many for him/her to cope. Key questions which could be put are:

- Is there sufficient time to cope with the demands of student teachers? Jacques (1992) has shown how some mentors have been surprised at the paucity of students' knowledge. In ITET courses which have been located primarily in schools, they have not always been able to find the amount of the time they would like to provide the necessary degree of assistance.

- Are there any strategies which could help you to manage time more efficiently?

- Are there other people to whom you can delegate some of your mentoring role? Delegation can often be helpful for ITET co-ordinators. In some schools in South-East Wales a senior co-ordinator works with assistant co-ordinators, each of whom assumes prime responsibility for students from one or more HEI. Again, in the organisation of seminars in educational and professional studies, co-ordinators can invite other staff with special expertise to address students.

(iii) *role development:* Some of the questions could be:

- Are you and your role partners satisfied with your role? If not, what forms of staff development can be employed to alleviate the problems identified?

- Have you developed a clear role relationship with your other partners, for example, tutors at the HEI?

- Can you negotiate new areas for inclusion in the mentoring programme?

- In what ways do you review your own performance and that of your various role partners?

〉 Issues for consideration

1. Read section I (*legal requirements in initial teacher education and training*) and use bullet points to summarise the current legal requirements which appertain to the course(s) of ITET offered at your school.

2. Briefly explain the meaning of: (a) *school-based initial teacher training:* (b) *school-centred initial teacher training* (SCITT).

3. Read section II (*the concept of mentoring*) and state what you understand the term 'mentor' to mean in the context of ITET.

4. Write a sentence to describe each of the following models of mentoring: (a) t*he apprenticeship model;* (b) *the competency model;* (c) *the reflective practitioner model.*

5. What in your view are the respective values of these models in the context of ITET at your school?

6. Consider some of the main mentoring activities which you have undertaken recently and categorise them in accordance with the assumptions of these three models: (a) *apprenticeship:* (b) *competency;* (c) *reflective practitioner.*

7. List what you would consider to be the most important aspects of the role of the mentor in ITET.

8. Read section III (*the concept of role*) and summarise the three conceptions of the term 'role' which are described.

9. Read section IV (*mentoring roles*) and list the chief mentoring roles which are performed at your school with a brief account of the principal duties associated with each.

10. Read sections V and VI (*issues in mentoring roles* and *the use of role maps*). With reference to your mentoring role at the school list your main role partners and complete the other boxes in the grid:

ROLE PARTNER	MAIN GOALS OF CONTACT	INDICATORS OF SUCCESS	PROBLEMS	POTENTIAL SOLUTIONS
1				
2				
3				
4				
5				

11. On the basis of the above analysis set out any recommendations you would make for improvements to the overall system of mentoring in your school.

Appendix 1

The standards defined in *Qualifying to Teach: Professional Standards for Qualified Teacher Status and Requirements for Initial Teacher Training* (**DFES-TTA, 2002**)*:*

1. Professional Values and Practice: Those awarded Qualified Teacher Status must understand and uphold the professional code of the General Teaching Council for England by demonstrating all of the following:

1.1 They have high expectations of all pupils; respect their social, cultural, linguistic, religious and ethnic backgrounds; and are committed to raising their educational achievement.

1.2 They treat pupils consistently, with respect and consideration, and are concerned for their development as learners.

1.3 They demonstrate and promote the positive values, attitudes and behaviour that they expect from their pupils.

1.4 They can communicate sensitively and effectively with parents and carers, recognising their roles in pupils' learning, and their rights, responsibilities and interests in this.

1.5 They can contribute to, and share responsibly in, the corporate life of schools.

1.6 They understand the contribution that support staff and other professionals make to teaching and learning.

1.7 They are able to improve their own teaching, by evaluating it, learning from the effective practice of others and from evidence. They are motivated and able to take increasing responsibility for their own professional development.

1.8 They are aware of, and work within, the statutory frameworks relating to teachers' responsibilities.

2. Knowledge and Understanding: Those awarded Qualified Teacher Status must demonstrate all of the following:

2.1 They have a secure knowledge and understanding of the subject(s) they are trained to teach. For those qualifying to teach secondary pupils this knowledge and understanding should be at a standard equivalent to degree level.

In relation to specific phases, this includes:

(i) For the Foundation Stage, they know and understand the aims, principles, six areas of learning and early learning goals described in the QCA/DFEE Curriculum Guidance for the Foundation Stage and, for Reception children, the frameworks, methods and expectations set out in the National Numeracy and Literacy Strategies.

(ii) For Key Stage 1 and/or 2, they know and understand the curriculum for each of the National Curriculum core subjects, and the frameworks, methods and expectations set out in the National Literacy and Numeracy Strategies. They have sufficient understanding of a range of work across the following subjects to be able to teach them in the age range for which they are trained, with advice from an experienced colleague where necessary:

History or Geography
Physical Education
ICT
Art and Design or Design and Technology
Performing Arts, and
Religious Education

(iii) For Key Stage 3, they know and understand the relevant National Curriculum Programme(s) of study, and for those qualifying to teach one or more of the core subjects, the relevant frameworks, methods and expectations set out in the National Strategy for Key Stage 3. All those qualifying to teach a subject at Key Stage 3 know and understand the cross-curricular expectations of the National Curriculum and are familiar with the guidance set out in the National Strategy for Key Stage 3.

(iv) For Key Stage 4 and post 16, they are aware of the pathways for progression through the 14-19 phase in school, college and work-based settings. They are familiar with the Key Skills as specified by QCA and the national qualifications framework, and they know the progression within and from their own subject and the range of qualifications to which their subject contributes. They understand how courses are combined in students' curricula.

2.2   They know and understand the Values, Aims and Purposes and the General Teaching Requirements set out in the National Curriculum Handbook. As relevant to the age range they are trained to teach, they are familiar with the Programme of Study for Citizenship and the National Curriculum Framework for Personal, Social and Health Education.

2.3   They are aware of expectations, typical curricula and teaching arrangements in the Key Stages or phases before and after the ones they are trained to teach.

2.4   They understand how pupils' learning can be affected by their physical, intellectual, linguistic, social, cultural and emotional development.

2.5   They know how to use ICT effectively, both to teach their subject and to support their wider professional role.

2.6   They understand their responsibilities under the SEN Code of Practice, and know how to seek advice from specialists on less common types of special educational needs.

2.7   They know a range of strategies to promote good behaviour and establish a purposeful learning environment.

2.8   They have passed the Qualified Teacher Status skills tests in numeracy, literacy and ICT.

3. Teaching:

3.1   *Planning, expectations and targets:* Those awarded Qualified Teacher Status must demonstrate all of the following:

3.1.1 They set challenging teaching and learning objectives which are relevant to all pupils in their classes. They base these on their knowledge of:

- the pupils
- evidence of their past and current achievement
- the expected standards for pupils of the relevant age range
- the range and content of work relevant to pupils in that age range.

3.1.2 They use these teaching and learning objectives to plan lessons, and sequences of lessons, showing how they will assess pupils' learning. They take account of and support pupils' varying needs so that girls and boys, from all ethnic groups, can make good progress.

3.1.3 They select and prepare resources, and plan for their safe and effective organisation, taking account of pupils' interests and their language and cultural backgrounds, with the help of support staff where appropriate.

3.1.4 They take part in, and contribute to, teaching teams, as appropriate to the school. Where applicable, they plan for the deployment of additional adults who support pupils' learning.

3.1.5 As relevant to the age range they are trained to teach, they are able to plan opportunities for pupils to learn in out-of-school contexts, such as school visits, museums, theatres, field-work and employment-based settings, with the help of other staff where appropriate.

3.2 *Monitoring and Assessment:* Those awarded Qualified Teacher Status must demonstrate all of the following:

3.2.1 They make appropriate use of a range of monitoring and assessment strategies to evaluate pupils' progress towards planned learning objectives, and use this information to improve their own planning and teaching.

3.2.2 They monitor and assess as they teach, giving immediate and constructive feedback to support pupils as they learn. They involve pupils in reflecting on, evaluating and improving their own performance.

3.2.3 They are able to assess pupils' progress accurately using, as relevant, the Early Learning Goals, National Curriculum level descriptions, criteria from national qualifications, the requirements of Awarding Bodies, National Curriculum and Foundation Stage assessment frameworks or objectives from the national strategies. They may have guidance from an experienced teacher where appropriate.

3.2.4 They identify and support more able pupils, those who are working below age-related expectations, those who are failing to achieve their potential in learning, and those who experience behavioural, emotional and social difficulties. They may have guidance from an experienced teacher where appropriate.

3.2.5 With the help of an experienced teacher, they can identify the levels of attainment of pupils learning English as an additional language. They begin to analyse the language demands and learning activities in order to provide cognitive challenge as well as language support.

3.2.6 They record pupils' progress and achievements systematically to provide evidence of the range of their work, progress and attainment over time. They use this to help pupils review their own progress and to inform planning.

3.2.7 They are able to use records as a basis for reporting on pupils' attainment and progress orally and in writing, concisely, informatively and accurately for parents, carers, other professionals and pupils.

3.3 *Teaching and Class Management:* Those awarded Qualified Teacher Status must demonstrate all of the following:

3.3.1 They have high expectations of pupils and build successful relationships, centred on teaching and learning. They establish a purposeful learning environment where diversity is valued and where pupils feel secure and confident.

3.3.2 They can teach the required or expected knowledge, understanding and skills relevant to the curriculum for pupils in the age range for which they are trained. In relation to specific phases:

(i) those qualifying to teach Foundation Stage children teach all six areas of learning outlined in the QCA/DFEE Curriculum Guidance for the Foundation Stage and, for Reception children, the objectives in the National Literacy and Numeracy Strategy frameworks competently and independently;

(ii) those qualifying to teach pupils in Key Stage 1 and/or 2 teach the core subjects (English, including the National Literacy Strategy, mathematics through the National Numeracy Strategy, and science) competently and independently.

They also teach, for either Key Stage 1 or Key Stage 2, a range of work across the following subjects independently, with advice from an experienced colleague where appropriate:

  - history or geography
  - physical education
  - ICT
  - art and design or design and technology, and
  - performing arts.

(iii) those qualifying to teach Key Stage 3 pupils teach their specialist subject(s) competently and independently using the National Curriculum Programmes of Study for Key Stage 3 and the relevant national frameworks and schemes of work. Those qualifying to teach the core subjects or ICT at Key Stage 3 use the relevant frameworks, methods and expectations set out in the National Strategy for Key Stage 3. All those qualifying to teach a subject at Key Stage 3 must be able to use the cross-curricular elements, such as literacy and numeracy, set out in the National Strategy for Key Stage 3, in their teaching, as appropriate to their specialist subject;

(iv) those qualifying to teach Key Stage 4 and post-16 pupils teach their specialist subject(s) competently and independently using, as relevant to the subject and age range, the National Curriculum Programmes of Study and related schemes of work, or programmes specified for national qualifications. They also provide opportunities for pupils to develop the key skills specified by QCA.

3.3.3 They teach clearly structured lessons or sequences of work which interest and motivate pupils and which:

- make learning objectives clear to pupils
- employ interactive teaching methods and collaborative group work
- promote active and independent learning that enables pupils to think for themselves, and to plan and manage their own learning.

3.3.4 They differentiate their teaching to meet the needs of pupils, including the more able and those with special educational needs. They may have guidance from an experienced teacher where appropriate.

3.3.5 They are able to support those who are learning English as an additional language, with the help of an experienced teacher where appropriate.

3.3.6 They take account of the varying interests, experiences and achievements of boys and girls, and pupils from different cultural and ethnic groups, to help pupils make good progress.

3.3.7 They organise and manage teaching and learning time effectively.

3.3.8 They organise and manage the physical teaching space, tools, materials, texts and other resources safely and effectively with the help of support staff where appropriate.

3.3.9 They set high expectations for pupils' behaviour and establish a clear framework for classroom discipline to anticipate and manage pupils' behaviour constructively and promote self-control and independence.

3.3.10 They use ICT effectively in their teaching.

3.3.11 They can take responsibility for teaching a class or classes over a sustained and substantial period of time. They are able to teach across the age and ability range for which they are trained.

3.3.12 They can provide homework and other out-of-class work which consolidates and extends work carried out in the class and encourages pupils to learn independently.

3.3.13 They work collaboratively with specialist teachers and other colleagues and, with the help of an experienced teacher as appropriate, manage the work of teaching assistants or other adults to enhance pupils' learning.

3.3.14 They recognise and respond effectively to equal opportunities issues as they arise in the classroom, including by challenging stereotyped views, and by challenging bullying or harassment, following relevant policies and procedures.

Appendix

2

The standards defined in *in Requirements for Courses of Initial Teacher Training* **(Welsh Office Circular 13/98):**

Students must, when assessed demonstrate that they:

(a) **Subject Knowledge And Understanding:**

- have a secure knowledge and understanding of the concepts and skills in their specialist subject(s) at a standard equivalent to degree level to enable them to teach confidently and accurately;

- have, for their specialist subject(s), a detailed knowledge and understanding of the NC PoS, LDs or end of key stage descriptions;

- for religious education specialists, have a detailed knowledge of the Agreed Syllabuses for RE;

- understand that, in Wales, pupils should be given opportunities, where appropriate, to develop and apply their knowledge and understanding of the cultural, economic, environmental, historical and linguistic characteristics of Wales (the Curriculum Cymreig).

- secondary students are familiar, for their specialist subject(s), with the relevant KS4 and post-16 examination syllabuses and courses, including vocational courses;

- understand, for their specialist subject(s), the framework of 14-19 qualifications and the routes of progression through it;

- understand, for their specialist subject(s), progression from the KS2 PoS;

- know and can teach the key skills required for current qualifications, relevant to their specialist subject(s), for pupils aged 14-19 and understand the contribution that their specialist subject(s) makes to the development of the key skills;

- cope securely with subject-related questions which pupils raise;

- are aware of, and know how to access, recent inspection evidence and classroom relevant research evidence on teaching secondary pupils in their specialist subject(s) and know how to use this to inform and improve their teaching;

- know, for their specialist subject(s), pupils' most common misconceptions and mistakes;

- understand how pupils' learning in the subject is affected by their physical, intellectual, emotional and social development;

- have a working knowledge of IT to a standard equivalent to level 8 in the NC for pupils, and understand the contribution that IT makes to their specialist subject(s);

- are familiar with subject-specific health and safety requirements, where relevant, and plan lessons to avoid potential hazards.

(b) Planning, Teaching And Class Management

(i) *Planning:*

- plan their teaching to achieve progression in pupils' learning through:

  - identifying clear teaching objectives and content, appropriate to the subject matter and the pupils being taught, and specifying how they will be taught and assessed;

  - setting tasks for whole class, individual and group work, including homework, which challenge pupils and ensure high levels of pupil interest;

  - setting appropriate and demanding expectations for pupils' learning, motivation and presentation of work;

  - setting clear targets for pupils' learning, building on prior attainment, and ensuring that pupils are aware of the substance and purpose of what they are asked to do;

  - identifying pupils who have special educational needs (including specific learning difficulties), are very able, or are not fluent in English (and Welsh, as appropriate), and knowing where to receive help in order to give positive and targeted support;

- provide clear structures for lessons and for sequences of lessons, in the short, medium and longer term, which maintain pace, motivation and challenge for pupils;

- make effective use of assessment information on pupils' attainment and progress in planning future lessons and sequences of lessons;

- plan opportunities to contribute to pupils' spiritual, moral, personal, social and cultural development;

- ensure coverage of the relevant NC PoS and examination syllabuses, as appropriate.

(ii) *Teaching and Class Management:*

- ensure effective teaching of whole classes, and of groups and individuals within the whole class setting, so that teaching objectives are met, and best use is made of available teaching time;

- monitor and intervene when teaching to ensure sound learning and discipline;

- establish and maintain a purposeful working atmosphere;

- set high expectations for pupils' behaviour, establishing and maintaining a good standard of discipline through well focused teaching and through positive and productive relationships;

- establish a safe environment which supports learning and in which pupils feel secure and confident;

- use teaching methods which sustain the momentum of pupils' work and keep all pupils engaged through:

  - stimulating intellectual curiosity, communicating enthusiasm for the subject being taught, fostering pupils' enthusiasm and maintaining their motivation;

  - matching the approaches used to the subject matter and the pupils being taught;

  - structuring information well, including content and aims, signalling transitions and summarising key points as the lesson progresses;

  - clear presentation of content around a set of key ideas, using appropriate subject-specific vocabulary and well chosen illustrations and examples;

  - clear instruction and demonstration, and accurate well-paced explanation;

  - effective questioning which matches the pace and direction of the lesson and ensures that pupils take part;

  - careful attention to pupils' errors and misconceptions and helping to remedy them;

  - listening carefully to pupils, analysing their responses and responding constructively to take pupils' learning forward;

  - selecting and making good use of textbooks, ICT and other learning resources which enable teaching objectives to be met;

  - providing opportunities for pupils to consolidate their knowledge and maximising opportunities, both in the classroom and through setting well focused homework, to reinforce and develop what has been learnt;

  - exploiting opportunities to improve pupils' basic skills in literacy, numeracy and ICT and the individual and collaborative study skills for effective learning, including information retrieval from libraries, texts and other sources;

  - exploiting opportunities to contribute to the quality of pupils' wider educational development, including their spiritual, moral, personal, social and cultural development;

  - setting high expectations for all pupils notwithstanding individual differences, including gender, and cultural and linguistic backgrounds;

  - providing opportunities to develop pupils' wider understanding by relating their learning to real and work-related examples;

- are familiar with the Code of Practice on the Identification and Assessment of Special Educational Needs and, as part of their responsibilities under the Code, implement and keep records on individual education plans for pupils at stage 2 of the Code and above;

- ensure that pupils acquire and consolidate knowledge, skills and understanding of the subject;

- evaluate their own teaching critically and use this to improve their effectiveness.

(c) Monitoring, Assessment, Recording, Reporting And Accountability

- assess how well learning objectives have been achieved and use this assessment to improve specific aspects of teaching;

- mark and monitor pupils' assigned classwork and homework, providing constructive oral and written feedback, and setting targets for pupils' progress;

- assess and record each pupil's progress systematically through focused observation, questioning, testing and marking, and use records to:

  - check that pupils have understood and completed the work set;

  - monitor strengths and weaknesses and use the information gained as a basis for purposeful intervention in pupils' learning;

  - inform planning;

  - check that pupils continue to make demonstrable progress in their acquisition of the knowledge, skills and understandings of the subject;

- are familiar with the statutory assessment and reporting requirements and know how to prepare and present informative reports to parents;

- where applicable, understand the expected demands of pupils in relation to each level description or end of key stage description, as well as the demands of the syllabuses and course requirements for GCSE, other KS4 courses and, where applicable, post-16 courses;

- where applicable, understand and know how to implement the assessment requirements of current qualifications for pupils aged 14-19;

- recognise the level at which a pupil is achieving, and assess pupils consistently against ATs, where applicable, if necessary with guidance from an experienced teacher;

- understand and know how to use national, local, comparative and school data, including NC test data, where applicable, to set clear targets for pupils' achievement;

- use different kinds of assessment appropriately for different purposes, including NC and other standardised tests, and baseline assessment, where relevant.

(d) Other Professional Requirements

- have a working knowledge and understanding of:

  - teachers' professional duties as set out in the current School Teachers' Pay and Conditions document issued under the School Teachers' Pay and Conditions Act 1991;

- teachers' legal liabilities and responsibilities relating to:

  - the Race Relations Act 1976;

- the Sex Discrimination Act 1975;

- the Health and Safety at Work Act 1974;

- teachers' common law duty to ensure that pupils are healthy and safe on school premises and when leading activities off the school site, such as educational visits, school outing or field trips;

- what is reasonable for the purposes of safeguarding or promoting children's welfare (Section 3[5] of the Children Act 1989);

- the role of the education service in protecting children from abuse (currently set out in DFEE circular 10/95 and the Home Office, Department of Health, DFEE and WO Guidance *Working Together: A Guide to Arrangements for Inter-Agency Co-operation for the Protection of Children from Abuse* 1991);

- appropriate physical contact with pupils (currently set out in DFEE circular 10/95);

- appropriate physical restraint of pupils (Section 4 of the Education Act 1997 and DFEE circular 9/94);

- detention of pupils on disciplinary grounds (Section 5 of the Education Act 1997).

- have established, during work in schools, effective working relationships with professional colleagues including, where relevant, associate staff;

- set a good example to the children they teach, through their presentation and their personal and professional conduct;

- are committed to ensuring that every pupil is given the opportunity to achieve their potential and meet the high expectations set for them;

- understand the need to take responsibility for their own professional development and to keep up to date with research and developments in pedagogy and in the subjects they teach;

- understand their professional responsibilities in relation to school policies and practices, including those concerned with pastoral and personal safety matters, including bullying;

- recognise that learning takes place inside and outside the school context, and understand the need to liaise effectively with parents and other carers and with agencies with responsibility for pupils' education and welfare;

- are aware of the role and purpose of school governing bodies.

2 The management of mentoring

In the previous chapter consideration was given to the meaning of 'mentoring' and to the role of various types of mentor. It is now proposed to focus upon the management of mentoring and the planning of a suitable programme for student teachers. It is assumed that this programme will incorporate ideas drawn from the apprenticeship, competency and reflective practitioner models of initial teacher education and training.

I: Establishing a management structure

Important factors to be taken into account include the following:

(a) **Whole-School Commitment:** As Brooks and Sikes note (1997, p. 61), it is essential that all staff in schools involved in ITET are committed to their role. It is suggested that:

- a whole-school policy for ITET should be established which covers the role of all staff working with students;

- a minimum student entitlement should be built into this policy;

- procedures for implementing the students' experience, for example, lesson observation, collaborative teaching and debriefing, should be clearly defined and observed;

- mentors should be carefully selected according to criteria which ensure their suitability for the task;

- all mentors should be fully aware of their roles and responsibilities. Hence, some form of mentor training is essential.

In some schools the provision for ITET is recognised as part of the school's development plan (Glover and Mardle, 1996).

(b) **Selection of Mentors:**

(i) *Selection Criteria:* Several studies have listed criteria for the selection of mentors (Corbett and Wright, 1994; Devlin, 1995; Brooks and Sikes, 1997; Geen, 2001c). These lists include such qualities as:

- an expressed interest and willingness to take on the role for a number of years;

- willingness to participate in initial and further training courses;

- a proven record as a successful classroom teacher who exhibits sound professional knowledge and practice and the ability to serve as a role model for students. The person should be able to offer advice on teaching techniques, provide clear explanations for practice and provide assistance in developing the standards required of trainee teachers;

- the ability to provide and organise activities which will broaden the students' range of experiences;

- the possession of good interpersonal skills, especially:

  - the ability to motivate students, to promote confidence and to raise self-esteem;

  - skills of communication, for example, being able to articulate practice, to provide oral and written feedback, to listen carefully and to challenge thinking;

  - skill in negotiating targets with students to advance their understanding and mastery of teaching techniques;

  - the ability to help students reflect upon their teaching, to review their progress and to resolve problems which arise within the role of the teacher;

  - the ability to provide advice without being overly judgemental,;

  - the capacity to be aware of the level of confidence of students and to provide them with critical comments without harming their motivation;

  - the ability to set boundaries and to help students make progress within those boundaries;

- the ability to reflect upon her/his teaching fluently and with enthusiasm and to realise that learning is a two-way process;

- flexibility in allowing for experimentation and the ability to respond to individual needs;

- sound skills of organisation, for example, in record-keeping and time-management;

- the ability to liaise effectively with colleagues, both in the school and at the HEI.

(ii) *Research Studies into the Selection of Mentors:* Ideally, clear criteria should be published for the selection of mentors within a school. Members of staff should then be invited to apply for the post, and a choice should be made in the light of the criteria. Research studies have shown that these procedures are rarely adopted.

(1) Headteachers quoted in the research of Moyles, Suschitzky and Chapman. (1998) into primary schools in partnership with Leicester University were able to offer no predominant reason for the selection of mentors for students or newly qualified teachers. Usually, the choice was made on the basis of requests from volunteers with about a third of headteachers over-riding the appointment of certain teachers if, for some reason, they were thought to be inappropriate for the role at that time. The usual reason for rejecting these staff members was that their workload would be excessive if they acted as mentors on top of their other duties.

In one school the head gave as the reason for his choice of mentor the desire to provide an experienced teacher with the chance to try something different; this, it was hoped, would enhance his professional development. In two cases the role of mentor was part of the job description for a team or year-group leader. At some schools staff did not volunteer because of workload.

(2) The research of Linda Devlin (1995) in the context of secondary schools in the Worcester College of Higher Education partnership found that the ITET co-ordinator was usually recruited on a voluntary basis. In ten of the twenty case study schools the post was occupied by the deputy headteacher, in six it was a senior teacher, in three a head of department and in one an unpromoted teacher. Very often the schools had been involved in initial teacher education and training for many years and the member of staff was continuing to fulfil a role which he/she had performed for some time. Some of these co-ordinators saw the post as a stepping stone for promotion, for example, moving into ITET at the HEI or providing evidence of management skills needed for headship through their involvement in the mentoring structure of the school. Others undertook the task because of enthusiasm for influencing the next generation of teachers. One commented: "There is nothing in it financially ... but I get a kick out of working with students and watching their development" (p. 86).

In many cases departments were selected for involvement in ITET by tutors at the HEI since they enjoyed a reputation for being successful and innovative. Usually, the head of department was known to college tutors, and that person acted as the subject mentor. Rarely were specific guidelines established by the HEI for choosing subject mentors. Nor did the head of department delegate the role in many cases. In appointing subject mentors - normally by invitation or by internal advertisement - headteachers and other senior managers tended to specify some experience of working with trainee teachers. Beyond this and the feeling that these people would 'do a good job', no specific criteria were adopted within the school.

(3) Research by Geen (2001c) of thirty-nine secondary schools in South-East Wales found that twenty-five ITET co-ordinators were deputy headteachers who undertook the role because it formed part of their job description. Others had volunteered or had been committed to ITET for many years and were thought by the senior management team to be the obvious candidates for the post. Only five – all heads of department – had applied for the position in response to an internal advertisement. Rarely were any selection criteria employed, since it was assumed that the qualities required of a deputy headteacher or departmental head would automatically be valuable for co-ordinating ITET arrangements and conducting tutorials with students.

In the case of the eighty-four subject mentors, selection procedures were highly arbitrary. At no school had any job specification been drawn up and applications invited. Seventy-three of these mentors were heads of department, thirty-six of whom performed the role because it was regarded as one of their managerial responsibilities. Twenty-one had volunteered and sixteen took on the commitment as the result of a long-term interest in ITET. At none of the schools had any standards for selection been set out in writing. As one mentor reported, appointments depended upon the subjective judgement of senior staff concerning a teacher's general suitability. In some cases there was little consistency in the selection process. At one school the practice varied with different departments. In some of these the prime consideration was the length of time a person had been teaching, whilst in others it was the tradition for the head of department to serve *ex officio* as the subject mentor, irrespective of her/his capability.

(c) **Building a Team:** There are many different ways in which mentoring can be organised. Some secondary schools have opted for a team approach based upon the following structure:

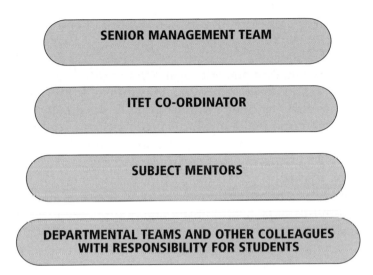

Others have appointed an overall ITET co-ordinator and assistant co-ordinators who take responsibility for students registered at different HEIs.

In the primary school, as Moyles, Suschitzky and Chapman (1998) show, the pyramid is usually flatter:

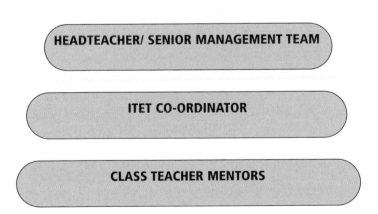

Within these structures team meetings can be held regularly to co-ordinate the school's mentoring programme. Initial meetings may focus upon aims, roles, responsibilities and practical issues such as the allocation of time for mentoring activities. Other issues may be:

- ensuring that the minimum student entitlement is being met;

- letting mentors know about any research assignments or other kinds of academic work which HEIs expect their students to undertake at the school;

- reviewing students' progress on a regular basis;

- conducting quality assurance surveys;

- deciding mentors' training needs.

Team work of this type is essential if all mentors are to have the same expectations of their students. Brooks and Sikes draw attention to bad practice in one school. Whereas the majority of staff had been helpful to trainees, one mentor " wasn't at all helpful, didn't observe him [the student], couldn't be bothered to look at his plans and then, when he did come in, he'd be negative and critical and didn't offer constructive advice" (p. 71). Research conducted at the University of Wales Institute, Cardiff (UWIC) during the academic year 2001-2002 has also identified inconsistencies in the quality of mentoring in various schools. In reply to a questionnaire in which students were asked to evaluate their school experience, one respondent bitterly complained that, though the ITET co-ordinator had promised to assess at least one lesson every week, in fact she had not written a single report. Another considered that visits from tutors at the HEIs were insufficient and that, as a consequence, 'schools get away with being less helpful'. Trainees also pointed to disparity among schools in terms of help with lesson preparation, feedback on teaching and the receipt of regular progress reports. One of them commented that her class mentor had conducted no debriefing sessions until the very end of her placement, at which point she had received a highly critical summative review. Where teams of mentors are formed and meet regularly to review the procedures adopted at their school, it is more likely that problems of this type can be noted and addressed. Murray (1991) believes that it can take at least three years for a school to establish a mentoring structure and to evaluate its effectiveness.

(d) **Timetabling Issues:** Researchers in the field of mentoring have frequently pointed to the problem of time. Carner and Hagger (1996), reviewing the University of Oxford's PGCE scheme, stress that a school's senior management team must realise that teachers' commitment to students is time consuming. Hence, they recommend that both ITET co-ordinators and subject/ class mentors have 'protected time' for working with students and for team meetings.

Research into the role of mentors in schools in partnership with UWIC has shown that lack of time is a major problem. For example, in one school the role of ITET co-ordinator was undertaken by a class teacher who was allocated only one hour a week for all duties relating to mentoring (Geen, Bassett and Douglas, 1998). Similarly, in a study of students' perceptions of ITET arrangements during the school year 2001-2002, the following comments were received:

> *My mentor read the 'crit' to me, but I felt that he just wanted to get rid of me so that he could finish other work.*

> *The mentors did not have the time to give advice at one of my schools. It was quite small and the staff had a lot of responsibilities.*

A further problem is that some schools receive students from as many as six different HEIs, each of which operates a totally different system of school experience for its students. Consequently, ITET co-ordinators may be expected to offer induction programmes and tutorials for groups arriving at various periods throughout the school year.

In the context of the primary school Cross (1999) refers to difficult decisions which mentors sometimes have to make, for example, how to deal with a distraught student whose confidence has been damaged in a disastrous lesson while having a class to teach at the same time. The issue of the availability of hours for mentoring has also been discussed by Field (1994a), Martin (1994), Jones (2000), Williams and Soares (2000) and Hayes (2001). One modern languages mentor in the study by Williams and Soares concludes that "time is a big problem; expectation placed on mentors is rather demanding. Teachers have different priorities – the first is the pupils" (p. 229). Moreover, if we agree with Elliott and Calderhead (1995) that mentors should be adept at the skill of 'listening', then considerable demands are made upon their time during debriefing and discussion with students.

The following suggestions may help to resolve some of the main problems identified in these studies:

(i) *Governors* should ensure that the funding transferred from HEIs to schools for ITET is actually devoted to that purpose. At present in England and Wales there is no obligation upon a school's governors to employ these resources on ITET. Research undertaken by Evans and Abbott (1997) of school-based and school-centred ITET schemes indicated that in some instances the money was absorbed into the general school budget. In others, part of it was added to the capitation allowance of departments which received students, while in only a small number of cases was it actually used to buy in teaching supply cover to release mentors from teaching duties. The advantages of buying in cover were clearly expressed by one respondent:

> *This coming year I have got the day off – we've got a part-timer who's come into the department and she's releasing me for the equivalent of one day. Last year I had money, but it's not the same. You do need the time to do the job properly (p. 140).*

Hence, it may be beneficial if legislation were enacted to make this a duty. In the meantime, it will be the responsibility of governors to check that departments and classes which receive students are allocated some funding to 'free up' time for mentors to meet with trainees, to help them plan lessons and to offer appropriate feedback on their teaching.

(ii) *Government:* Another desirable policy is for partnerships to be funded directly by central government with a sum specifically allocated for the creation of tutorial time. The Green Paper *The BEST for Teaching and Learning* (Welsh Office, 1999) suggested the provision of funds to partnerships rather than HEIs. This is a recommendation which many mentors have welcomed.

It is also generally acknowledged that partnerships have been under-funded (Griffiths and Owen, 1995). If government wishes ITET to be school-based or school-centred, the necessary resources have to be provided.

(iii) *HEIs:* It would be helpful if all the HEIs in partnership with the same schools could reach an agreement concerning the timing of their students' school experience. If this were done, mentors would no longer be faced with the prospect of having to repeat the same seminars and tutorials for the benefit of discrete groups of trainees attending different universities or colleges.

Moreover, it may be possible to operate a system whereby education departments at HEIs 'buy in' only those central services which are actually relevant to students pursuing ITET courses. As trainees spend much of their time off the university campus, this would result in savings which could be passed on to schools.

(iv) *ITET Co-ordinators:* Co-ordinators could undertake a realistic assessment of the time required by staff at their schools to fulfil their responsibilities towards students and use this calculation as a basis for discussion with HEIs about the transfer of funds. Negotiations could then follow with their school's timetabler in order to secure sufficient non-contact time for all teachers involved in ITET to fulfil their mentoring responsibilities.

(v) *Economies in ITET provision:* Economies can also be made in schools' expenditure on photocopying where mentors produce a CD-Rom summarising all the information needed by students. Savings made in this direction can again be devoted to the provision of time for mentoring.

II: Planning and co-ordinating the students' experience

Key issues to be addressed are:

(a) **Provision of Relevant Information about the School:** Much of the information students need can be sent to them before they attend the school. Often this takes the form of a school handbook with details of such major policy areas as:

- the names of all mentors;

- timetables for school experience;

- relevant documents concerned with students' experience, for example, focused observation sheets and report forms used for the monitoring of students' lessons and summative assessment;

- regulations relating to ITET, for example, the QTS standards;

- a copy of the staff handbook;

- a statement of the aims of the school;

- details of the organisation of the curriculum;

- an account of the academic organisation of the school, for example, faculties and departments in secondary schools;

- guidelines on the provision of pastoral care;

- expectations made of the school staff, for example, dress code;

- policy concerning discipline and school rules;

- policy concerning rewards and sanctions;

- assessment procedures;

- policy concerning special educational needs;

- equal opportunities policies;

- health and safety guidelines;

- an account of the role of the school governors;

- the admissions policy and catchment area;

- a plan of the buildings;

- administrative procedures, for example, reporting absences from school.

However, there is the danger, as students at UWIC have pointed out, that newcomers to the school will be inundated with information. Accordingly, it is valuable for the co-ordinator to talk to them on their first day about their forthcoming school experience and to summarise as efficiently as possible the main issues with which they need to be familiar. The areas of most immediate relevance are the organisation of the induction programme, assessment procedures and the expectations of school staff. Some co-ordinators also organise a tour of the school's catchment area, which is usually appreciated by students.

It is important for the mentoring team to ensure that the information provided to students is kept as up to date as is possible.

(b) **Establishing Criteria for the Students' Experience:** Important criteria are:

(i) *to secure a well-planned induction.* It is essential that the first classroom experiences are positive and that students are not required to undertake responsibilities for which they are not yet ready. As one ITET co-ordinator has stated, " the start is important. They shouldn't be chucked in at the deep end; they should be given time to progress from sound, positive experiences in the classroom" (Hagger, Burn and McIntyre. 1993, p. 20). Thus, it is important for students in their first weeks in the school to engage in activities which allow for a gradual initiation before they take on responsibility for teaching a full class. These activities will include observation and forms of collaborative teaching.

(ii) *to ensure progression in the students' programme:* As confidence develops, students can gradually be given greater responsibilities. Shaw (1995) observes that expectations of what students can accomplish depends upon:

- their level of experience;

- the progress they have made; and

- their familiarity with the school.

These factors will affect the demands made of them at any stage and the opportunities they are offered. Hence, a programme of school experience should be sufficiently flexible to accommodate change in the light of perceived needs. This means that it is important that students' performance is regularly monitored and that mentors liaise with the link and subject tutors at the HEI. A typical example of the need to modify a programme to foster progression is given by a mentor in the study of Hagger, Burn and McIntyre (1993):

> *A couple of years ago the student I had was very quick to learn. She took observation seriously, got on well with everyone and was very enthusiastic about becoming a teacher. She was really alert to what was going on in classrooms and she used to ask us very searching questions. I did some collaborative teaching with her with two of my classes, one in year 7 and the other in year 9. Within a few weeks it was clear from what I was seeing as well as from what my colleagues were saying about her that I needed to adjust the programme as she was learning so quickly and well. To start with we changed the way we worked together with the two classes - she became the senior partner and I moved more into the background. Then, with another teacher she began to take complete lessons so that she took the class twice a week while he took their other three lessons (p. 29).*

(iii) *to offer a variety of experiences:* To obviate the problem of 'cloning' which can arise when students work exclusively with one teacher, it is desirable to ensure that they experience a range of teaching skills, styles and perspectives. This is often arranged during the early stages of school experience where they 'shadow' a class and observe all the members of staff who normally teach it.

(iv) *to ensure that the programme is structured and coherent:* Students' learning activities need to be interconnected and sequenced for cross-reference and progression. For example, observation needs to be carefully guided and focused. As Tomlinson notes, "whether pedagogy and broader issues are studied within an integrated approach to subject teaching or involve separate course components, there is obvious advantage if such coverage can dovetail with experiences in teaching and students' 'research activities' such as pupil tracking" (p. 205).

(v) *to plan a timetable of realistic proportions:* ITET co-ordinators must ensure that students are not given a timetable in the early stages which will make too many demands of them. The amount of teaching they undertake will, of course, vary with experience and progress. Mentors need to appreciate that time is also needed for planning lessons, collecting resources, undertaking assignments and reflecting upon experience. In many partnerships students begin with a fifty per cent timetable and gradually move during their second term to seventy-five per cent.

In planning the students' timetable it is also important to take into account the needs of pupils. For example, in the case of year 11 GCSE classes, having the student teacher work alongside small groups of pupils who want to revise particular topics can be valuable, since additional help may be offered to individuals.

On the other hand, it is necessary to check that classes are not overloaded with student teachers. In one survey conducted at UWIC (Geen, Bassett and Douglas, 2000) mentors pointed to the problems which can occur when pupils are taught for a substantial number of lessons by people who are still striving to achieve QTS. There can be lack of continuity in their learning as they have to adjust to new procedures and different standards. Students who rely exclusively upon a restricted range of teaching strategies or fail to maintain discipline are especially problematic. As one co-ordinator argued, committed though his school was to the training of new teachers, he had to deal with parents who took the view that the interests of their children were paramount and that inadequate classroom performance should not be tolerated from any quarter.

(vi) *to provide opportunities for students to develop their professional knowledge:* In order to meet the QTS standards students need to acquire an understanding of a wide range of educational issues beyond subject-specific teaching. This may involve observation of such areas as the school's internal organisation, its links with the community and its relationships with parents.

During tutorials with the ITET co-ordinator and other mentors students should be able to discuss in a structured manner any assignments they have been set and/or observation exercises which relate to these wider professional issues. Ideally, the tutorials should develop themes which have been explored within the educational and professional studies course offered at the HEI. Examples of topics are listed in chapter six.

(vii) *to give students clear directions about the expectations made of them:* Students should be given clear directions about the activities they are expected to undertake during their non-contact time. In the same way, they should fully understand the focus of any observations in which they engage. Other issues such as participation in the extra-curricular life of the school should be explained at the outset of their placement.

(viii) *to encourage students to monitor and evaluate their progress:* In many schools both the ITET co-ordinator and mentors timetable weekly meetings with students in which they can review their progress. During these sessions evaluations may take place of lessons which have been given, and the teaching of topics to classes over the following weeks can be planned. Usually, these reviews culminate in the setting and recording of targets for the student. It is highly desirable that strategies associated with the reflective practitioner models of ITET are practised at this stage.

(ix) *to ensure that mentors understand their responsibilities and have the requisite skills to perform their role:* Difficulties arise if mentors have unrealistic views of what students can accomplish. This again points to the need for a team approach in which all teachers working with students:

- understand what can reasonably be expected of trainees;

- understand the nature and principles of the scheme of ITET in operation;

- are kept informed of the student's programme and progress;

- are supported in their work with students and helped to develop the skills needed for the work.

It is inappropriate for students to be based with a teacher who is totally disillusioned with her/his work and who does not accept the philosophy of ITET operated in the school. Comments made by UWIC students during the academic year 2001-2002 reveal some of the problems which can occur.

Although all the mentoring procedures for the school were handed to me and looked great on paper, in practice no advice or help was given at all. I felt the procedures were just a paper exercise to which the teachers had no commitment at all.

When on my second placement I asked for advice about classroom management with a class that was giving me trouble, I was simply told to go home and forget about it.

Collaborative teaching worked well with one teacher, but with the actual mentor I felt as if I were intruding and that she did not want me to be in the room at all.

III: Outline of a student's programme

(a) **Before Students Arrive:** Before the commencement of any placement it is essential for the ITET co-ordinator to ensure that all arrangements are in place to make the student's experience as valuable as possible. Attention needs to be paid to the following items:

(i) *the provision of information:* It is advantageous for mentors to send students details about the school before the commencement of the placement. Examples of information have been given in section II (a) above.

(ii) *administrative arrangements:* The ITET co-ordinator's role includes the organisation of a series of seminars and tutorials with students. This means that she/he must be familiar with the course offered by the HEI and with any school-based assignments or tasks that students are required to complete. Possession of this information enables the mentor to plan school-based activities which will help the student tackle these exercises.

Other tasks include: deciding details of the scheme for inducting student teachers into the school as a whole and into their respective class or department; establishing a system whereby they can be informed about communication networks, for example, having their own pigeon-holes; and making sure that they are clear about such issues as access to photocopying and other resources.

(iii) *liaison with mentors:* The co-ordinator must ensure that all teachers who will be working with trainees fully understand their responsibilities. Thus, all relevant materials concerning initial teacher education and training produced by the HEI will be passed to them.

He/she will liaise with them to check that they are all aware of the programme of induction agreed by the mentoring team and that adequate arrangements are at hand for the introduction of students to departments or classes. It is necessary to ensure that no overlap exists between the whole-school induction programme and that organised by the subject or class mentor.

As soon as they are available, a student's *curriculum vitae* and application form for the course (where this information is provided by the HEI) can be given to the appropriate mentor so that he/she can learn about the trainee's background and acquire some 'feel' for her/his interests and needs.

(b) **Induction to the School:** Feedback from students at UWIC suggests that Shaw (1995) is justified in making the comment that " first impressions count" and that a warm, friendly welcome to the school is essential. At one school they felt that they were 'really wanted'. During induction they were impressed with the enthusiasm with which they were greeted by staff and pupils. Lunch with the headteacher and mentors was described as 'welcoming'. Unfortunately, at another school students' experience was very different, as they were given the strong impression that they were merely an additional burden to hard-working teachers.

Induction arrangements vary. In most cases the ITET co-ordinator takes responsibility for the induction of student teachers into the school as a whole, while the subject or class mentor retains responsibility for induction into the department or class. Whatever the practice, it is important that at some early stage - whether in the HEI or in the school - students are made fully aware of the objectives of their school experience, including the standards which they must achieve during their time there. Consequently, they need in summarised form an account of the requirements of *Qualifying to Teach* (DFES-TTA, 2002) or Welsh Office Circular 13/98 (Welsh Office, 1998). In many partnerships and SCITTs a summary of the standards is printed on the lesson feedback sheets given to students.

The following programme, which operates at a comprehensive school in South Wales, is offered as an example of an induction system which has been well received by student teachers:

Day 1:

9.00 a.m. - 9.15 a.m.: Welcome by the headteacher

9.15 a.m. - 10.25 a.m.: Meeting with the ITET co-ordinator. Brief information is given about the school's ethos and organisation. Students are allocated to form tutor groups and given a tour of the school, seeing samples of pupils' work displayed around the building. They learn the location of mentors and their respective form tutor rooms.

10.25 a.m. - 10.45 a.m.: Break. Students have the opportunity to meet subject mentors and form tutors.

10.45 a.m. - 11.00 a.m.: Students meet librarian, reprographics technicians and appropriate support staff.

11.00 a.m. - 12.20 p.m.: Students are based in their departments with subject mentors for observation.

12.20 p.m. - 1.10 p.m: Lunch.

1.15 p.m. - 3.30 p.m.: Students are located with their subject mentors in departments for discussion and observation. Timetables are allocated.

3.30 p.m.: Meeting with the co-ordinator for a review of the first day. Students have the opportunity to seek further information and guidance where necessary.

Day 2:

9.00 a.m. - 9.15 a.m.: Registration in form rooms with assigned tutor group.

During the course of the morning, students meet heads of year to discuss their roles and the pastoral needs of different year groups.

In the afternoon they attend lessons in personal, social and health education with two different year groups.

Day 3: Focused 'pupil trails':

9.00 am. - 9.15 am: Registration in form rooms. Students shadow two or three children in their tutor group throughout the day.

9.15 a.m. - 3.30 p.m.: Pupil Trails: Students shadow the pupils and complete a 'structured observation sheet' for some of the lessons visited. They are expected to make brief notes about their experiences for discussion with the ITET co-ordinator in the educational and professional studies seminar later in the week.

In some schools students are given strands from the QTS standards, for example, ways of promoting active and independent learning that enables pupils to think for themselves, and they record examples used by teachers in the lessons observed.

Day 4: The day is spent in departments under the guidance of subject mentors. The programme for the remainder of the period of school experience is finalised and observation begins of other staff in the department.

Day 5:

9.00 a.m. - 9.15 a.m.: Registration

9.15 - 3.30 p.m.: Normal school day as timetabled by subject mentors.

At the end of the day students meet the ITET co-ordinator to discuss their observations and review the events of the first week. Towards the end of the second week they are required to submit to her a short assignment reflecting their observations.

(c) **Departmental/Class Induction:** Induction will concentrate upon the following:

(i) *Colleagues:* Students should be introduced to all staff with whom they will come into contact, including, where appropriate, laboratory assistants, teacher assistants and other ancillary staff.

(ii) *Facilities and resources:*

- Students need to be shown around the teaching area, and the use of any special work and preparation surfaces should be explained to them.

- They should be informed of the location of resources and procedures for the use of such items as class sets of books, the photocopier, the television and the video.

(iii) *Routines and practices:* They must be informed of any important routines and practices, for example, arrangements for pupils' movement around the building or coffee/tea making facilities in the teaching area.

(iv) *Class or Departmental Policies:*

- Students should be given a brief introduction to policy on such matters as grouping pupils, assessment, recording and reporting.

- They must be provided with appropriate schemes of work.

(v) *Expectations and plans:*

- The role of the mentor and other staff involved in ITET should be clarified.

- The mentor must explain what is expected of student teachers in terms of commitment, reliability and enthusiasm. Issues such as the time of their arrival at the school and dress code need to be addressed at this point. It is also helpful for mentors to learn about students' previous experience, for example, the courses they have taken in higher education, and to encourage them to talk about what they are hoping to gain from their placement at the school.

- Specific targets for the initial period of school experience should be set at this point.

- A preliminary programme should be discussed with them, and they should be informed of the ways in which they will be working with mentors.

- An account should be given of important events and calendar dates relevant to students. They need to be informed of the meetings they should attend, for example, regular debriefing sessions, weekly review sessions to discuss their overall progress, teacher meetings, full staff meetings and parents' evenings.

(d) **Early weeks:** Major aims at this stage are to:

(i) offer a broad picture of class routines;

(ii) make trainees aware of the QTS standards;

(iii) help them focus on different aspects of teaching;

(iv) encourage them from the outset to reflect critically upon their teaching and to understand that experienced teachers are also reflective practitioners;

(v) provide a general introduction to whole-school issues and areas of school organisation outside classroom teaching;

(vi) build their confidence.

A possible approach to the early weeks will involve the following activities:

- *The student observes lessons* and the mentor guides and helps him/her to make sense of what has been observed.

- *The student takes a small group of pupils:* The mentor involves the student in the lesson planning, the student teaches a limited number of children in the class and the two of them evaluate the outcome. Even at this early stage the mentor should expect the student to reflect upon the lesson and make reference to some of the QTS standards.

- *The student takes the whole class for parts of the lesson:* The mentor discusses with the student the skills upon which he/she should focus, assists with the lesson planning and provides diagnostic feedback. Once again, the student will be expected to present her/his own ideas on the strengths of the lesson taught and ways in which it could have been tackled differently.

- *Collaborative teaching:* The mentor and student jointly plan, carry out and evaluate the lesson.

- *The student teaches the class with mentor support:* At this point the student takes the lead in the planning, while the mentor offers advice, observes the student's teaching, invites him/her to analyse the lesson and provides diagnostic feedback .

- *The student teaches the whole class unaided:* The mentor advises on the lesson plan in the light of the overall scheme of work, observes, encourages self-reflection and provides diagnostic feedback intermittently and at agreed times during the rest of the placement.

In offering feedback the mentor will ensure that her/his comments relate to the standards and that every encouragement is given to the student to evaluate the extent to which the lesson objectives were achieved. Some of the models described in the last chapter can be utilised within collaborative teaching, for example, Schon's 'follow me' and 'hall of mirrors'.

(e) **Subsequent Experience:** After the period of gradual initiation into teaching, students assume greater responsibility for teaching unassisted. Nonetheless, it is helpful for them to continue with some observation and collaborative teaching, especially where:

- they have, to use the terminology of Furlong and Maynard (1995), reached a 'plateau' and need to be stimulated to try more ambitious approaches. Observation of a number of experienced teachers can be helpful in offering them new ideas;

- they are encountering difficulties and need to learn from observation;

- they wish to embark upon new strategies with which they have had little experience previously and are not fully aware of the best ways of proceeding, for example, using role play, negotiated learning or discussion techniques. Working with teachers who regularly employ these strategies can offer them ideas for their own lesson planning.

It is also important to:

* ensure that they work with the full age range, including classes which are more difficult to motivate. It is, of course, for the mentor to decide what is most appropriate for their development at any one stage, and teaching less motivated pupils may be postponed until they have gained some experience and have acquired a degree of confidence;

* allow them to study key aspects of the teacher's role outside subject teaching, for example, administrative duties and in-service meetings;

* provide a range of activities. As Brooks and Sikes note, there can be an element of negotiation in deciding the student's timetable. Some may wish to become involved in certain extra-curricular activities or examine in some detail an area of especial interest, for example, SEN, ICT or equal opportunities policy;

* discuss with students any assignments or projects they are required to undertake on teaching strategies, classroom management, assessment techniques, etc.;

* help them reflect upon their reading and other forms of experience in relation to teaching and educational issues.

(f) **Monitoring Progress:** Both ITET co-ordinators and mentors need to keep careful records which chart students' progress. It is helpful for class/subject mentors to:

* offer feedback on at least one lesson each day;

* meet students at least once a week to review their progress against the standards. In many schools specific targets are set for students in weekly reviews. Target setting will be discussed in a later chapter;

* maintain a profile of students' progress. Modes of profiling are discussed in chapter twelve;

* inform the ITET co-ordinator if a student experiences any especial problems.

The ITET co-ordinator should:

* liaise with class/subject mentors regularly concerning students' progress;

* maintain contact with students during the weekly seminar/tutorial sessions;

* keep in touch with the HEI link tutor and draw attention to any problems as soon as these are identified;

* moderate the judgements of class/subject mentors by observing at least one lesson given by each student in the school;

• discuss each student's general progress towards the end of the placement.

(g) **Later Stages:** Current government regulations state that students involved in systems of ITET based upon partnership must attend at least two schools during a one-year PGCE course. Those pursuing BEd or BA/BSc (Ed) courses attend several schools.

When students transfer to a different school it is vital that there is a smooth transition and that the programme offered ensures progression and continuity. In most partnership schemes it is the practice for ITET co-ordinators or mentors to send a profile on the student to the school which he/she will be attending for the next placement. The receipt of this profile helps the staff there to understand the stage the trainee has reached. They are then able to plan a sequence of activities based upon this knowledge which is suited to her/his immediate needs.

Research conducted at UWIC over the academic year 2001-2002 has noted that some students encounter problems when they transfer schools:

(i) Whereas the majority were satisfied that they received policy statements, observed lessons and attended seminar classes with the ITET co-ordinator in their first period of experience, it was noted that the same opportunities were not always offered when they attended their second school. This could be due to the belief that by this phase of their PGCE course students have acquired sufficient knowledge and experience and do not need the same degree of support. Alternatively, it may be because some schools receive trainees from a number of HEIs at different points within the academic year and do not have time to design a suitable programme for each separate cohort.

(ii) Some students who have found a pedagogic strategy to be particularly successful in their first school try to 'import' it into the second where it is unfamiliar to their pupils. Problems can arise if they refuse to modify their approach and are loathe to try other techniques. Consequently, it is important in their induction period at the second school, before they take on responsibility for teaching a full class, that there is full discussion of their previous experiences and the expectations of staff at the second school. In this way they can be guided either by the ITET co-ordinator or the mentor to adopt a range of suitable strategies from the outset.

IV: Monitoring and reviewing the programme

The mentoring team needs constantly to review the progress of the provision made at the school. Possible approaches are:

(a) **To Issue Students with Questionnaires** to ascertain their views on the quality of the mentoring offered at the school and to invite them to make constructive suggestions for improving provision. A typical questionnaire could ask students to rate on a one to four scale, where four indicates 'highly satisfactory' and one 'totally unsatisfactory', such items as:

(i) *The Role of the ITET Co-ordinator in:*

• providing relevant documentation.;

- organising a tour of the school, an introduction to its management structure, an attachment to a form tutor (in the secondary sector) and observation of teachers other than those with whom they are normally located;

- enabling students to attend relevant meetings, for example, in-service training, and to take part in appropriate extra-curricular duties;

- meeting students regularly for seminars and tutorials relating to whole-school and wider educational issues;

- ensuring that these classes correlate with the topics undertaken at the HEI;

- monitoring students' progress by observing at least one lesson and holding a formal review meeting to discuss overall performance.

(ii) *The Role of the Class/Subject Mentor in:*

- providing a suitable framework for school experience, for example, providing a timetable to allow students to teach a range of ages and abilities, holding regular lesson debriefings, signing students' registers and being available each week for a formal review and the setting of targets;

- serving as a role model, for example, allowing students to observe lessons, demonstrating a variety of teaching styles, allowing students to undertake focused lesson observations, and working with them in collaborative teaching;

- coaching students in the standards, for example, helping them to set challenging teaching and learning objectives and to use these to plan lessons, to follow the requirements of the National Curriculum, to differentiate their teaching to meet the needs of pupils, to use ICT in their lessons, to establish a clear framework for classroom discipline, and to assess pupils' achievements;

- encouraging students to become reflective practitioners by expecting them to evaluate strengths and areas for improvement in their teaching, to move from reflection-in-action to reflection-on-action, to derive theory from experience, and to consider the wider educational issues and ethical principles underlying their teaching;

- practising interpersonal skills, for example, clear communications, challenging students' thinking without demoralising them, explaining the basis for their judgements and helping them to resolve problems arising in the classroom;

- interrelating school and college-based components of the ITET course, for example, using the HEI's criteria for lesson evaluation and showing the application to school practice of topics covered at the university.

(b) **Skills Audits:** The ITET co-ordinator can provide a checklist of key skills and organise an audit on the part of subject or class mentors of their capabilities in the light of these skills. Typical skills are discussed in chapters seven and eight. Information derived from this source may be used to supplement the feedback received from students.

(c) **Review of the Mentoring Programme:** In the light of the questionnaires and audit the mentoring team, led by the co-ordinator, can review the effectiveness of the programme offered and plan any suitable staff development to meet the needs of both the institution and individual mentors. Devoting one in-service day each year to activities of this type may be beneficial.

V: Professional development for mentors

The following strategies are suggestions for the professional development of mentors:

(i) *internal meetings of members of the mentoring team to share good practice.*

(ii) *courses organised to meet specific needs identified in skills audits.* These can be conducted by the ITET co-ordinator or HEI tutors.

(iii) *the use of software to provide information on partnership.* In some surveys (e.g. Booth, 2001; Geen, 2001c), mentors have expressed the view that professional development sessions organised at HEIs are dominated by instructions relating to the completion of forms and documentation on students. Much of this information can be given to schools on a CD-Rom or downloaded from an HEI website. This allows greater time within professional development courses to be devoted to the acquisition of such areas as reflective practice and mentoring skills.

(iv) *the attendance of mentors on courses which lead to the award of a higher degree.* As Williams and Soares (2000) show, the government is currently concerned to extend support for teachers' professional development with such schemes as sabbaticals, professional bursaries and Best Practice Research Scholarships (DFEE, 2000b, DFEE 2001a), and HEIs have a major role to play in these programmes. It is certainly possible for school staff to embark upon courses of study in the field of mentoring which confer upon them a postgraduate qualification (Stierer, 2000).

(v) *the establishment of 'professional development' schools:* Mentors could plan and undertake research into good practice, either independently or in collaboration with HEI tutors. Eighty-six per cent of respondents in a survey into mentor training (Geen, 2000c) expressed enthusiasm for the concept of the 'professional development' school pioneered in the United States of America, in which school-HEI parternships are established not only to train student teachers but also to conduct appropriate research (Grossman, 1992; Fullan, 1993; Edwards and Collison, 1996). The introduction of a similar system in England and Wales would encourage them to explore innovative strategies and allow them to disseminate their findings. In this way the quality of ITET would be enhanced by school staff directly involved in the training and education of student teachers.

(vi) *the creation of a national professional qualification for mentors:* In the same piece of research three-quarters of respondents favoured the idea of a national professional qualification on a par with those offered to subject leaders, advanced skills teachers and headteachers (TTA, 1998). For each of these roles a set of standards, set out in terms of knowledge, skills and understanding, has been defined. A similar practice could be adopted for mentors, and courses could be organised nationally to meet these standards. Examples might be:

- *knowledge* of the philosophies of mentoring and their implications;

- *skills,* for example, motivating students, helping them to evaluate their teaching, counselling and target setting;

- *understanding* of strategies such as Schon's 'hall of mirrors'.

The successful completion of such a course would then lead to the award of a recognised qualification along the lines of the National Professional Qualification for Headteachers. Not only would this improve the quality of mentor training, but it would also raise the status of the mentor in the school.

Issues for consideration

1. Read section I (*establishing a management structure*) and list the main conditions which you feel are essential to ensure a whole-school commitment to ITET.

2. Write down what you consider to be the main qualities which should be taken into account when mentors are chosen for their role.

3. What advantages can be claimed for a team approach to mentoring?

4. Describe the management system in operation at your school with reference to the factors discussed in section I. Consider:

   (a) *whole-school policy;*

   (b) *the selection of mentors;*

   (c) *the provision of time for school staff to fulfil their mentoring duties;*

   (d) *a team approach.*

5. In the light of your reading record the *strengths* of the managerial system used at your school for mentoring in relation to the issues raised in section I of the chapter and suggest any strategies by which it might be *further developed.*

6. Read section II (*planning and co-ordinating the students' experience*) and describe the steps which are taken at your school with respect to the following items:

   (a) *providing relevant information to students;*

   (b) *planning induction;*

   (c) *ensuring progression;*

(d) *providing a variety of experience;*

(e) *ensuring that the programme is structured and coherent;*

(f) *guaranteeing that the student's timetable is of realistic proportions;*

(g) *providing opportunities for students to develop their professional knowledge;*

(h) *giving students clear instructions about the expectations made of them;*

(i) *encouraging them to monitor and evaluate their own progress;*

(j) *ensuring that colleagues have realistic perceptions.*

7.   With reference to these criteria record what you consider to be the major strengths of the provision offered at your school and suggest any *further developments* which could be beneficial.

8.   Read section III (*outline of a student's ptogramme*) and describe the arrangements made at your school for:

(a) *planning before the student arrives;*

(b) *the induction of the student to the school;*

(c) *the induction of the student to the class or department:*

(d) *the strategies used in the early weeks of school experience;*

(e) *arrangements made during the bulk of the placement to ensure that progress is maintained, that students extend their experience and that they reflect both upon that experience and upon wider educational issues;*

(f) *monitoring progress;*

(g) *making arrangements to ensure a smooth transition to their second placement.*

9.   Read section IV (*monitoring and reviewing the programme*). What systems are in place at your school:

(a) *for reviewing the effectiveness of the mentoring programme?*

(b) *for planning change in the light of this review?*

10. In the light of your reading state what you consider to be the strengths of your school's practice in relation to the issues in questions 8 and 9 above and note any changes which you feel could be beneficial.

11. (a) What forms of professional development are available to mentors at your school?

(b) How often are professional development activities conducted in the field of mentoring?

(c) Which of these activities are organised internally and which are conducted under the aegis of an HEI?

(d) Suggest any steps which could be taken to improve the professional development available to mentors at your school.

Students' classroom observation

I: Students' observation of lessons

In most ITET schemes students' school experience begins with classroom observation in which they focus attention upon the interaction of teachers and their pupils. This is often seen as a good example of the apprenticeship approach, since the student is then able to model her/himself on the class teacher. Nonetheless, opportunities exist for mentors to employ the other approaches to ITET outlined in the first chapter by making reference to the QTS standards and encouraging reflective practice in discussion of a lesson.

A number of issues have been raised in literature on students' observation:

(a) Tomlinson (1995) advocates the 'PAMR' model in which teachers who are observed discuss with students the following issues:

- their *lesson planning* and its underlying rationale;

- their *attempt* to put their lesson plan into action;

- their *monitoring* of the lesson;

- their *reflections* upon the effectiveness of the lesson and their thoughts on strategies by which it might have been improved.

The subject mentor's role, therefore, is to:

- 'unpack' or explain with reasons the planning for the lesson;

- guide the student's observation of the action of the lesson in the light of the planning;

- discuss with the student after the lesson the extent to which the objectives were attained and ways in which they might have been more effectively achieved.

This model combines tenets of the apprenticeship approach with the reflective practitioner philosophy. It is important in the PAMR system that mentors take a critical stance with respect to their own teaching.

(b) Teaching on the part of experienced staff sometimes looks easy to people who lack any experience in the classroom. Teachers are in control and their classes are used to routines, rules and methods of working. Lessons therefore progress smoothly, and the student is not aware of all the strategies which these teachers have employed to bring about this state of affairs, for example, establishing rules when they first meet a new class, acquiring knowledge of individual pupils and making clear their expectations. The author makes much use of videotapes of lessons with ITET students at an early stage in their course and has frequently received from them the superficial judgement that the lesson shown was "good because the teacher had an easy class". It is not until they have acquired some understanding of the need for careful preparation and techniques for maintaining an orderly, purposeful classroom environment that they fully appreciate the strengths demonstrated in the videotaped lessons they have seen. One important aim in observation, therefore, is to make them aware of the actions practitioners take to bring about successful learning.

(c) Feiman-Nemser and Buchmann (1985) point out that, in their early stages, many students tend to regard the lessons they observe from the point of view of the pupil. They write that "looking at teaching from the perspective of a pupil is not the same as viewing it from the pedagogical perspective, that is, the perspective of a teacher" (p. 257). Observation, therefore, can be helpful in enabling students to think from the point of view of the teacher.

(d) Frequently, trainees at the inception of their school experience have strong ideas about the type of teacher they wish to become. In a study by Furlong and Maynard (1995) of primary and secondary students at the University of Wales in Swansea it was clear that many wished to be seen by their pupils as 'warm', 'friendly', 'caring', 'enthusiastic' and 'popular' teachers. In some cases, they then judged experienced teachers harshly because they fell short of the student's ideals - ideals which they usually abandoned in the light of subsequent school experience. As Furlong and Maynard write, some students believed that they had little to learn from that "miserable old cynic in the corner of the staffroom" (p. 74). Again, observation and discussion of the lessons viewed can help them understand teachers' thinking and the underlying rationale for actions they take.

(e) A not uncommon problem is that students are often keen to embark upon teaching by themselves and to learn from their own experience rather than from observation. They, therefore, tend to dismiss observation as a technique of secondary importance and do not gain as much from it as they could.

(f) In some ITET courses students have sat at the back of the class and made notes without any clear guidelines for their observation. Fish (1995b) feels that observation in a 'naturalistic' manner with no pre-determined criteria can be useful at the outset of school experience. The student watches with an open mind, sees what happens and learns something of the teacher's general role. However, she stresses that this approach is unlikely to have very much value if utilised for too long, and can degenerate into a pointless activity. Without guidance, knowledge of what they are looking for and discussion with staff after the lessson, it is unlikely that they will learn very much.

In view of these problems Shaw (1995) argues that "both trainee and mentor need to receive careful training and preparation early in the school-based period in order to ensure that observation is truly developmental" (pp. 106-107).

II: Students' perceptions of observation

In a small-scale research study undertaken at the University of Wales Institute, Cardiff in January 2002, sixty students following the secondary PGCE route into teaching were asked to complete a questionnaire on their experiences of observation during the first term of their school placement. The main findings are reported under the headings: what students hoped to gain from observation; the procedures they experienced in their schools; the benefits they gained from observation; and the principal constraints. This account will be followed with discussion of good practice in the organisation of students' observation.

(a) **What Students Hoped to Gain from Observation:** The following were the aims which these trainees identified for their observation:

(i) *to observe good practice* in order to help them solve problems they either had or were likely to encounter in teaching their subject. Ninety-three per cent of students felt that this was the principal gain to be acquired from observation.

(ii) *to identify a range of different teaching techniques.* Ninety per cent expressed the view that, through observation of a number of experienced school staff, they could develop their knowledge of teaching methodologies and strategies such as starting and ending lessons, planning and carrying out group work and setting differentiated activities.

(iii) *to understand key aspects of the teacher's role:* Eighty-nine per cent stated that observation was valuable in helping them learn about the role of the teacher. This covered not just the teaching of classes but the pastoral and administrative duties which they would be expected to undertake.

(iv) *to focus upon specific teaching skills:* It was noted by eighty-six per cent of the sample that observation was an excellent means of enabling them to concentrate upon particular skills. From their own experience as pupils they usually realised that teaching involves such techniques as questioning. Observation culminating in discussion with an experienced practitioner enabled them to appreciate the different questioning techniques which can be used, for example,

- reasons for putting questions (to motivate pupils at the beginning of a lesson, to consolidate learning, to uncover incorrect ideas and assumptions, to promote cognitive skills, to acquire feedback and clarify the learning which has taken place, to allow the lesson to proceed at a pace suited to the pupils, to maintain order, to promote personal relationships between the teacher and the pupils and to provide a variety of activities);

- the use of lower order questioning (recall and comprehension) and higher order questioning (application, analysis, synthesis, evaluation);

- questioning skills such as pausing, re-direction and prompting;

- ways of using pupils' responses;

- the use of open and closed questions;

- criteria for an adequate response;

- the need to consider the distribution of questions among members of the class and the involvement of non-volunteers;

- the need to establish routines for pupils' answering so that responses can be clearly heard, for example, requesting pupils to raise their hands if they wish to answer a question and not to speak until they have the teacher's permission.

(v) *to gain insight into ways of organising pupils:* Observing procedures relating to the orderly entry of pupils to the room, seating arrangements and the distribution and collection of equipment were important to eighty-four per cent of students.

(vi) to *gain an understanding of teachers' professional knowledge:* Sixty-five per cent understood that not every aspect of a lesson would be clear to them, because they might not be fully aware of the teacher's philosophy, intentions and aims. Hence, they welcomed the opportunity to talk to the teachers whose lessons they observed and to put such questions as: "Why did you do ..... at that stage in the lesson?" Discussion following observation which leads staff to 'open up their practice' (Hagger, Burn and McIntyre, 1993, p. 41) can be of great value for students.

(vii) to *analyse what is happening in classrooms:* Sixty-four per cent considered that observation, as well as helping them concentrate in detail upon specific teaching skills such as questioning, allowed them to take a wider view of the factors which need to be taken into account in planning and teaching a lesson.

(viii) to *move from a pupil to a teacher perspective:* Observation can help students become aware of major aspects of the teacher's role which they otherwise would take for granted, for example, the need for careful preparation, organisation, control and supervision. By focusing upon pupil activity and behaviour they are able to acquire some understanding of the overall demands of the role. Sixty-three per cent the students saw this as an important aspect of observation.

(ix) to *acquire an understanding of the teacher's standards and expectations:* Fifty-seven per cent of the students believed that an important aim of observation was to familiarise themselves with the standards of conduct and work which their mentors considered to be acceptable. As Brooks and Sikes (1997) note, "students need ... to be helped to observe classrooms from the point of view of the teachers teaching in them" (p. 97). Observation can enable them to understand the relationship between expectations in terms of standards and the amount of work which can reasonably be set in the light of the age and ability of different classes.

(x) to *understand more clearly the standards for qualified teacher status:* Although students identified many advantages in the competency model of ITET, they did not wish in the very early stages of school experience to be overwhelmed with a list of some seventy-six standards set out in Welsh Office Circular 13/98 (Welsh Office, 1998). Consequently, just half the sample saw observation as an opportunity to develop further their knowledge of the QTS standards.

(b) **The Procedures Adopted in Schools for Students' Observation:** Unstructured observation can be used to advantage in the earliest stages of school experience. Its main function is to encourage learning about the overall demands made upon the teacher and to enable newcomers to the profession to "get the feel of the classroom". However, if trainees are to gain the maximum benefit beyond that stage, it is important that they:

- are given a particular focus for their observation. In the survey of UWIC students, examples of focused observation included: the maintenance of an orderly environment; teaching styles; and the ability levels of pupils;

- realise that they are analysing classroom practice with the aim of applying their learning to their own performance with classes;

- are provided with the requisite information about a class and documentation to enable them to make sense of what they observe;

• understand the expectations made of them during the lesson. For example, they may be asked:

    - to write down answers to specific questions,

    - to concentrate upon an agreed section of a lesson only;

    - to observe just one group of pupils.

In the UWIC study eighty-nine per cent of students were able to observe lessons taught to the full age and ability range at their schools. They were all expected to make written records of their observations. Ninety per cent completed these records during the lesson; the remainder made only rough jottings and produced a tidier draft later the same day. In some cases, records were merely brief notes on any useful 'tips' they had acquired. Elsewhere, the following procedures were reported:

(i) *the use of TALLY SYSTEMS,* where the student records all the events which take place in the classroom over a period of time, e.g.

The teacher asks questions. /////////////////////	20
The teacher uses instructions. /////	5
The teacher intervenes in the work of a group of pupils. ///////	7
The teacher revises an important theme in the lesson. ///	3
The teacher uses the board to summarise the main points. ///	3

This type of activity may be useful in the early stages of observation to draw attention to the main aspects of the teacher's role. Sixty-five per cent of students practised this form of recording their observations. In a more sophisticated system described by Wragg (1999, p. 37), a number of teacher activities is listed on the left hand side of the page, while on the right hand side there is a series of boxes representing segments of time, for example, three minutes. The student then ticks each item in the order in which it occurs, so that he/she has a complete chronological record of the events of the lesson.

(ii) *the use of TIME LINES:* Where the focus is timing, pacing or lesson structure, time lines can be helpful. The student draws a line across the page, representing the length of time spent on the activity being studied. Graph paper can be useful in this exercise. Thus, in a modern foreign language lesson, if the focus is *speaking*, a time line could be:

The teacher speaks. _____	_____
An individual pupil speaks. _____	_____
There is teacher-pupil conversation. _____	
There is conversation involving pairs of pupils.	_____
There is conversation involving groups of pupils.	_____
No-one talks. _____	

In the survey of UWIC students it was found that fifty per cent made use of this technique.

(iii) *TARGETING PUPILS:* It is sometimes difficult for students to observe all the activities or contribution of thirty or more pupils, who in the course of the day could be engaged in hundreds of interactions with their teachers and peers. Consequently, it is beneficial for them to select a group of about six pupils chosen from high, medium and low abilities in the hope that they will be representative of the overall class. Each group is then observed in turn or a tally system is utilised to show which pupil is involved in any particular event.

Half the sample used this strategy. Observation was directed at either individuals or groups of up to four children.

(iv) *the use of RATING SCALES:* For example, the student uses the scale: 1= never/almost never; 2 = rarely; 3 = sometimes; 4 = often; 5 = always. He/she then scores items by means of this scale. Examples are:

The teacher uses rapid-fire questions. _____	1 2 3 4 5
The teacher uses redirection in questioning. _____	1 2 3 4 5
Pupils' answers are repeated and developed. _____	1 2 3 4 5
The teacher uses prompting techniques. _____	1 2 3 4 5
The teacher praises a correct answer. _____	1 2 3 4 5
The teacher puts a question directly to a pupil who has not volunteered an answer. _____	1 2 3 4 5
The teacher offers opportunities for pupils to put questions on anything they have failed to understand. _____	1 2 3 4 5
The teacher uses lower order questions. _____	1 2 3 4 5
The teacher uses higher order questions. _____	1 2 3 4 5

Only one fifth of students had any experience of rating scales.

(v) *the use of LOGS.* Logs offer excellent opportunities for focusing observation. The following are examples given by Wragg (1999, pp. 84-85):

Explanations: Write down two explanations given to the whole class, a small group or an individual pupil. Describe the context, the strategy used and the result.

Explanation 1: ....

Explanation 2: ....

Explaining to different pupils: Write down an explanation given to a more able and a less able pupil during the day. In each case note the context, the strategy used and the outcome.

Explanation to more able pupil: ....

Explanation to less able pupil: ....

Sequences: Write down a sequence of between two and five questions that belonged together and followed each other. Record the actual words asked and write brief notes about the reasons behind the sequence and the actual outcome.

Question 1..

Outcome ....

Question 2 ....

Outcome ....

Less than one per cent of the sample had been able to use logs of this type.

(c) **The Benefits of Observation:** Students clearly found many benefits in lesson observation. The main areas in which they felt they had learned were:

- establishing an orderly and purposeful learning environment (all students);

- planning lessons (all students);

- setting activities commensurate with pupils' abilities (ninety-three per cent);

- selecting suitable teaching strategies (eighty-five per cent);

- establishing appropriate teacher-pupil relationships (eighty-two per cent);

- monitoring the pace of a lesson (eighty per cent);

- setting objectives for lessons (seventy-nine per cent);

- planning coherent lesson structures (seventy-nine per cent);

- grouping pupils (sixty-five per cent);

- conducting assessment of pupils' achievements (sixty per cent).

Other benefits reported by individual students were:

- being able to see classes which they were not likely to teach, for example, examination classes;

- being able to learn pupils' names at an early stage in school experience;

- understanding how different teachers operate, especially with respect to pedagogic practice and management strategies;

- appreciating that experienced teachers often face difficulties themselves. One student commented that, after watching the mentor, he was aware that he was not the only person to experience problems with certain classes. This, he added, "was comforting because I knew that the difficulties I encountered were not all my own fault";

- being able to observe a range of lessons taken by one class for a day. As one respondent wrote, it gave him "a real feel for the classroom";

- being able to build up a relationship with a class before they started to teach it. This helped to create a degree of confidence;

- understanding the amount of work pupils could be expected to complete in the course of one lesson;

- acquiring specific ideas for teaching a topic which students subsequently used in their own lessons.

In terms of the apprenticeship model of ITET, UWIC students clearly benefited much from their lesson observation, and similar conclusions have been drawn in research undertaken at schools in partnership with other HEIs. For example, in the survey conducted by Drever and Cope (1999) trainees felt that observation provided a standard at which to aim. It assisted them to identify good practice and to adopt it within their own teaching. Again, Burn, Hagger, Mutton and Everton (2000) show how students' thinking about the complexity of learning and the range of conditions they need to take into account when planning a lesson has been developed over the years by the system of partnership. Trainees, it is argued, are better prepared by their tutors and mentors to undertake observation and, consequently, they derive greater benefits from it. They write that "the staged programmes of observation and teaching tasks in school, combined with structured support in the university to help them analyse their observations and experiences, meant that the student teachers quickly came to appreciate the complex nature of teaching" (p. 276).

(d) **Constraints:** As well as reporting the advantages to be gained from observation, the UWIC students drew attention to a number of constraints:

(i) *the provision of relevant information:* Not all of them were provided with information about the lesson they were expected to observe. Thus, severe limitations were imposed upon their understanding of the contexts within which these classes were conducted. The following chart reveals the respective percentages of students who received relevant items of information:

Item of Information	Percentage of students
• the ability of the class	71
• the specific objectives for the lesson	43
• the overall aims of the unit of work of which the lesson formed part	36
• rules which the teacher had established with the class at the beginning of the school year	34
• the strategies the teacher intended to adopt in the lesson	28
• the structure the lesson would take	15
• previous work which the teacher had undertaken with the class	14
• ways in which the teacher would demonstrate the standards for qualified teacher status	10

It is disconcerting to note that few mentors drew attention to the standards. Whereas students do not wish to be confused with too many aspects of lesson planning in their first days in a school, it should be possible to make reference to some of the main headings, for example, planning, expectations and targets, monitoring and assessment, teaching and class management. Again, understanding can only be enhanced by discussion before the lesson of its main objectives, their relationship to prior learning, the overall structure of the lesson and the pedagogic strategies the mentor intends to employ.

(ii) *the focusing of observation:* Only twenty-eight per cent of students reported that their mentors had set a focus for their observation. Examples of topics upon which they were expected to concentrate were: timekeeping; assessment strategies; the beginnings and ends of lessons; giving the class instructions; using the target language in modern foreign language classes; different learning strategies; and class management. All those students who assumed a focus of this type found the exercise to be advantageous.

(iii) *post-lesson observation discussion:* Fifty-seven per cent of students discussed their observation with the mentor. The others missed the opportunity to put questions, to report their perceptions about the lesson or to engage in reflective dialogue. To a large extent, this is the result of insufficient time allocation for mentors to fulfil their role adequately, a problem which was highlighted in the last chapter.

(iv) *the apprenticeship model:* UWIC students considered that their observations did help them to understand what was happening in the classroom. In the research of Drever and Cope (1999), however, some trainees stated that observation by itself did not always make clear to them the rationale underlying teachers' actions. They sometimes found it difficult to interpret what they saw. Thus, one wrote that "an incident such as shouting out an answer ... was met with a different reaction by each teacher ... sometimes a different reaction in the same classroom depending entirely on which class was being taught. This made my task very hard" (p. 102).

(v) *the competency model:* Of the UWIC student whose mentors did engage in dialogue with them after the lesson, not one reported that the discussion related directly to the QTS standards.

(vi) *the reflective practitioner model:* All the mentors who engaged in post-lesson analysis with their students encouraged them to ask questions, but only thirty-six per cent of students considered that there had been genuine reflection on their part and less than one per cent felt that their mentors had been prepared themselves to reflect critically upon their teaching. Just fifteen per cent of students were required to consult any notes they had made during the observation, and the same small percentage stated that their mentors had made reference to wider educational issues or linked the observation to aspects of teaching covered in the course taken at the HEI.

(vi) *poor practice:* In a few cases students did not consider their mentor to be an ideal role model. One commented that she had witnessed bad behaviour on the part of pupils, which the teacher had failed to correct, and she had been uncertain whether to intervene or not. She also found it very difficult to write an honest appraisal of the lesson for fear of offending this teacher if he read her notes.

(vii) *problems with pupil relationships:* Eight students were unhappy to sit in classes as observers, especially when they were timetabled to teach those classes at a later stage.

Their main fear was that observation would reinforce their role as 'the student'. Three comments received in reply to the questionnaire were:

Pupils know you are a trainee because you observe them.

Sometimes, I felt I was in the way during the lesson, and this made me feel uncomfortable.

The pupils were unclear about my presence in the classroom, and it was hard for me to explain it.

III: Good practice in student observation

(a) **The Need for Clear Aims:** Mentors need to be aware of their aims in providing classroom observation. The list given in section II of students' expectations could be used by members of the mentoring team as the basis for a discussion of their fundamental goals and purposes.

(b) **The Provision of Relevant Information Prior to the Observation:** In order to help students gain the maximum benefit from their observations, mentors need to provide all relevant background information about the classes they will be watching. This will include details of the work the pupils have been undertaking previously, the aims underlying the sequence of lessons, the objectives for the specific lesson to be observed, pertinent details concerning individual pupils, the lesson plan and the principal strategies which will be adopted.

(c) **The Planning of General Observation:** UWIC students agreed that at the very outset of their school experience non-focused observation was valuable in enabling them to reflect upon important elements of the teacher's role and to consider situations which would confront them once they started teaching. To help them in their early observations it may be useful to offer a set of questions to guide their thinking. The following are suggested as examples:

- What are the objectives for this lesson?

- How did the teacher try to achieve these objectives?

- What provision was made for differentiation?

- How was the lesson topic introduced? Did it relate to previous sessions with this class?

- What activities did the pupils undertake?

- What was the role of the teacher during these activities?

- What feedback was offered to the pupils?

- How did the lesson end? Were there opportunities for the consolidation of learning?

- To what extent did the teaching strategies relate to the practices used when I was a pupil?

- If I had taken this lesson, what would I have done that would have been different and why?

- If I had been taking this lesson, what problems would I have encountered? From what I have seen of this teacher's practice, what have I learned that would assist me to avoid those problems?

(d) **The Planning of Focused Observation:** Mentors must agree the focus of the observation with students and consider the ways in which they will record their observations, using tally systems, rating scales, timelines, logs, questionnaires or some other suitable format. Areas for focused observation need to be decided by the mentor and student well in advance of the lesson. Examples are:

- structuring a lesson, for example, strategies used at the outset to arouse interest and motivation, the sequencing of material for the lesson, the transition from one section to another, the nature of the activities set, closure techniques and ways of reinforcing learning;

- lesson objectives, for example, statements of aims which cover the whole unit of work, objectives which establish the outline of the lesson, the relationship between the objectives and the aims, categories of objectives (for example, cognitive, affective and psychomotor), objectives which define deeper learning intentions (for example, researching information, applying previous learning, analysis, synthesis, evaluation), and strategies by which teachers ascertain the extent to which their objectives were achieved;

- the nature of teacher-pupil interaction, for example, listening to pupils' comments, analysing their responses and replying in such a way that learning is developed, types of teacher contact with individual pupils, (for example, whether the contact was initiated by the teacher or the pupil and the subject of the communication);

- activities which develop key skills, for example, exploiting pupils' basic skills in literacy, numeracy and ICT and setting work which requires them to solve problems and to work with others;

- activities which promote thinking skills, for example, information-processing, reasoning, enquiry, creative thinking and evaluation;

- the structuring of information in a lesson, for example, indicating the lesson objectives, signalling transitions, giving clear illustrations of difficult points, explaining complex terminology, summarising key points as the lesson progresses, and checking that pupils have understood the lesson content;

- the nature of differentiation and the ways in which suitable activities are set for pupils of differing ability ranges;

- the nature of feedback to pupils, for example, the use of constructive criticism, ways of developing pupils' ideas and setting appropriate targets to advance learning;

- pupil grouping, for example, the size and composition of groups, any variety in the grouping employed during the lesson, activities conducted by the groups, and the rationale for forming the groups (for example, to set by ability, to develop social skills such as communication and working in a team, to enable pupils to use expensive, specialist equipment in rotation, to encourage peer tutoring, or to allow teachers to concentrate their time on pupils who require support while others practise or consolidate steps previously learned);

- timing and pacing covering the development of the lesson at all stages, for example, entry, settling the pupils down, the time devoted to each section of the lesson, the rules and procedures employed, the nature of the work undertaken by the pupils, the techniques used to supervise pupils' progress throughout the lesson, the types of teacher intervention used where pupils are not working to capacity, methods of clearing away, and exit phases;

- strategies by which teachers endeavour to inculcate in their classes the ability to work independently, for example, setting clear instructions and guidelines for the pupils to follow, providing clear examples, answering pupils' questions and entering time plans on the board.

The nature of the topics depends upon the programme offered by the school and HEI. The suggestion of Mercer and Abbott (1989) that students negotiate topics with their mentors is helpful, Although the focus in their model is upon mentors' assessment of lessons given by students, the same principle can apply to trainees' observation of experienced teachers. Thus, students may negotiate with their mentors a particular focus which they feel will be most valuable to their needs at any given point. This can be especially useful at later stages in a course where they wish to develop expertise in a skill which is relatively unfamiliar to them.

A valuable word of warning is offered by Fish (1995b), who argues that mentors should avoid constructing schedules and checklists for observation which have too many categories, with the result that the student is overwhelmed with detail and cannot 'see the wood for the trees'. Nor, she contends, should observation be focused so tightly that the student loses sight of other important events which may arise in the lesson and merit discussion but which are not listed in the observation schedule.

(e) **Discussion at the End of the Observation to Promote the Benefits of the Three Models of ITET:** It is essential that time is found to enable all mentors to discuss the lesson observed with their students. Areas on which they may concentrate are:

- any questions which the student may wish to put;

- analysis of the lesson. Hagger, Burn and McIntyre suggest discussion which centres upon:

- the teacher's successes or achievements;

- the actions taken by the teacher to achieve her/his objectives;

- the teacher's reasons for taking the action he/she took. This is an important part of any analysis because it allows mentors to 'unpack' their knowledge and to explain not just *what* they did but *why* they did it. In the UWIC research, one mathematics graduate reported that he had experienced difficulties of control with a certain class and had had the opportunity to watch his mentor teach these pupils. Although the lesson proceeded in an orderly fashion, the mentor was quite unable to explain the reasons for this or to suggest ways in which the student could obtain the same outcomes. As a result, he learned nothing of substance and felt that the entire observation had been waste of his and the mentor's time;

- the circumstances and conditions which led the teacher to make a particular decision.

It is, however, also important that:

- reference is made during the evaluation to the main headings of the QTS standards;

- questions are put by the mentor to help the student to reflect. To set an example of good practice, mentors could take the lead by appraising their own teaching along the lines suggested in the first chapter. Students could them be invited to contribute their own observations and judgements, backed up by evidence from events in the lesson. It was noted above that many students found that their mentors were not prepared to analyse their own performance. Perhaps more training is needed in this field so that they are aware of the distinction drawn by Elliott (1991, pp. 309 -318) between 'infallible experts' and reflective practitioners. Infallible experts, it is argued,

- require students to defer to their superior knowledge in identifying, clarifying and resolving the problems they face;

- practise one-way communication. They prescribe courses of action for the student which he/she is expected to adopt. Whereas the student may ask questions to clarify issues, there is little scope to question the superior wisdom of the mentor;

- handle the situation confronting them by the use of specialised knowledge which they have acquired over time. This knowledge can be divided into specific categories;

- apply this specialist knowledge mechanistically in an intuitive manner rather than through reflection.

  Reflective practitioners, on the other hand, who characterise 'the new professional images':

- work in collaboration with their students to identify, clarify and resolve their problems;

- realise the importance of dialogue and empathy with their students to understand the problem from their point of view;

- emphasise holistic understanding of the situation rather than reacting to problems by the application of knowledge subdivided into separate categories;

- reflect upon their own performance.

"Learning to be a reflective practitioner," writes Elliott, "is learning to reflect about one's experience of complex human situations holistically. It is always a form of experiential learning." This is the type of teacher who will best serve the needs of students in the early stages of a school placement.

(f) **Observation to Help Students Solve Problems:** It has been argued that observation can be valuable not just at the outset of an ITET course but at any stage where students experience problems or need to be made aware of a wider range of teaching strategies. In these circumstances it may be useful for them to observe a number of teachers and several different classes. At the end of the observation, with guidance from mentors, they may reflect upon:

- variations and common expectations manifested by the staff they have observed;

- ways in which their own practice has fallen outside the normal range;

- strategies by which they can modify, improve and develop their own teaching skills.

To take an example, at one school in partnership with UWIC, difficulties were encountered by a mature history student who believed that her education at a grammar school, based upon the dictation of notes and regular testing of pupils' ability to memorise facts, was the only approach to teaching the subject. This led to problems of class management, as a diet of instruction and recall questioning failed to maintain the interest and motivation of the younger children. To help the student, the mentor demonstrated the use of group work and the setting of activities in which classes were able to examine historical documents. In dialogue with the student at the end of the lesson he explained the higher quality of learning involved in researching documents, sharing ideas, critically appraising what was read, drawing conclusions and justifying judgements to other people. From this observation and discussion the student revised her views and acquired an understanding of methodologies more conducive to the work of the department.

(g) **The Use of Video Programmes:** Wragg (1999, p. 83) suggests that, as well as observing actual lessons, students may watch videotapes of lessons illustrating specific aspects of a lesson. One approach he favours is the 'interrupted story' where a scene is shown of a critical incident in a classroom and students are required to select one out of three or four options to bring the incident to a satisfactory resolution. Thus, a scene may show a pupil misbehaving, and at the end of the film sequence the viewers are asked to make a choice, for example,

- ignoring the behaviour;

- punishing the pupil;

- re-involving the pupil in her/his work;

- discussing the misbehaviour with the pupil concerned and others.

Once the choice has been made, the students can see on film the outcomes of the course of action which they have prescribed.

(h) Observation Outside the Student's Specialism: Trainees are frequently expected to observe aspects of the school's work other than lessons in their own specialism or age range, for example, teaching strategies employed in a number of subjects and classes or teachers' contact with parents. Observation of this nature is discussed in chapter six.

(i) Record Keeping: Use of the Journal: It can be valuable for students to maintain a record or journal of their observations. This can encourage them to begin to grapple with the task of reflecting upon and learning from experience. As John Loughran (1996, p. 8) writes, "it is anticipated that by writing about experiences, actions and events, student teachers will reflect on and learn from these events. ... [The] purpose of journal writing is to help the writer look back on (or forward to) an event in the hope that it will be a catalyst for reflection".

(j) Code of Professional Practice: Several writers on students' observation have suggest that students be made familiar with a code of professional practice to obviate the problem of their giving offence to teachers by seeming to criticise their lessons. The following draft draws upon several codes practised in primary and secondary schools:

- Both students and mentors should understand that there is no one 'right' approach to teaching any subjects. It is possible that staff in the same school will have different philosophies concerning the interaction of teachers and pupils. Pupil discussion may seem to one teacher to be an excellent vehicle for decision making and the development of team work. Another may judge the same lesson to be 'too noisy'. Some teachers may prefer to explain a point orally on the grounds that instruction is economic in terms of time. Others may consider that it is far more important for children to discover some principle for themselves. Again, a lesson which proceeds at a good pace in the opinion of one mentor may be deemed by another to be too brisk and to fail to offer pupils sufficient time to reflect.

- Students should be fully aware that their presence as observers is a strategy intended to help them develop knowledge and understanding of classroom practice and teaching. If, for any reason, they disagree with what they see their teachers model, they should realise that these teachers have greater experience and that, whereas they are prepared to answer questions about their practices, it is not fitting for them to be criticised in a negative manner by newcomers to the classroom.

- It is beneficial for students to record any questions they wish to put to mentors at the end of a lesson. They can read through this list carefully before discussing the lesson with the teacher. This process of recording may help to ensure that no questions are put to which school staff will take exception. Examples of acceptable questions are:

  - Why did you do ....?
  - What were you seeking to achieve?
  - Did you feel that you achieved what you intended?
  - How else might you have achieved your aims?

- Lesson observation should be confidential between the student, mentor and pupils. In highly exceptional cases, it may be the student's professional duty to report what he/she sees, but in such cases, the ITET co-ordinator should be consulted in the first instance.

- Students should be aware of the overall programme of ITET and understand that they will begin with general, unfocused observation to acquire a 'feeling' for the classroom. After this stage, they need to concentrate upon one or two carefully defined areas linked to their learning targets. They should understand the relationship of what they observe to the QTS standards.

- Agreement between student and mentor should be reached on the ways in which the observation is to be conducted before it actually takes place. Thus, the student should decide, in consultation with the mentor, where he/she is going to sit and whether he/she is to intervene in the lesson at any point.

- At the end of the observation it is only polite for the student to thank the mentor for allowing him/her to be present.

(k) **Deciding When Students Should Move On:** It is important that students are not expected to spend too long a time during their course on observation and that opportunities are provided for them to move to other activities. In the research study undertaken with students at UWIC during the academic year 2001-2002, there was little evidence to suggest that mentors were reluctant to allow them to start teaching once they had undertaken classroom observation. In a survey conducted by Hayes (2001), however, certain trainees located in primary schools felt a sense of frustration because they were expected to continue to observe for a whole half term or more, and believed that they were ready to begin planning and conducting lessons, if only in collaboration with the mentor. Comments received from these students included the following statements:

> *We spent a lot of time up to half term observing and I didn't feel involved. I desperately wanted to have a go* (p. 15).

> *The class teacher was quite receptive to start with, but, as soon as we wanted to plan our own lessons, she was quite hostile and intransigent with such comments as: 'This is my class and my children'* (p. 16).

❯ Points for consideration

1. Read section I (*students' observation of lessons*) and summarise the main problems which have been identified in research into students' observation of lessons.

2. Read section II (*students' perceptions of observation*) and state what you consider the principal aims of student observation to be.

3. Describe the practice at your school with respect to the following items, taking into account the factors discussed in the text.

(a) *observation designed to help the student understand good practice;*

(b) *observation geared to help the student identify a range of teaching and learning techniques;*

(c)   *observation planned to enable the student to understand major aspects of the teacher's role;*

(d)   *observation offered to enable the student to focus upon specific teaching skills;*

(e)   *observation offered to promote understanding of ways of organising pupils;*

(f)   *observation geared to developing an understanding of teachers' professional knowledge;*

(g)   *observation intended to help students analyse what is happening in classrooms;*

(h)   *observation geared to help the student move from a pupil to a teacher perspective;*

(i)   *observation set to develop a sense of the standards which teachers expect;*

j)   *observation linking to the standards for QTS.*

4.   Describe any procedures used at your schools for: (a) students' general observation; (b) students' focused observation, including the use of tally systems, time lines, targeting pupils, rating scales and logs.

5.   Consult students at your school on the advantages and constraints of observation. To what extent do their comments correlate with the list given by the trainees from UWIC? Comment on:

(a)   *the types of observation they found most helpful;*

(b)   *the areas/ standards about which they learned most from observation;*

(c)   *the stage in their course in which the observation took place;*

(d)   *the provision of relevant information about the class;*

(e)   *the focusing of the observation;*

(f)   *the quality of post-observation discussion;*

(g)   *reference to the QTS standards;*

(h)   *the opportunity for reflective practice;*

(i)   *any problems reported with respect to pupil relationships.*

6.   Read section III (*good practice in student observation*) and suggest any strategies which could be utilised at your school to enhance the quality of students' observation of lessons.

7.   List some of the key areas in teaching your subject which could form the focus of students' observation.

8.   Select any *three* of these areas and devise appropriate guidelines which could be issued to students to guide their observation. Where appropriate, make reference to tally systems, rating scales and the other techniques discussed in the text.

9. With reference to your school set out a code of professional practice to guide students' observation of lessons.

10. In the context of your work as a mentor consider the principal advantages and problems associated with the use of video cassettes and audio cassettes in the process of students' observation.

Collaborative teaching

4

a) **From Observation to Collaborative Teaching:** The activities described in the last chapter are beneficial in focusing students' attention upon classroom practices and serve as an excellent introduction to school experience. However, many trainees comment that they find observation more valuable when they can combine it with actual teaching. As Brooks and Sikes (1997, p. 106) note, guided observation of experienced teachers offers the opportunity to develop professional perceptions by analysis and reflection about what happens in specific classroom situations. Collaborative teaching then takes this process further by permitting students to work alongside practitioners and share in the planning, conduct and evaluation of lessons. They can still observe, but now they also assume some personal responsibility for teaching classes.

(b) **Definitions:** The term 'collaborative teaching' can be used in different ways. Examples of techniques commonly used in ITET are:

(i) *Students Teaching in Partnership with Mentors:* Hagger, Burn and McIntyre (1993) define collaborative teaching as "any lesson that has been jointly planned and taught by a mentor and student teacher" (p. 61). In this sense it is a form of team teaching (Geen, 1985).

The degree of collaboration can vary considerably, and Peter Tomlinson (1995) refers to the concept of *progressively collaborative teaching* (PCT) "in which the student engages in teaching with another, usually a more experienced teacher-mentor, initially staying very much within the mentor's framework and undertaking limited aspects of teaching with support, but progressively trying out and taking on a wider range of more extensive aspects" (p. 51).

Whatever the precise role of the student may be, the key elements are that:

• both mentor and student are involved in planning the lesson;

• both are involved in delivering the lesson;

• both have clearly defined roles and responsibilities within that lesson;

• both are involved in an evaluation of the lesson.

(ii) *Students Teaching with other Students:* Various schemes have been implemented in which pairs or small groups of students work together to teach the same class. In some schools students at the same stage of the ITET course have been brought together; elsewhere teams have been created which incorporate trainees from different years, for example, the first and the fourth year of a BEd degree course.

(c) **Underlying Philosophies of Collaborative Teaching:** Maynard and Furlong (1995) argue that collaborative teaching is an excellent example of the *apprenticeship* model of ITET outlined in the first chapter, as the student models him/herself upon the mentor and learns, at least in part, by imitation of that mentor. This is perhaps to ignore the important role which it can play within the other models of ITET - competency and reflective practice. Where students and mentors jointly plan a series of lessons, it is possible for them to make reference to the QTS standards and for the mentor to act as a professional 'coach' by offering guidance and advice derived from her/his experience (Geen, Bassett and Douglas, 1999b).

Many opportunites are also available for mentors to put into practice techniques associated with the reflective practitioner philosophy. Students' understanding can be promoted by requiring them critically to analyse their own performance and that of other practitioners (Schon, 1983; Schon, 1987; Calderhead and Gates, 1993). Schon, for instance, considers that 'reflection-on-action' can best be achieved in contexts in which students and mentors work together in the classroom and jointly evaluate the outcomes. In his 'follow me' model the mentor not only responds to a student's attempts to imitate qualified teachers but also helps him/her by means of skilful questioning to construct meaning from action. Similarly, within his 'hall of mirrors' the teaching of both parties is constantly analysed. (Schon, 1987, p. 298).

In collaborative teaching it is also possible for mentors to practise some of the reflective strategies described by Fish (1995b), Loughran (1995), Arthur, Davidson and Moss (1997) and Ghaye and Ghaye (1998). Indeed, one of the greatest advantages of collaborative teaching is that it enables mentors to set a good example of critical reflection of this type from their earliest contact with students. If they can demonstrate from the outset that analysis of their teaching is something which experienced teachers regularly undertake, it is more likely that students will begin to acquire the characteristics of the reflective practitioner.

In this chapter an account is offered of some of the approaches to collaborative teaching. This is followed by discussion of the main advantages and problems which students have experienced when they embark upon the various models employed in schools. Reference is made both to a survey conducted at UWIC involving undergraduate and postgraduate ITET students and to research conducted at other institutions.

II: Collaborative teaching involving the mentor and the student

(a) The Planning of Collaboratively Taught Lessons: It is important that both the mentor and student are fully involved in making decisions about the aims, objectives, content and teaching strategies to be adopted in the lesson. This process enables the student to:

(i) *realise that lessons need thorough planning.* In the early stages of school experience some students assume that, because experienced teachers do not always set out elaborate lesson notes, planning is an irrelevance. Often, this is reinforced by their naive beliefs about the teaching process. Thus, one student commented in Furlong and Maynard's research (1995) into attitudes on ITET courses that teachers "just teach English, maths and geography - they just get on and do it." Where students have to work together with mentors in planning, they come to understand the need for thorough preparation and the construction of a lesson plan which takes account of the QTS standards.

(ii) *learn from the mentor what he/she takes into account in the planning process,* for example,

- the characteristics and needs of a particular class;

- the time pupils are likely to take to complete a set assignment;

- specific activities which are popular with the class.

(iii) *play a larger part in the decision making process as her/his experience increases.* In the early stages, the mentor is likely to take the lead in the planning process. As the period of school experience develops, the student should take on a more extensive role.

It is of paramount importance that, when planning is undertaken, both mentor and student are fully aware of their respective roles and duties. They need to be clear about which of them is responsible for each section of the lesson and for discipline and control at any particular time. To help them plan, Hagger, Burn and McIntyre (1993) suggest the use of a sheet which incorporates a number of headings: (*See opposite page*)

(b) **Teaching the Lesson: Modes of Organisation:** During the course of the lesson the student should have the opportunity:

- to observe the mentor teach in accordance with the guidelines offered in the previous chapter;

- to teach sections of the lesson him/herself with the mentor in the room to add support;

There is no one standard form of collaborative teaching. Several studies have been made (e.g. Arthur, Davison and Moss, 1997; Geen and Harris, 2002) of the most popular models which appear to be:

(i) *the linear sequence mode,* where the lesson is compartmentalised into discrete sections for each of which either the mentor or the student takes sole responsibility. An example is given by Burn (1992) where the lesson topic is the sinking of the *Lusitania*. The class consists of thirty pupils in year 9.

1. The student settles the class and calls the register. A question and answer session is held to provide a recapitulation on the previous lesson's work - the factual detail of how and when the ship was sunk, and the British press reports of the sinking as 'the foulest act of murder'.

2. The mentor interrupts the student to challenge this interpretation.

3. The student and mentor engage in structured argument, alternating to present different claims, each based on a specific piece of primary evidence.

☐ CLASS:

☐ DATE:

☐ TOPIC:

☐ CONTEXT OF THE CLASS: (i.e. previous relevant knowledge)

☐ LESSON OBJECTIVES/LEARNING INTENTIONS:

☐ TIME:

☐ ACTIVITY:

☐ MENTOR'S ROLE:

☐ STUDENT TEACHER'S ROLE:

☐ RESOURCES NEEDED:

☐ WHOSE RESPONSIBILITY:

☐ FOCUS OF OBSERVATION:

☐ TIME AGREED TO EVALUATE THE LESSON:

The student represents the British viewpoint that the *Lusitania* was an innocent passenger ship unjustly attacked, while the mentor advocates the German viewpoint that the *Lusitania* was carrying arms and was therefore a perfectly legitimate target.

4. The mentor explains that the pupils' task is to complete a chart recording each piece of evidence, the claims it makes and the extent to which it may be regarded as reliable.

5. The student and mentor distribute sheets of evidence to pupils. They circulate to help or advise individuals as necessary.

6. The mentor sums up, explaining that both sides had very different perceptions of the same event and that both sought to exploit it for their own advantage.

7. The student sets the homework: to design a propaganda poster from either the British or the German perspective, using the sinking of the ship to justify their own position and to recruit support.

It is suggested by Hagger, Burn and McIntyre (1993, p. 68) that lessons of this type can be planned in such a way that the mentor has the opportunity to provide brief feedback to the student in the course of the actual lesson, for example, when the class has settled down to an assignment.

(ii) *the teacher and classroom assistant mode,* where the mentor leads the teaching and the student assists (or *vice versa*). The person acting as classroom assistant can then support small groups or individual pupils.

(iii) *the class division mode,* in which the class is divided into two groups which are then taught separately by the mentor and the student for periods ranging from parts of a lesson to the time taken to teach the whole unit of work.

These last two approaches often allow the trainee to participate in micro-teaching, which is an attempt to scale down the normal regime so that he/she can develop and practise a limited range of teaching skills by working with a smaller number of children than is possible in the traditional class of thirty or more. Micro-teaching has been practised in ITET for many years (Olivero, 1970; Brown, 1975; Yeany, 1976). One pattern, outlined by Allen and Ryan (1969), involves the following stages:

1. PREPARATION: The student prepares a short lesson, concentrating upon specific teaching and learning skills in collaboration with the subject mentor.

2. SKILLS: The mentor and the student decide the focus of the lesson, for example, clarity of exposition, questioning technique or class management.

3. CLASS SIZE: They also decide the size of the group, which may vary from three pupils to half the class.

4. TIME UNIT: Decisions are reached concerning the amount of time the student will teach. This could be five minutes to twenty minutes.

5. TEACH PHASE: The student teaches the group and this is recorded on videotape.

6. FEEDBACK: The student receives feedback about the teaching from the mentor, a fellow student or from pupils' response in a questionnaire.

7. RETEACH PHASE: The student has a second opportunity to teach the same topic, taking into account the conclusions reached in the feedback session and any targets which have been set as a result of that session. The lesson is then taken again with a parallel group of children drawn from the same class.

8. DEBRIEFING: Once the student has completed the full cycle, he/she has the opportunity to discuss what has been learned and to reflect upon future strategies.

Two further, slightly different approaches to collaborative teaching described by Arthur Davison and Moss are:

(i) *the pre-teaching observation mode,* where the student watches the mentor teach and then uses the same material with another class. It is highly desirable that this be undertaken with more than one teacher and that the student be fully involved in the planning if the problem of 'cloning' and the worst aspects of the apprenticeship model are to be avoided.

(ii) *the planning/teaching split mode,* where either the mentor or the student plans a lesson which the other teaches. Schon's 'follow me' approach can be adopted where the mentor serves as the role model.

(c) **Debriefing:** At the end of the lesson the mentor and student jointly review and evaluate the lesson, paying particular attention to:

- the extent to which the lesson objectives were achieved;

- the student's teaching skills;

- the mentor's professional knowledge and underlying philosophy. As the period of school experience develops, the mentor will discuss in greater depth her/his rationale for the strategies which were adopted, especially if these deviated from the initial lesson plan;

- issues arising from the discussion which need to be addressed in the planning of subsequent lessons and targets for the student to achieve.

It is important that such discussion be organised as soon as possible after the lesson has concluded. The actual content of the debriefing will depend upon the needs of the student and her/his stage of development. Mentors need to make reference to the QTS standards and to encourage critical reflection of the discursive type. The model devised by Ghaye and Ghaye (1998) can be of advantage, as it takes students through the following five reflective stages:

- descriptive reflection, which is personal and retrospective;

- perceptive reflection, where students recount their feelings about their teaching;

- receptive reflection, where their views are discussed in the light of the judgements of other people. 'Deconstruction' is the process of putting questions to help the mentee become aware of what he/she is doing and why the lesson developed as it did;

- interactive reflection, where discussion centres on the implications of the analysis of the lesson for future action;
- critical reflection, where individual teaching is considered within wider contexts, for example, government demands of teachers and the political structure existing with the school.

(d) **Matching Students' Involvement to their Stage of Development:** The ways in which collaborative teaching are used should vary with the student's experience. In many partnership schemes the following timetable is followed:

(i) *First Weeks of School Experience:* Tomlinson (1995) feels that in the very early stages of school experience mentors and students could begin with the demands of the National Curriculum and the *long term planning* involved in a sequence of lessons (for example, over the current term or half term) and then concentrate upon the lessons immediately ahead, some of which the student would systematically observe and monitor.

In the next phase the student might carry out *restricted aspects* of the teaching. Collaborative teaching offers a protected environment in which he/she can develop the necessary teaching skills. At this stage the mentor is most likely to retain responsibility for the main part of the lesson. The student's role may involve:

- working with individuals

- working with pairs of pupils at a time

- supervising small groups of pupils, e.g.

 - providing tuition for slow learners;

 - providing extension activities for and working with the more able pupils;

- taking short sections of the lesson, for example,

 - introducing the topic and setting targets for the lesson;

 - organising and/or chairing a short whole-class discussion;

 - questioning the class on some section of the work;

 - providing feedback to the class on group activities.

In the early stages mentors need to consider:

- that the student is provided with the opportunity to practise a range of teaching skills;

- that the student's programme of collaborative teaching progresses in a clear sequence and that an array of relevant skills is being acquired;

- that the programme matches the expectations of the partner university or college;

- that the QTS standards are being developed.

(ii) *Later Stages:* As students acquire a greater range of skills and gain in confidence, they are able to take a more positive role in the planning and teaching. The principal aim at this point is not so much to offer a protective element as to enable them to extend their repertoire of teaching skills, for example,

- experimenting with specific teaching strategies such as 'hot seating' in the teaching of drama. Some of these may be strategies which the student has observed experienced teachers utilise. He/she can then plan their inclusion in lessons given in collaboration with the mentor. At the end of the session, the two jointly review the student's ability to adopt these strategies. This type of exercise can be repeated with different teaching styles and techniques.

- joining with other teachers in planning course material for use in a department or with a primary school class. This can be useful as a preparation for a student's role within a school during the induction year.

- developing their own ideas on teaching strategies in collaboration with experienced colleagues.

Again, it may be advantageous for them to engage in collaborative teaching at a later stage in their school experience where this is to the advantage of pupils, for example, having two teachers to lead different sides in a debate or illustrating a conversation in a modern foreign language.

The actual stages adopted in collaborative teaching and the student's progression to individual teaching depend upon such factors as:

- the length of the ITET course;

- the subject area (for example, in science the need to take into account safety in the laboratory);

- the capability and needs of the individual student.

III: Collaborative teaching involving pairs or groups of students

(a) **Pair Work:** Pair work has been employed in a number of university ITET courses in the UK (e.g. Oxford, Swansea, Bangor). Usually, it involves two students from the same course. In some schemes they choose their partners. Elsewhere, HEI tutors decide the grouping. Pair work can be applied to:

(i) *classroom practice* where the students engage in collaborative teaching activities. The usual mode of organisation is to devote one period of school experience to collaborative work and a second to the more conventional system whereby a single student is located with one subject mentor.

In the Swansea University model pair teaching has involved the following:

- *Stage 1:* The students plan jointly, each of them taking responsibility for a part or parts of the lesson.

- *Stage 2:* One student leads and the other acts as an assistant.

- *Stage 3:* One student leads and the other works with individual pupils.

- *Stage 4:* One student teaches and the other observes.

During the lessons specific QTS standards and experiences are targeted, and students work with a wider range of classes than is normal in the early stages of a school placement, for example, SEN groups and years 11, 12 and 13.

(ii) *lesson evaluation:* Where students work in pairs, it is argued (Burt, 1985) that they can exchange ideas and comment on each other's performance, for example, use of body language and terminology. Wragg (1999) strongly advocates this approach. In *An Introduction to Classroom Observation* he gives the example of 'reciprocal pair work' where one student observes the teaching of another in some specific context. Examples are:

- *eye contact:* One student for ten minutes watches the other's use of her/his eyes, for example, to scan the class or make eye contact with individual pupils. The observer makes appropriate notes.

- *pupils who are not engaged in the task at hand:* One student looks for pupils who, for whatever reason, are not tackling the work set. He/she studies one of these for five minutes and makes a record of the activities being undertaken by that pupil.

After the agreed period of time for each observation, the student who has been observing discusses her/his findings with the trainee who has been conducting the lesson. They then exchange roles (Wragg, 1999, pp. 86-87).

(iii) *research*, for example, joint enquiry of some aspect of educational and professional studies or a classroom issue such as evaluating a particular pedagogic strategy.

(iv) *presentations in the college:* Pairs of students can explore and report on educational issues in seminars given either at the school or at the higher education institution.

The philosophy underlying pair work, writes Burt, is that "as student teachers we cannot be taught how to teach, but we can be put in situations where we can learn - particularly from each other". Working in partnership with a colleague in the school is therefore described as "potentially an especially rich framework for exchanging and testing various approaches to teaching. The hope is that, having undergone both kinds of practice, we shall be more aware of own performance and able to evaluate it, more conversant with alternative ideas and techniques and more willing to share our own with our present and future colleagues" (Burt, 1985, p.16.).

(b) **Buddy Systems:** Glover (1996a and 1996b) describes a system employed at the University of Sunderland whereby second year students on a BA(Ed) course in technology were paired with and acted as 'buddies' to less experienced students on the university's PGCE programme. The aim was for the second year students, who had already undertaken school experience, to provide the PGCE students with advice, guidance and support.

(c) **Group Teaching in Discrete Subjects:** In some schemes of ITET small groups of students work in collaboration in the classroom. Thus, Andrews (1997) recounts the experience of mathematics students at Manchester Metropolitan University who operated in groups of three and four. This allowed one to act as the principal teacher, whilst the others served as teachers' aides and general supervisors.

An account is given by Salmons (1997) of another system in which groups of students have worked in collaboration in the teaching of modern foreign languages in schools in partnership with the University of Manchester.

(d) **Group Teaching in Integrated Subjects:** In a pilot project launched at UWIC during the academic year 2000-2001, a number of art and science graduates worked together with primary school pupils on activities designed "to lead to experiential and creative explorations of a range of natural and made phenomena" (O'Neil, 2000). Typical themes were: 'the environment'; and 'growth and decay'.

IV: Research into collaborative teaching: benefits and constraints

Research was conducted at UWIC into the experience of sixty-six undergraduate and 198 postgraduate students of collaborative teaching during the academic year of 2000-2001 (Geen and Harris, 2002). The table below reveals the various models in which they participated:

Percentage of Students	Undergraduate N= 66	Postgraduate N=198
• practising some form of collaborative teaching	100	67
• experiencing the linear sequence approach	77	75
• experiencing the class division approach	74	67
• experiencing the classroom assistant approach	47	53
• engaging in collaborative teaching with the mentor or class teacher	86	84
• engaging in collaborative teaching with another student (pair teaching)	36	55
• engaging in collaborative teaching with more than one student (group teaching)	9	25
• engaging in 'buddy systems'	9	0

The students were asked to comment on the main benefits and difficulties they encountered. Their observations are recorded below:

(a) **Benefits:**

(i) Collaborative teaching with a mentor offers an 'easy way' into school experience, since the student works closely with an experienced practitioner in the initial stages, receives guidance and help in planning, is supported during the actual lesson and has the opportunity to discuss the lesson at the end. Eighty-six per cent of the UWIC sample found it re-assuring to know that the regular teacher was present in the room and that advice and assistance were always available in their early encounters with classes.

(ii) Collaborative teaching offers trainees the opportunity to plan their lessons carefully with a teacher and to understand the factors which they need to take into account. The mentor's thinking is made clear to them, and they can acquire planning skills by working closely with that teacher.

(iii) The teacher and classroom assistant mode was thought by ninety per cent to be an excellent vehicle for learning at first hand about teachers' professional understanding. Where they had been permitted to plan and teach with several members of the school's staff, they were able to experience different approaches and to extend their knowledge of pedagogic styles. Hence, one student commented:

> *I found it useful to teach with experienced teachers and to observe their techniques for dealing with different situations. I was then able to use many of these techniques when I was teaching alone.*

Similarly, one student in the study by Andrews (1997) stated:

> *I observed colleagues with differing styles of teaching and benefited tremendously"* (p. 10).

(iv) The class division model was considered by eighty-nine per cent to be especially helpful as it allowed them to work with small groups and to discover more about the learning process as a result. This advantage has been reported by students in other surveys. One student who was training to teach mathematics within the Manchester Metropolitan partnership stated:

> *With regard to children's learning of mathematics, working with small groups enabled me to observe the children's problem-solving mechanisms and therefore understand their specific misconceptions. As the number of kids in each group was small, it gave opportunities for myself to pick up the more subtle messages of success, exasperation and confusion of the kids* (Andrews, 1997, p. 9).

(v) UWIC students felt that the class division model facilitated the task of memorising pupils' names.

(vi) Over four-fifths of the sample pointed to the advantage that within the linear sequence model they could acquire skills in a progressive manner. In the first weeks of their school placement they were able to focus upon specific parts of a lesson and still take a holistic view of pupils' learning. As their confidence increased, they could plan with the mentor a more extensive role and practise a wider range of skills. This gradual initiation into classroom procedures was particularly appreciated, since they could concentrate upon any standards which they felt they especially needed to develop, while receiving the requisite support. For example, some drama students found it difficult to assess pupils' performances consistently. Collaborative teaching offered them the opportunity to discuss marking criteria with the mentor, to observe members of the department when they evaluated pupils' performance and to have their own judgements moderated.

The opportunity for students to develop skills in a progressive manner has been stressed by other researchers. Tomlinson (1995) points to the advantages of *scaffolding* whereby support is provided which is gradually removed only as the student becomes independently capable. Hagger, Burn and McIntyre (1993) give the example of a student's acquisition of skills in questioning. The questions which she was going to put were discussed in considerable detail, particularly their relationship to pupils' previous knowledge and the level of language with which they could cope. This discussion allowed the student to learn from her mentor about the class's capacity to cope with different types of questions and helped in her planning. Consequently, in a lesson delivered at the beginning of her experience, she had sufficient questions to ensure that she did not 'dry up', as had been feared. Nor did she encounter a sea of blank faces, as she was able to pitch the material at the appropriate level.

Skills which can be the subject of focus in the linear sequence model include:

- speaking to the whole class – clarity of exposition inthe setting of appropriate tasks;

- organising a practical activity;

- supervising and/or chairing a whole class discussion;

- planning for smooth transitions between the sections of the lesson;

- working with slow learners;

- providing extension activities and working with the abler pupils;

- managing a small group discussion;

- questioning;

- using audio-visual materials.

(vii) Where students have concentrated upon a specific teaching skill in a collaborative situation, they are in a relatively strong position to discuss the teacher's philosophy and professional knowledge after the lesson. As the student has actually practised that skill and been involved in planning the whole lesson, he/she is better able to question the teacher than would be the case after observation of the type described in the last chapter.

(viii) As well as being of benefit to themselves, eighty-six per cent of UWIC students affirmed that collaborative teaching had been advantageous to their pupils. The presence of more than one adult in the classroom meant that a more extensive array of teaching strategies could be employed than was normally the case. It was possible for mentor and student to lead opposing sides in debates on controversial topics, inviting pupils to contribute their views. In language classes, smaller groups had been formed and a greater number of pupils had engaged in conversation directly with a teacher.

(ix) Collaborative teaching can be of value to mentors, helping them with their own professional development by giving them the stimulus and time to reflect upon their own classroom teaching. In a survey of the main benefits and costs of partnership involving seventy-five mentors, ninety per cent put professional development as the principal advantage. The evaluation of lessons, whether taught by themselves or by students, was seen to be an excellent vehicle for reflecting upon good practice. Where classes were taken jointly with trainees and discussion followed of the rationale underlying the approaches adopted, mentors had to justify their thinking and in some instances this led to a re-appraisal of policy (Geen, Bassett and Douglas, 2000).

(x) Of the students who engaged in pair and group teaching with their peers, seventy-nine per cent appreciated the opportunity to share ideas during lesson planning, which, they claimed, helped them refine their thinking about the delivery of a topic, while seventy-two per cent felt less apprehensive about facing a class at the commencement of their school experience when there was at least one other student in the room.

Similarly, one ITET co-ordinator in partnership with UWIC commented that the main benefits of this approach for students were:

- stress reduction;

- the opportunity to pool resources and ideas;

- the sharing of the workload;

- the provision of peer support and reassurance, which could help build confidence; and

- the detection and resolution of classroom problems as the result of enhanced supervision.

(xi) Seven of the nine respondents who participated in 'buddy systems' found the experience to be valuable. Where they worked with older trainees, they were able to learn from their more extensive experience. One first year drama student paid tribute to the fourth year student who helped her settle in by giving helpful guidance on "everything from class management to getting along with the mentor". Nor were the advantages of the 'buddy system' confined to the less experienced members of the pair or group. Undergraduates in the last year of their course stated that acting as advisers to total newcomers to the classroom had required them to clarify their own thinking about lesson objectives, teaching strategies and modes of assessment. It had also helped them develop their communication skills.

(xii) The project in which art and science specialists worked together in the primary school was judged by the majority of participants to have been an exciting learning experience for their pupils. Knowledge, it was noted, does not always divide into neatly separate compartments and topics such as 'the environment' and 'growth and decay' can be investigated from the perspective of both these disciplines. Agreement was expressed with the proposition that in science "illustrations are not frills or summaries; they are foci for modes of thought" (Gould, 1991, p. 171). Furthermore, as a result of this teamwork many students extended their own knowledge of concepts and validation procedures pertinent to curricular areas other than those in which they had been formerly trained.

(b) **Constraints:**

Despite these encouraging comments, it was apparent that a number of problems could be identified. These can be most conveniently categorised under four main headings.

(i) *Failure of mentors to exploit the benefits of collaborative teaching:* In a significant number of schools the programme of collaborative teaching was not well organised with the result that the strengths associated with the apprenticeship, competency and reflective practitioner models were not always exploited. Specific problems were:

- About a third of students felt that certain of the school staff with whom they engaged in collaborative teaching did not always share their professional knowledge. Whereas trainees' presence in the classroom had been welcomed, they had been treated primarily as an 'extra pair of hands' rather than learners. Discussion during planning and evaluation sessions was brief and peremptory, and, although these students were allowed to work with and observe experienced teachers, their mentors often neglected to discuss with them the rationale underlying their choice of methodologies. Observation without interpretation, as Burn (1992) has noted, can be of only limited value.

- A significant number of teachers failed to model good practice. A quarter of PGCE and forty-four per cent of undergraduate students reported that their mentors did not plan lessons adequately, which created difficulties since important details of content and organisation had not been determined beforehand. One teacher seemed to be reluctant to prepare lessons, his policy for classes taken on a Friday afternoon being to distribute photocopies of texts which the pupils were required to read for the entire lesson. Such activities are unlikely to extend students' understanding of effective learning and teaching.

- At a small minority of schools staff expected students to become 'clones' of themselves. One undergraduate claimed that her mentor rigidly imposed his views and was reluctant to accept that any ideas other than his own could be valid. Another mentor had given the strong impression that she deemed it an impertinence for newcomers to the classroom to suggest approaches which she had not herself previously adopted. This attitude had created an unpleasant atmosphere and discouraged the trainee from contributing further to lesson planning. A third respondent was left in little doubt that the receipt of a positive lesson evaluation was dependent upon close imitation of the teacher's classroom style.

- Two-thirds of the sample believed that they did learn about teaching skills, but in only fifteen per cent of schools did their mentors regularly make reference to the QTS standards set out in Welsh Office Circular 13/98. Moreover, opportunities were lost in many schools for students to work with the full ability range, although this was an expectation of the Circular (Welsh Office, 1998, p. 11). Just over half were directed in the class division approach to concentrate their attention upon groups of pupils with special educational needs. Far fewer (twenty-six per cent), however, were able to undertake extension work with abler children, even though the provision of a curriculum designed to challenge the most talented is currently an educational priority (DFEE, 2001b, p. 51).

- Nor was the students' programme always organised in a progressive manner or designed to meet the needs of individuals. Fifty-five per cent reported that, where they had reached a plateau and needed to experiment with fresh ideas, they were given little incentive in joint lesson planning to consider alternative strategies.

- As for critical reflection, fifty-eight per cent of mentors did expect students to review collaboratively taught lessons, but only thirty per cent asked specific questions or encouraged systematic analysis. Over half the respondents considered that the school staff with whom they worked were not keen to submit their own teaching to any form of evaluation by students and even fewer mentors were prepared to reflect upon their own specific contribution to the lesson. Of the practices advocated by Schon, less than half the students had experienced the 'follow me' approach and thirty-eight per cent 'hall of mirrors'. Only twenty-one per cent had been able to participate in discursive as opposed to pragmatic dialogue. Where initial planning had been of an *ad hoc* nature, lesson evaluation tended to be dominated by discussion of deficiencies which could have been avoided with greater forethought, and little time was left for probing deeper educational issues. One student described a highly unfortunate experience:

> *My mentor was unwilling to give advice before the lesson or help with the planning, but seemed to enjoy evaluating my part of the lesson and picking up on the problems afterwards. Many of these difficulties could have been avoided if we had prepared properly beforehand. Often you feel as if all you receive is criticism and negativity.*

(ii) *Time constraints:* In many instances, though mentors set a good example themselves and were anxious to engage with students in collaborative activities, they lacked the time to provide the degree of support they considered to be desirable. At just over half the schools provision was made within mentors' timetables for meetings with students in which joint planning and lesson analysis could take place; elsewhere discussion had to be squeezed in between lessons or held whenever both parties were free. Since the majority of mentors were either heads of subject departments or members of the senior management team who had to attend to other administrative duties, severe limitations were imposed upon the time they could devote to sessions with trainees.

(iii) *Students' relations with mentors and pupils:* Although they were aware of the advantages of collaboration, some students were evidently uncomfortable when they were required to teach with another adult in the same room. Sixty-eight per cent admitted that they considered the presence of the mentor in the vicinity to be inhibiting and stated that they preferred to work by themselves from the very outset. One respondent acknowledged that she felt nervous and lacking in confidence whenever she shared a lesson with her mentor, adding that her teaching invariably improved the moment that person left the room. Others pointed to the tendency of some pupils to view them merely as assistants, even when they assumed sole responsibility for the entire class.

A further cause of concern was that, where lesson planning had been rushed, pupils were sometimes uncertain whether the regular teacher or the student was in charge. As one postgraduate noted, many younger children need a definitive authoritative figure to whom to respond and wished to know which adult was assuming that role. Again, it was apparent that the expectations of certain students concerning pupils' behaviour, in terms, for example, of the amount of noise permitted, differed substantially from those of the mentor.

In a few extreme cases the impression was formed that trainees were not really welcome in the department. Thus, one undergraduate wrote that:

> *My mentor had very little time for students. He was*
> *unco-operative and stubborn, and so there was never*
> *any proper planning in collaborative teaching. I did*
> *not really know what I was supposed to be doing in*
> *a lesson. He would start it off and then tell me to take*
> *over. I had to improvise and think on my feet all*
> *the time. I can't say that I learned very much from the*
> *experience except the importance of planning*
> *beforehand.*

Two others were unhappy that mentors constantly interrupted them during those sections of the lesson which had been assigned to them or undermined their authority by contradicting them in front of the class.

(iv) *Problems in pair and group teaching:* Several issues were raised:

- Difficulties arose when students working in pairs or groups failed to co-operate. Disagreement about aims and strategies created stress and hindered progress. Hence, one student commented that the planning involved in a group practice took far longer and was much more complex than the preparation she had undertaken on other placements where she had taught independently. Similar findings are reported by Burt (1985, p. 28) and Andrews (1997, p. 8). Typical comments received from students in Andrews's survey were:

> *The planning kind of fell apart with one person taking*
> *over and everyone else not exactly giving up, but not*
> *being allowed to join in.*

> *Group planning can get bogged down in discussions*
> *and differences of opinion.*

- Occasionally, trainees believed that there had been an unfair distribution of labour. One undergraduate had been expected to produce all the plans for a series of lessons simply because he possessed a computer. As a result, once the class arrived, he felt that he was well prepared, but his partners were not always sure of the direction the topic was to take and this led to unsatisfactory delivery. Certain students, it was alleged, sought to allocate to the other members of the group those aspects of a lesson which they did not themselves wish to teach.

- The presence of a very weak student was another source of anxiety. A member of one team, it was reported, sometimes abandoned his contribution after only a few minutes. This meant that the others had to intervene and assume roles for which they had not prepared.

- At some schools, once a lesson was underway, an element of unhelpful competition could be discerned and certain pupils, sensing this, had tried to play one student off against another.

- Where groups contained trainees from different years of undergraduate courses, some of the older students felt that they were under pressure to prove themselves to be superior teachers. The younger group members also experienced a degree of confusion when they were offered advice by these students which contradicted the guidelines they had received from their subject mentors. Students participating in 'buddy systems' in schools in partnership with the University of Sunderland have reported similar findings (Glover, 1996b).

- An ambitious project carried out by one group required a considerable degree of planning and preparation, but the members of that group lived too far apart to meet in the evenings or at weekends on a regular basis. As a result, they felt that the unit of work they taught was less effective than they would have liked.

- Whereas the collaboration of PGCE art and science students was welcomed in principle, difficulties were encountered in determining the topics which the pupils were to pursue since the two groups, as the result of logistical and timetabling constraints, did not commence their primary school placements at the same time.

- It was noted that fewer students seem to have undertaken detailed evaluation of their teaching when they were involved in pair and team teaching than when they taught with school staff. Whereas sixty-one per cent assessed lessons taken with mentors and fifty per cent judged this activity to have been of value, the respective percentages for lessons shared with their peers were only forty-one and thirty-two.

V: Recommendations for future practice

In order to develop further the strengths of collaborative teaching and to alleviate the constraints recounted by the students in this sample the following strategies are recommended.

(i) *The preparation of mentors:* It is of vital importance that collaborative teaching is organised in schools in such a way that students gain the maximum benefits claimed for the three philosophic models of ITET. To achieve this goal all mentors need to understand these models and the ways in which techniques of collaboration can be employed to best effect. Accordingly, it is suggested that, when mentors make decisions about the programme to be initiated for the early stages of students' school experience, they should take account of the following principles:

- At the very outset collaborative teaching should enable students to observe their mentors modelling good practice. Subsequent dialogue should be a genuine learning experience for students. Hence, mentors should be prepared not just to offer advice and 'teaching tips' but also to discuss their professional knowledge analytically and to examine the deeper educational thinking which underpins the procedures they demonstrate.

- Due attention must be paid to the standards required by central government during lesson planning and evaluation. Mentors need to understand that, whatever criticisms have been advanced of the competency model of ITET (McCulloch, 1994; Richards, 1999), the vast majority of students valued the establishment of criteria which pinpoint the skills they are required to master. Students commended the practice of those mentors who organised the appraisal of lessons taught jointly with them under the headings of Welsh Office Circular 13/98.

- The programme of collaborative teaching should ensure the gradual and progressive acquisition of knowledge and skills. As students' expertise develops, they should be able to play a more extensive role in the planning of lessons and experiment with a range of learning strategies. Where the class division model is employed, they should be encouraged to gain experience of teaching groups of widely differing abilities. When students are based with one teacher for a lengthy period of time, there is the danger that they may model themselves too closely on that one person. Ideally, they ought to engage in collaborative teaching with at least two different teachers who demonstrate contrasting styles.

- From the first lesson mentors should set an example of reflective practice by ensuring that their own contribution is fully evaluated as well as that of the student. It is highly desirable that they possess some knowledge of 'hall of mirrors' and other practices which are designed to promote reflection-on-action. There is evidence from this and other surveys reported in later chapters to suggest that the majority of mentors have very limited understanding of the literature available on reflective practice and that opportunities for stimulating students' learning through critical thinking about their teaching are lost.

- During collaborative teaching students should be offered a supportive environment in which they feel comfortable when working with school staff. The attitude of teachers is as important as the implementation of formal procedures for students' experiences, especially at the beginning of an ITET programme when many trainees are lacking in confidence.

Several options are available for improving the quality of mentoring along these lines. Courses can be organised by tutors at higher education institutions (HEIs) for at least one mentor from each partnership school who can in turn offer appropriate training to her/his colleagues. Alternatively, school staff can take the initiative and the ITET co-ordinator can arrange in-service provision for mentors. Again, training materials of the type produced by the Local Education Authorities in Association with HEIs (1993a and 1993b) can be used to advantage.

(ii) *Allocating time for mentors:* Lack of time is one of the key constraints upon the role of the mentor. Joint planning and evaluation which result in genuine reflection and deep understanding cannot be accomplished without the provision of adequate 'protected time'. This has resource implications and brings us back to the suggestions which were advanced in the second chapter for improving the current regime

(iii) *Selection and briefing of students:* Where schemes of pair and group teaching are employed, it is important that the students involved are carefully chosen and given clear instructions concerning the need to define precise responsibilities, to rotate roles and to ensure that everyone makes a worthwhile contribution. One group of PGCE students considered that their group practice had been especially valuable since they had undertaken meticulous preparation, deciding who should lead each lesson and checking that every other member of the team was fully occupied in a subsidiary role. In another placement, a team of art students had taken advantage of the fact that each of them possessed a different area of expertise within the subject; their planning had ensured that these skills had been fully integrated into the activities which were set for the pupils.

To assist students working in pairs and groups, a programme has been implemented by mentors at one school in South Wales (Smallwood, 1997). In the first sessions trainees learn about each other's backgrounds, the courses of study they have pursued and their general interests. The ITET co-ordinator helps them to understand what the role of the teacher entails and stresses that teamwork is one of the QTS standards. Discussion then ensues of conflicts which can arise over teaching styles and preferred ways of working and difficulties which are created when students overrun their time in a short lesson. Consideration is also given to ways of handling annoyances and frustrations with partners, listening to other students' viewpoints, sharing ideas and supporting each other.

In this school, the importance of joint evaluation at the end of lessons taught by pairs or groups is very much emphasised, and, to promote this aspect of collaborative teaching, specific guidelines are offered on the nature of feedback. Trainees are instructed to begin with the positive and to focus, in the early stages, upon those aspects of the lesson which can be fairly easily assessed, for example, timing, eye contact and clarity of exposition. Later on, they are expected to consider such deeper issues as the quality of pupils' learning and the inculcation of desirable attitudes to learning. They are also instructed to provide evidence to support any judgements they make about their colleagues' teaching. Careful supervision of all pair and group teaching is undertaken by the school's mentors, who then discuss its progress in their weekly meetings with the co-ordinator.

(iv) *The need for flexibility:* A degree of flexibility is essential in any system of collaborative teaching. The actual programme to be offered to the student is dependent upon such factors as her/his knowledge, level of skills and capability. The degree of autonomy required by trainees also varies, and to insist upon a rigid pattern can sometimes be counter-productive. As one UWIC student commented:

> *Using collaborative teaching at the beginning of my school experience was extremely helpful, but, as I grew in confidence and so did my partner, we were ready to go our separate ways. We felt that four weeks of pair teaching would have been just right. Six weeks was too long.*

Consequently, it is desirable for mentors to consult students and to negotiate with them the activities which best suit their needs.

> Issues for consideration

1. Read section I (*collaborative teaching in ITET*) and define in one sentence the meaning of 'collaborative teaching'.

2. Read section II (*collaborative teaching involving the mentor and student*) and devise a lesson in your area of expertise which could be developed by you and a student together at an early stage in the student's school experience. Use the headings indicated:

(a) *planning:* overall course aims; lesson objectives: pupils' previous relevant knowledge; differentiation; demands of the National Curriculum (where appropriate); quality of learning issues; resources; risk assessment; lesson structure (introduction, development, and closure);

(b) *your aims for the student's development in the lesson;*

(c) *the respective roles fulfilled by yourself and the student in the lesson;*

(d) *key points you would stress to the student in planning this lesson* (e.g. any characteristics and needs of the class, timing issues, class management, specific activities which are popular with the class);

(e) *key issues you would expect to address in debriefing.*

3. Describe the practice adopted at your school with reference to:

(a) *students working with individuals:*

(b) *students working with pairs of pupils.*

(c) *students supervising small groups of pupils:*

(d) *students taking short sections of the lessons:.*

4. In the light of the criteria for progressively collaborative teaching (e.g. that the student is provided with the opportunity gradually to extend her/his teaching skills), list any changes which could be made to your school's programme.

5. Briefly describe any strategies adopted at your school for collaborative teaching in the case of students who are at the later stages of their school experience.

6. Read section III (*collaborative teaching involving pairs or groups of students*) and in the context of your school list any advantages and limitations you can identify in adopting these practices:

(a) *pair teaching;*

(b) *buddy systems;*

(c)   *group teaching in discrete subjects;*
(d)   *group teaching in integrated subjects.*

7.   State any advantages for mentoring in your subject area which you can identify in the different models of collaborative teaching discussed in this chapter.

8.   Read section IV (*research into collaborative teaching: benefits and constraints*) and section V (*recommendations for future practice*), and, in the light of the arguments presented, set out what you consider to be the optimum model for collaborative teaching for the students to whom you act as mentor.

9.   Read the following statements made by students involved in pair teaching. If you were a mentor with responsibility for these students, what steps would you take to resolve the tensions they report?

(a)   ***My partner is unco-operative and cannot take criticism; he fails to bring me into the planning, but instead says the ideas are in his head, and writes them down an hour before the lesson. We had an argument before going to school when I criticised his original plan ... His other ideas weren't much better. ...the main problem regarding team-teaching between NH and myself, I think, is that NH works hard and ferrets out basically good ideas from the literature, but does not discuss these ideas with me so (a) the idea is not as well-planned and developed as it could be, (b) there is not as much harmony between us as there should be, (c) the class-presentation is not as professional as it should be.***

The failure of NH to discuss the idea with me is difficult to understand; there may be some kind of personality clash going on under the surface. Maybe he's too touchy over any kind of criticism. Maybe he's never experienced this kind of co-operation before (Burt, 1985, p. 28).

(b)   ***Faced by a pair team-teaching situation, my colleague and I began by working together closely in our preparation for a full lesson. ... However, after days of exhausting lesson preparation we regretfully decided that, although the pupils no doubt had a lot to gain from this integrated approach, we just hadn't the time or patience to work so closely together without fraying our tempers*** (Burt, 1985, p. 32).

(c)   ***I found that I had planned the team taught lessons, but my partner was happy to take all the credit for them. This was very frustrating since I felt that I was carrying that person. I appreciate that we should learn to work with people we don't get on with, but***

we are eighteen or nineteen and on our first school placement (UWIC undergraduate student).

5 Supporting students' teaching

I: Research into students' experiences

After engaging in observation and collaborative teaching, students begin to teach whole classes themselves under the supervision of their mentors. Progress is to be assessed in the light of the QTS standards. Over the last few years, several research studies have been published which highlight difficulties they frequently face. This chapter begins with a summary of some of these studies, since they raise important issues of which mentors need to be aware.

(a) **Class Management:** Trainees sometimes encounter problems for the following reasons:

(i) They begin their school experience with unrealistic perceptions of the nature of teaching and class management. Furlong and Maynard (1995) suggests that many embark upon an ITET course at the stage of 'early idealism'. Their ideas are fragmentary, simplistic and based upon notions derived from their own experience as pupils. Often, they have formed an opinion of what constitutes good teaching on the basis of memories of teachers who influenced them most. These views are usually highly idealistic.

Other studies have reached similar conclusions. Thus, one student quoted in the survey of Arthur, Davison and Moss (1997) gave the following as a reason for wanting to teach: "If I can inspire pupils to be amazed by what a fantastic world they are part of, to enjoy their lives no matter what they are or become, then I might start considering myself as a teacher" (p. 79). Again, Calderhead and Shorrock (1997) in research focusing upon twenty PGCE primary students noted that their conception of the teacher's role was often coloured by a strong sense of social justice.

(ii) Most teachers establish their authority at the outset of the school year before the students begin their placement, and so trainees do not have the opportunity to observe or to be involved in this process. By the time they join the school, their mentors have explained, justified and enforced their rules, and are at a stage where they are able to enjoy a more relaxed relationship with their classes. Trainees, perhaps unaware of the importance of establishing rules at the beginning of the year, immediately try to emulate this warm relationship, and this leads to problems once they start to teach without assistance from the mentor. Students in a survey conducted at UWIC over the academic year 2001-2002 pinpointed as a constraint the fact that they were not always aware of the rules and routines teachers had established at the start of the term. As a consequence, they were not clear about the expectations they should have for their classes in terms of behaviour, and were unsure which rules they ought to impose. Nor were they always able to anticipate the ways in which children were likely to respond to their instructions.

(iii) Many UWIC students stated that they were not informed by their mentors of pupils in their classes who had been statemented for emotional and behavioural difficulties. Nor were they given copies of any appropriate individual education plans. This created problems in the management of classes containing children with special educational needs.

(iv) Whereas most teachers realise the need to become 'larger than life' on their first encounters with a class and of putting over their rules in a business-like manner, students often feel inhibited because of their lack of experience. Sometimes, the presence of the regular teacher is a further factor which prevents their adopting this business-like approach in their first lesson with a class. As one student stated, "you're conscious of asserting your authority all the time because the teacher's there and you think - that's her responsibility" (Furlong and Maynard, 1995, p. 108). Similarly, whereas experienced teachers use a whole range of strategies to maintain a purposeful working environment other than merely establishing classroom rules, for example, the use of body language, intonation, pauses or the use of the right word, students are often unfamiliar with techniques of this type or are reluctant to employ them, feeling that they are the 'property' of that teacher. There is, therefore, sometimes a degree of reluctance to imitate established teachers.

(v) Although students are often advised not to be too friendly, at least in the early stages of a school placement ("Don't smile at them until Christmas"), many find this precept difficult to follow.

(vi) Furlong and Maynard show that in the stage of early idealism many students genuinely want to be seen as 'warm', 'friendly', 'enthusiatic' and 'popular'. However, where they begin by being too friendly and pupils take advantage of them as a result, they react with anger and frustration. Some students in the Swansea research complained to bored children that they considered them to be ungrateful for failing to respond to all the trainee's hard work. One commented: "I feel very insecure and angry. ... It's because you're being ignored. It's the fact that you're there - you're speaking to them and they're all carrying on ... they can't do this to me."

Some students become annoyed with pupils for making them assume a personality they do not find attractive. Thus, one stated: "You do scare yourself sometimes with what you can do." In certain cases they argue that they will not abandon their ideals of friendliness, but they will "postpone them" for the time being.

(vii) Where mentors have not prepared them adequately, common mistakes made by students are:

- adopting an overly confrontational style which has a negative effect upon the class;

- enforcing their rules inconsistently. Some students state their rule that pupils should be silent when they, as teachers, are speaking, remind offenders of it when it is broken on the first and perhaps second occasion, and then ignore further breaches of the rule. The class gradually becomes more and more disorderly, and, when the noise is unbearable, they again seek to impose a rule which has been repeatedly broken throughout the lesson;

- making demands which their teachers do not feel are acceptable, for example, threatening to keep the whole class in at break every day for a week for the misdemeanours of a small number of pupils;

- making idle threats;

- becoming engrossed with the work of individuals and failing to scan the class to detect problems before they become serious;

- embarking upon the introduction to their lessons before all pupils are listening;

- being unsure when to intervene. Furlong and Maynard show that some students in their sample tended to ignore pupil misbehaviour, while others constantly 'nagged' a class by insisting upon too many rules;

- failing to analyse the problems they face and trying to rationalise disruptive behaviour with comments such as: "This class is naturally disruptive. I don't think it is me."

(b) Teaching Strategies:

(i) Some students begin with false assumptions about teaching and learning. They take a very simple-minded view of the teaching process, believing that it consists primarily of instruction. Effective learning is thought to be recall and remembering. Typical comments in Furlong and Maynard's survey were:

> *I thought teaching was about standing at the front,*
> *because that's what I remembered.*
>
> *I'm doing pollution; so I'll look it up in all these books*
> *and now I'm an expert on it. So I'm going to tell you*
> *... it's definitely there.*

As Calderhead and Shorrock (1997, p. 162) note, understanding about children's learning can be a slow process. Whereas most students understand the importance of motivation, the following problems are not uncommon in the early stages of their teaching:

- failure to take account of pupils' prior learning and to differentiate accordingly;

- inability to create contexts in which pupils can see the relevance of the learning;

- the imposition of students' own structure of understanding on pupils and failure to help them to make sense of what is being taught;

- inability to break a concept down into simpler parts and to explain and illustrate principles with meaningful examples at an appropriate level;

- failure to structure material in a logical sequence or to make cross-reference to knowledge the pupils have acquired in other contexts;

- the tendency to rush through whole-class exposition without giving sufficiently explicit instructions about the tasks to be undertaken. The pupils are then left confused, because they do not comprehend the student's expectations;

- failure to use pupils' responses in a structured manner so that clear conclusions can be reached;

- the tendency to be over-prescriptive in their expectations, as a consequence of which pupils are sometimes unable to learn in their own way.

(ii) In some instances students are overly influenced by their experiences as pupils. At one school in partnership with UWIC, the ITET co-ordinator has described the difficulties which can arise when certain mature student believe that the education they received, usually at selective schools, is the only possible approach and must be applied to all the pupils they meet. One of these endeavoured to impose upon a class of low ability children a regime of discipline which would have been more acceptable in the 1950s, and openly criticised mentors who tried to offer her constructive advice, branding them as 'progressive' and 'trendy'.

(iii) Because of the disciplinary problems they encounter, some students are reluctant to deviate very far from the teaching methods of instruction and close supervision of individual work. In this way, they can feel they can maintain control more effectively, as the children are either paying attention to them or working directly under their observation. Hence, they tend to dominate the lesson and severely restrict the range of learning opportunities offered to pupils.

(c) **Assessing Pupils' Achievements**: Research was undertaken by Geen, Bassett and Douglas (2001) during the school year1998- 1999 of students' ability to meet the standards for assessment outlined in Welsh Office Circular 13/98 (Welsh Office, 1998). The sample involved 230 secondary PGCE students at UWIC and the same number of students pursuing primary PGCE and BA(Ed) courses. Evidence was also submitted by 102 mentors. In addition interviews were held with twenty-one mentors and further information was acquired from analysis of teachers' written reports of thirty-four lessons and seventeen oral debriefings of trainees' teaching recorded on audio-cassette. The key findings were:

(i) *Achievement of the Standards:* Most mentors felt that by the end of the course their students were successful in the following standards. These were also the standards in

Percentage of students meeting the standard:		
	Primary	Secondary
• applying the school's assessment procedures for marking classwork and homework	88%	88%
• providing valuable feedback, both orally and in writing	80%	79%
• recording pupils' progress	81%	79%

(ii) *Difficulties and constraints:* Some difficulties were noted with respect to the other standards and it is possible to link these to five main causes:

(1) OPPORTUNITIES WHICH WERE NOT AVAILABLE TO STUDENTS: Some secondary students had been unable to meet all the standards because their placement schools did not cater for pupils beyond the age of sixteen-plus or the range of syllabuses on offer was limited. Thus, only thirty-one per cent acquired first-hand experience of assessment within examination courses for pupils aged sixteen to nineteen, and a mere four per cent gained familiarity with the newer vocational courses. The timing of school placements did not allow more than six per cent of secondary and twenty-four per cent of primary students to play a part in the preparation of reports for parents.

(2) RESOURCE ISSUES: THE TIME FACTOR: Standards in which students were judged to have experienced problems are shown in the table below:

Percentage of students meeting the standard:	Primary	Secondary
• setting appropriate learning targets based upon assessment of pupils' acheivments	36%	37%
• using records to inform lesson planning	30%	38%
• using the outcomes of assessment to intervene purposefully in pupils' learning	47%	42%

These were areas in which less guidance had been offered by mentors. Indeed, over a third of them admitted that they had made little or no reference to these standards, and eighty-three per cent had offered no advice on reporting to parents. Thirty-nine per cent of secondary and forty-eight per cent of primary students had not been able to attend tutorials on a regular basis with mentors at which questions on assessment could have been raised. The time factor was most frequently mentioned as the reason for this. Thus, mentors argued that:

> *Where students and mentors mark the same piece of work and then discuss their findings and grades, this provides an excellent sense of involvement on the student's part, and is a good approach to learning, but it does make great demands on our limited time.*

> *Teachers have work to assess and cannot always find time to explain every mark to the student.*

At a fifth of secondary schools the problem was made worse, since they were in partnership with several HEIs, all operating different systems of school experience. Very few mentors had time to repeat a tutorial on assessment to groups of students from different HEIs.

(3) RECENT INNOVATIONS: It was found that only twenty-six per cent of secondary and thirty-eight per cent of primary students were thought by their mentors to have shown evidence of meeting the standard of using national, local, comparative and school data to set targets for pupils. The main reason for this was that the legislation on target setting (sections 19-20 of the Education Act 1997 and sections 6-7 of the School Standards and Framework Act 1998) was recent and many teachers were still in the process of establishing targets during the school year 1998-99.

(4) DEFICIENCIES IN MENTORING PRACTICE: The following deficiencies were noted:

• When the oral debriefings recorded on the audio-cassette were analysed, it was found that assessment and reporting accounted for just four per cent of the average number of responses per five minutes in formal evaluations of students' teaching. The respective percentages for teaching strategies and class management stood at thirty-six and forty-two. Eleven per cent of comments related to administrative issues (for example, arranging the next lesson observation), four per cent to subject knowledge and three per cent to other aspects of professional development. Most comments on assessment were concerned with the quality of students' responses to answers given in class rather than the role of assessment in making decisions about future lesson objectives. This was often because many mentors considered that the priorities in debriefing were teaching methodology and control. Assessment did not always form the principal focus, particularly in the early stages of school experience. Often mentors began debriefing by asking students for their impressions of the lesson and this established the order of priorities.

- Some schools did not have a consistent policy on assessment. This is an issue to which the inspectorate in Wales has drawn attention (OHMCI, 1997 and 1998b).

- Only forty-eight per cent of secondary and fifty-three per cent of primary students received a copy of the whole-school policy on assessment.

- Some mentors were reluctant to give students responsibility for assessing classes' work, while others assumed that they were experts in this field as a result of studies during their HEI course and, consequently, offered little advice.

(5) STUDENT PERCEPTIONS AND UNDERSTANDING:

- Seventy-nine per cent of secondary and fifty-three per cent of primary mentors were pleased with students' ability to employ statutory assessment under the National Curriculum. Nonetheless, seventy-seven per cent of all trainees considered that assigning level descriptions was one of the most difficult tasks they faced.

- Mentors cited cases where they set standards which were either too low for fear of discouraging pupils or too high, because they failed to realise that pupils lacked their specialist knowledge of the subject.

- Some students, at least in their first encounters in the classroom, believed that assessment consisted only of marking assignments and failed to understand its formative role.

II: Helping students to meet the QTS standards

The following approaches are suggested to help resolve some of the problems which have been identified in the research studies. The overall framework is based upon the analysis of the mentor's role given in the first chapter:

(a) **Providing a Suitable Framework for Students' Experience:** Important issues of which mentors need to take note are:

(i) *Class Management:*

- to ensure that all students have policy documents on the rules and procedures imposed by the teachers with whom they are based and that they are made aware of the standards of behaviour which are deemed to be acceptable. This documentation should include a statement of the rewards and sanctions which are available. In a survey conducted by Geen, Bassett and Douglas (1999b), it was noted that most of the 223 UWIC students who competed a questionnaire during the academic year 1997-98 did receive the requisite information. Eighty-one per cent had access to a written policy on discipline and eighty per cent understood procedures with respect to rewards and sanctions.

- to inform them of the techniques which have been used to establish class rules and to make clear that they have the same authority as other members of the school staff.

- to provide them with full information on individual pupils they will meet who present particular behavioural problems.

(ii) *Teaching:*

- to provide guidance on learning and teaching. This can be achieved during weekly tutorials which form part of the 'coaching' function of the mentor.

- to offer a timetable which permits them to teach a range of ages and abilities and to develop their skills.

- to ensure that they receive oral and written feedback on their teaching and are able to attend a weekly review at which targets are set.

In the UWIC survey ninety-four per cent of students stated that they had taught a timetable which allowed them to meet the full age and ability range, eighty-five per cent received copies of the teacher's schemes of work and eighty-four per cent were very satisfied with the advice offered on lesson planning. However, thirty-nine per cent did not always receive written comments on lessons they had taught and forty-one per cent were not set targets on a weekly basis.

(iii) *Assessment:* Responses from the UWIC students suggested that they received less help with assessment than class management and teaching. For example, forty-one per cent had no guidelines on assessment policy and forty per cent were given no feedback on the quality of their assessment. Accordingly, the following strategies are suggested:

- Recognising that not every secondary school can provide experience of a wide variety of courses in all subjects, especially those devised for the fourteen to nineteen age group, tutors at HEIs need to compile a register of the syllabuses available in their partnership schools and use this information to ensure that all students have by the end of their training encountered as many of them as is feasible.

- Within the schools it is important that mentors consult the list of assessment standards and plan a programme designed to develop expertise in the greatest number possible. Where a class or department provides only limited facilities, structured observation and other relevant exercises involving different groups of pupils can be organised, for example, profiling pupils within tutorial classes, writing mock reports in consultation with class teachers and preparing statements for parents' evenings. Visits to schools in the locality where recent initiatives have been introduced may also be considered.

- Providing a framework for students to use when they plan their lessons. From the outset of their placement they should be guided to take account of the assessment standards. Where printed lesson formats are used, a section could be included with the heading *'opportunities for assessment'* together with a short reminder of the main provisions of the standards. Under this heading they would be expected to record *all* forms of assessment, recording and reporting pertinent to that lesson, for example, formative assessment through supervision and questioning, apportioning marks according to a specific scheme of grading and recording pupils' progress with reference to the level descriptions of the National Curriculum.

- When they assess pupils' work, students should be required to follow a standard format. A marking proforma could be devised to make reference to the following items:

☐ SUBJECT:

☐ NATURE OF ASSIGNMENT:

☐ CRITERIA FOR ASSESSMENT:
  1
  2
  3

☐ RELATIONSHIP OF THE ASSESSMENT CRITERIA TO THE LEVELS OF THE NATIONAL CURRICULUM OR EXAMINATION SPECIFICATION:

☐ COMMENTS ON STRENGTHS IN THE PUPIL'S WORK IN RELATION TO THE CRITERIA FOR ASSESSMENT:

☐ AREAS FOR IMPROVEMENT IN RELATION TO THE CRITERIA FOR ASSESSMENT:

☐ TARGETS SET FOR THE PUPIL:
  1
  2
  3

☐ LEVEL AT WHICH THE PUPIL IS WORKING (WHERE APPROPRIATE):

☐ IMPLICATIONS FOR FUTURE LESSONS:

(b) **Modelling Good Practice:** To a large extent this can be achieved by organising observation of lessons and through the provision of collaborative teaching along the lines discussed in the previous chapters. In the UWIC survey eighty-five per cent of students observed a variety of teaching styles, but only fifty-eight per cent observed teachers as they assessed pupils' work. To help students cope with assessment issues, the following model can be adopted (Stephens, 1996):

(i) *explaining policy:* At an early stage the mentor explains the class or departmental policy on assessment.

(ii) *observation:* Students watch teachers when they mark homework, coursework and tests and when they write school reports, and have the opportunity to ask questions concerning procedures and the rationale behind the grades awarded. Offering students some form of 'running commentary' during assessment is valuable so that they can understand the criteria teachers employ in evaluating children's work.

 It is also helpful for students to shadow lessons where:

- formal assessment takes place;

- assessment is informal, for example, when verbal comments are given to pupils on their work as it proceeds.

(iii) *discussing pupils' work with the student,* for example, looking at representative samples of pupils' marked work and offering a full explanation of the reasons why certain grades or comments have been given.

(iv) *establishing good practice in assessment:* Some of the guidelines listed by Stephens are:

- to encourage students to enter comments which emphasise pupils' achievements relative to their personal prior best rather than to that of their peers (i.e. ipsative assessment);

- to ensure that comments entered on pupils' assignments are legible, clear and meaningful rather than bland (for example, "fair effort");

- to encourage students to employ forms of assessment which identify strengths and highlight areas needing improvement;

- to ensure that their assessment is fair and objective at all times.

(v) *allowing students to mark pupils' work:* The teacher selects pieces of work for assessment and allows the student to mark them, following the agreed assessment criteria. Stephens suggests that trainees write all their comments and calibration of scores and grades on separate sheets rather than in the pupils' exercise books. The teacher does the same, and the results are compared. Once a reasonable degree of parity has been achieved between the two, the student is allowed to transfer her/his comments to the pupils' book. If the mentor disagrees with the student's assessment, it is important that he/she gives clear reasons for this and allows the trainee to undertake further evaluation of pupils' work until the correct standard has been reached.

This type of exercise can be continued for several weeks until the teacher is happy that the mentee's marking is at the appropriate level. At that stage he/she can be entrusted with responsibility for marking a quota of assignments and putting marks/grades and comments directly on the pupils' work. Random selection cross-marking by the teacher can continue through the school placement.

Where criterion-referencing forms the basis of assessment, a portfolio of work can be compiled to illustrate the standards associated with each of the various levels. Subsequently, written justification on the part of students for the levels they award may serve as a valuable basis for dialogue about standards in marking.

(c) **Coaching:** This can take various forms:

(i) *Tutorials in which mentors offer basic advice pertinent to the standards.* Key issues which need to be considered include:

- teaching strategies, for example, the respective role of instruction, questioning, supervised practical work, heuristic ('discovery') learning strategies, investigative assignments, experiential learning, discussion, creative activity, negotiated learning, team teaching and contexts where whole class teaching, group work and individual tuition are most appropriate. Reference can also be made to the Hay McBer report (2000) on research into effective teaching and learning.

The majority of UWIC students considered that the advice they received with respect to planning and teaching was valuable (Geen, Bassett and Douglas, 1999b). The main areas on which mentors needed to concentrate were the use of ICT and ways of involving pupils in planning and assessing their own learning. The following chart summarises the percentage who expressed satisfaction with mentors' coaching in each of the standards:

Standards	Percentage
• planning appropriate demanding tasks	92
• presenting subject content in a clear and stimulating manner	90
• setting suitable lesson objectives	89
• timing and pacing of lessons	88
• utilising National Curriculum programmes of study in their teaching	86
• ensuring continuity and progression between lessons	86
• employing a range of teaching strategies	81
• consolidating and reinforcing learning	79
• questioning technique	75
• planning for differentiation	74
• using appropriate teaching aids	73
• using a range of teaching methods	69
• involving pupils in planning and assessing their own learning	58
• using ICT in their teaching	53

- techniques of classroom management, for example, establishing and justifying class rules and routines, strategies for enforcing them, the consistent use of rewards and sanctions, general guidelines on the management of classes, for example, scanning the class, anticipating possible problems, deciding seating arrangements, and familiarising themselves with the whole-school policy on discipline, including the members of staff to whom they can turn if they experience major problems. Again, eighty-eight per cent of UWIC students felt that their mentors had been helpful in enabling them to create and maintain an orderly environment and eighty-five believed that they learned how to maintain interest and motivation.

Useful books on class management which mentors can use in their tutorials with students include: Docking (1987); Gray and Richer (1988); Charlton and David (1989); Robertson (1989); McGuiness (1993); Smith and Laslett (1993); Wragg (1993); Lund (1996); McPhillimy (1996); Olsen and Cooper (2001); Blandford (1998); Chaplain (1998); MacGrath (1998); Cowley (1999 and 2001); Porter (2000); Rogers (2000); Visser (2000), Olsen and Cooper (2001); and Wright (2001).

- assessment issues, especially types of assessment (for example, formative, summative and ipsative), modes of assessment (norm-referenced and criterion-referenced including competence testing), differentiation, assessment under the National Curriculum, the use of level descriptions, techniques of assessment (for example, the use of objective questions), National Curriculum testing, examination specifications, the use of profiles, and the writing of reports for parents, carers, other professionals and pupils. Mentors may also draw attention to recent research studies in the field of assessment such as the work of Black and Wiliam (1998).

(ii) *Advice on Lesson Planning:* Giving advice about the range of strategies available to students and helping them plan and teach their lessons are key functions of the mentor. In the survey conducted by Arthur, Davison and Moss (1997) of sixty-five mentors in two hundred schools, it was found that in some cases students were presented with model lesson plans to illustrate the type of approach deemed most suitable at those schools. Basic areas on which subject mentors are likely to advise students are:

(1) CRITERIA FOR PLANNING LESSONS: These include:

- planning lesson objectives (or learning outcomes) which accord with the aims of the class teacher's unit of work to ensure progression and continuity between lessons;

- relating teaching to the appropriate programmes of study, attainment targets and level descriptions of the National Curriculum;

- selecting suitable learning activities which take into account differentiation;

- utilising appropriate teaching aids, deploying resources and making the best use of information and communication technology;

- looking for opportunities to involve pupils in planning, conducting and assessing their own learning;

- planning the development of the lesson to arouse motivation from the outset and to make clear to pupils the targets they are to achieve in the lesson;

- setting a series of suitable learning activities so that pupils will achieve the learning outcomes;

- choosing a variety of activities to obviate boredom - especially with younger and less able/motivated classes;

- ensuring logical sequencing in the development of the lesson so that there is a smooth transition between the different activities in the lesson. Mentors may offer advice to students to help them avoid such problems as 'jerkiness' - interrupting one activity unnecessarily with another;

- ensuring that their explanations to the class are as clear as possible, and that terminology is at a suitable level for the age and ability of the pupils;

- planning the main questions that they will put and techniques of questioning, for example, the distribution of questions, pausing, prompting, redirection, developing responses and the use of open and closed questions;

- paying attention to timing, pacing and supervision;

- considering the most appropriate closure technique to draw the lesson to a satisfactory end, for example, reviewing the extent to which targets have been achieved and pre-viewing the work of the next lesson;

- considering strategies for applying, consolidating and reinforcing learning;

- looking for opportunities for the assessment of pupils' work, the establishment of assessment criteria which are made clear to pupils, the provision of positive feedback on their progress and the setting of targets to guide future learning.

In planning lessons students may need help in taking into account the quality of the learning, for example,

- the progress made in the development of knowledge, understanding and skills set out in the current statutory Orders of the National Curriculum, including communication, number and information and communication technology;

- such learning skills as observation and information seeking, looking for patterns and deeper understanding, communicating information and ideas in various ways, posing questions and solving problems, applying what has been learned to unfamiliar situations and evaluating completed work;

- promoting such desirable attitudes to learning as interest and the ability to concentrate, co-operate and work productively.

(2) WRITING LESSON NOTES: Research by Sarah Tann (1994) concludes that most of the students in her survey were concerned about the quality of their files. Typical questions to mentors and tutors were: "Are my lesson plans OK?", "Do I have to do all the objectives every time?" Practice varies, but the following headings are suggested as important considerations for students in writing lesson plans:

- *GENERAL ORGANISATION*: Students need to file their lesson plans in order, so that the notes for each class (year 4, year 5, year 6, etc.) are kept together. The use of file dividers is strongly recommended.

- *PLANNING FOR EACH UNIT OF WORK:* Students need to set out: the *title* of the unit of work, the *year* for which it is intended, the *duration* of the unit of work in weeks, pupils' *previous experience* and *relevant knowledge*, any important *key skills*, for example, communication, number and ICT, and the *aims* for the unit of work. Aims are long-term and cover the whole unit of work. The degree of success in attaining them cannot usually be measured by the end of one or two lessons. They can be expressed by means of the formula: "By the end of this unit pupils should be able to ....."

Reference should also be made to the relevant *programmes of study* of the National Curriculum, and a brief description should be given of the main learning activities which will be employed and of the ways in which differentiation has been taken into account. Students need to address the principal modes of class organisation which will be used (for example, individual, group, whole class teaching), the assessment procedures which will be employed for the unit of work and the resources needed, including the use of ICT.

- *SPECIFIC LESSON PLAN.* Basic information needed to help students plan lessons adequately includes:

  - the DATE, CLASS, PERIOD and DURATION OF THE LESSON.

  - the TITLE OF THE UNIT OF WORK.

  - the LEARNING OUTCOMES/OBJECTIVES for the lesson, i.e. "By the end of the lesson pupils should know/be able to: ..." Objectives should be short-term, measurable, achievable, realistic and time-bound. Hence, by the end of the lesson the student should be able to ascertain the extent to which they have been accomplished. Examples from the area of food technology would be:

    - *identify* pieces of large equipment used in the kitchen;

    - *list* four types of oven;

    - *label* a diagram to illustrate the parts of a cooker;

    - *answer questions* orally and in writing on the cooking methods associated with parts of the oven; etc.

It is also important that students consider the relationship of the objectives for a specific lesson to the aims of the entire unit of work. By the time that the pupils have achieved all the objectives for each lesson in the series, they should have mastered the overall aims for the entire unit of work. If students bear this relationship in mind, there will be continuity and progression in their teaching.

In planning objectives it is necessary to take into account the level of ability of the pupils. In the case of many mixed ability classes, it can be helpful to set out objectives in the following manner:

By the end of this lesson, all pupils should be able to ....

By the end of this lesson, most pupils should be able to ....
By the end of this lesson, some pupils should be able to ....

- RELATIONSHIP TO THE NATIONAL CURRICULUM OR EXAMINATION SPECIFICATION: Students need to indicate the relationship of their lesson objectives to the programmes of study of relevant National Curriculum Orders, for example, KS1: Sc1 (h) to (j); KS2: Sc4 (3) (a) to (c); KS3 Sc3: 2(c) (o).

- KEY SKILLS: Where a lesson provides opportunities for pupils to develop and apply key skills (communications, application of number, ICT, problem solving, working with others and improving one's own learning and performance) or thinking skills (information processing skills, reasoning skills, enquiry skills, creative thinking skills and evaluation skills), these should also be recorded. Students pursuing the National Curriculum in Wales will need to consider the common requirements -ICT, communication, Cwricwlwm Cymreig, problem solving, creative skills and personal and social education.

- LESSON STRUCTURE: ACTIVITY SEQUENCE: Overall lesson structure may be organised under the headings: *introduction* (for example, links to previous learning, points raised from homework, presenting some artefact as a focus for discussion); *development*, which covers the main part of the lesson in which learning is extended; and *closure* where the main strands of the learning are drawn together, homework may be set, and the work of the next lesson is pre-viewed.

- LESSON STRUCTURE: TEACHING STRATEGIES: Under this heading students decide the strategies to be employed (for example, instruction, investigative activity, questioning, group discussion) and such organisational considerations as the distribution and collection of equipment.

- TIMING: In many lessons it is highly desirable for students to set out the times they anticipate that each activity in the lesson will take.

- ASSESSMENT PROCEDURES: Students often need to be guided to ensure that the opportunities for assessment identified in their planning relate to the learning outcomes/ objectives for the lesson. They also need to take into account the standards for assessment, especially using the level descriptions of the National Curriculum, providing feedback to support pupils as they learn, recording the outcomes of assessment, involving pupils in reflecting on, evaluating and improving their own performance, and using the results of assessment to inform future planning and teaching.

- RESOURCES, including the use of ICT.

- RISK ASSSESSMENT: Where this is relevant, they should identify any risks which pupils may incur during the lesson in terms of health and safety, (for example, use of potentially dangerous equipment, the danger of accidents) and devise an appropriate action plan. This plan will cover the steps they must take to minimise the dangers, for example, warnings to the whole class and careful supervision. They may require small groups to use certain apparatus and then only with the permission of the teacher.

- CONTINUITY. This points to homework and any issues which will be taken up in the next lesson. Consideration of this criterion helps ensure continuity and progression in lesson planning and delivery.

(iii) *Pre-Lesson Discussion:* This involves discussion concerning preparation for a specific lesson. The student applies the knowledge acquired about teaching strategies, class management and assessment to a given context. Tomlinson (1995) suggests that the mentor's role at this stage will include the following:

(1) EXPLORING THE STUDENT'S IDEAS AND INTENTIONS: The mentor listens to the student's ideas and prompts him/her to explain the objectives, the strategies to be employed to achieve them and any alternative courses of action which may be relevant. The mentor needs to check that:

- what the student intends is pedagogically appropriate and that the teaching strategies are likely to achieve the lesson objectives;

- what they intend is realistic when account is taken of the pupils' abilities, the context, the time available and the resources at hand;

- the student has thought through the lesson content in sufficient detail. It is sometimes useful to prompt thinking where it appears that some aspect of the lesson has not been considered in sufficient depth. Examples of questions are:

What precisely do you think you will do at this point?

How do you intend to explain that?

- the student is capable of executing the planned strategies in the context of the class.

(2) KEEPING THE DISCUSSION PROACTIVE AND AVOIDING REACTIVE CRISIS MANAGEMENT SITUATIONS: Students should be encouraged to anticipate problems and to consider potential solutions before the start of the lesson. However, as Tomlinson notes, there is always the danger that students will become over-anxious and bogged down in a "What if ...?" series of questions in which the worst nightmare situations are dreamed up. Sometimes, their fears about class management are acute, and so he recommends that mentors point out to them:

- the power of a positive stance by making clear the rules which the class is expected to obey from the very outset;

- the school's policy on discipline;

- the support which is available to them if their worst fears are realised.

(3) ALERTING, EXPLAINING AND CHALLENGING WHERE NECESSARY: Where mentors believe that there are problems in a student's lesson plan, they must alert her/him to the problem and give a clear explanation. It is, of course, important not to appear to be totally dismissive of a trainee's ideas or to create a closed climate of authority. The requisite skill, Tomlinson feels, is to question and probe the student's thinking about the activities planned for the lesson. Mentors, he maintains, need to have a sense of the whole picture before they can decide which aspects need to be challenged.

Examples of questions will can help clarify thinking on lesson planning are:

Do you think that you can accomplish all this in one lesson? Let us discuss the amount of time they are going to take to carry out this first activity.

How exactly are you going to organise the distribution and collection of equipment at this point?

I am not fully clear what the pupils are going to do in this section of the lesson plan. I can see that Group A is fully involved, but what are the other groups supposed to be doing?

So, each group discusses these points and records its conclusions. How do we ensure that all their ideas are reported to the whole class?

On occasions it may be desirable to challenge more directly, especially where mentors have greater knowledge of a class's capabilities then the student:

I understand what you are planning, but I really do not think that this class will complete so much by 11.00 a.m. My experience of these pupils is that they will take at least fifteen minutes to complete your first activity.

(4) NEGOTIATING, SUGGESTING AND INFORMING: Where the student's planning reveals major gaps or he/she has problems in deciding between options, the mentors may suggest specific activities. Tomlinson stresses that it is sometimes difficult to decide the exact degree of detail to provide and warns against the danger of overloading students with advice. He therefore suggests that a 'top-down' approach be utilised whereby the mentor starts with the overall phases of the lesson and the major learning strategies to be employed and then goes only into those details which the student wishes to pursue.

(iv) *advising on strategies for monitoring and evaluating lessons:* Mentor need to provide students with a framework for evaluating and reflecting upon their lessons. This aspect of the role is discussed in detail in chapter nine

(d) **Taking Account of Students' Skills Acquisition:** Mentors need to take into account the stage reached by each student and offer appropriate support and advice. The analysis of stages given by Furlong and Maynard, which was summarised in the first chapter, can be useful, though it must be appreciated that students do develop at different rates. The research by Tann (1994) showed that, in the early stages of their school experience, most students expressed needs which were 'survival-oriented'; they wanted tips and easy solutions to problems usually relating to class management. Once they had gained confidence and felt less vulnerable in terms of discipline, they showed greater interest in varying strategies of teaching and developing their role in extending pupils' learning experiences.

One problem which can arise is that some mentors expect students from their first lesson to perform with the proficiency associated with experienced teachers. This happened at one school in South Wales, where students' concern at the unrealistic assumptions of some of their mentors became apparent to the ITET co-ordinator. In order to resolve this difficulty, he devised a series of 'pen portraits' to illustrate the standards which can reasonably be expected of students at each phase of their teaching. This proved to be extremely successful, and is a practice which may with advantage be adopted in other schools.

(e) **Supervision and Practising Mentoring Skills:** Mentoring skills are discussed in later chapters. However, specific courses of action which mentors can take to help their students in the classroom are:

(i) *to be sensitive to the student's situation:* They should not introduce a student to a potentially difficult class by threatening the pupils with sanctions if they fail to behave themselves with Mr/Ms X "who is a student". It is better to introduce Mr/Ms X as someone "who will be teaching you this year. Sometimes we will teach together, sometimes separately". Similarly, as the term progresses, mentors need to resist the temptation to let pupils address them as "the teacher" and automatically to turn to them if they experience a problem. Where this occurs, the student's status, authority and confidence can be drastically reduced.

(ii) *to provide students with a clear framework for school experience:* Students in the research published by Hayes (2001) were unhappy when they were put in a situation where their lesson timetable was constantly being changed and they were unable to teach the lessons they had agreed with their mentors. It is, of course, impossible in any school for plans to be written in tablets of stone, but, nonetheless, mentors must realise that students can make progress only if there is a clear structure in which they can plan, teach and evaluate lessons.

(iii) *to prompt the student to carry out planned activities* before the lesson begins. The mentor may remind the student about important advice given in previous debriefing sessions. There may have been some serious problem, and the discussion may have culminated in the compilation of an action plan. The mentor now needs to have the student recall what was agreed, so that the key points in that action plan can be implemented during the lesson.

(iv) *to ensure that a supportive mentor figure is present during the lesson:* In the early stages of students' school experience, this can be beneficial, as the presence of the mentor in the classroom is seen by some students as a safety net - someone at hand to help in case trouble breaks out. Mentors need not be present formally to observe the lesson, but, for many trainees, the knowledge that the teacher is in the area can be comforting.

(v) *to monitor progress and diagnose* any necessary interventions to assist the student, providing that this does not undermine her/his authority in front of the class.

(vi) *to provide the student with important information* about aspects of the lesson which he/she is too inexperienced to notice, for example, that certain pupils are being left out of a discussion or that others are not concentrating on the work set. This can often be done outside a formal observation of a lesson. The mentor may be in the room for part of the lesson and at an appropriate point draw the student's attention to some specific issue ("I think you will find … is happening because of …").

(vii) *to offer advice and suggestions for tactics:* If, in the course of the lesson, the student seems unsure of the optimum way to proceed because of some unforeseen contingency, the mentor can provide guidance and advice on the spot.

(viii) *to review lessons/parts of lessons with the use of audio-recording equipment:* In the Leeds University School Partnership Scheme (Tomlinson, 1995) use has been made of hand-held cassette tape recorders. Small machines can be worn in a pocket with an extension microphone attached to a buttonhole or lapel so that the student's speech and voice can be recorded. The mentor can then listen to these recordings and use them as the basis for debriefing sessions. Shaw (1995) likewise believes that video and tape recordings have a valuable role to play in helping mentors discuss lessons with students, provided that this is agreeable to both parties. Such an approach, she contends, allows mentors and students to reflect upon the use of language, voice projection, questioning techniques and body language.

(ix) *to give encouragement and positive feedback:* Positive feedback and praise are very important in boosting students' morale. They are vital where trainees are lacking in confidence or are very self-critical. It is, of course, important that the comments made are realistic. In the survey by Hayes (2001) one student stated:

> **I could have done with more feedback, as I needed to understand how I am doing. This helps my confidence, as I may appear to be confident on the outside, but I'm pretty shaky on the inside.** (p. 18).

(x) *gradually to increase the scope and difficulty of the teaching activities:* ITET co-ordinators need to ensure that none of their colleagues adheres to such outdated and pernicious philosophies as: "The only way to teach is to be thrown in at the deep end". As has been argued in previous chapters, the optimum programme for the majority of students involves a gradual transition from observation to individual teaching.

III: Observation of students' lessons

(a) **Pre-Observation Considerations:** In many partnerships mentors are requested to ensure that at least one lesson given by a student each week is assessed, while ITET co-ordinators are to moderate their judgements by observing at least one lesson during the period of school experience. Brooks and Sikes (1997) refer to the view of some teachers that there should be an element of surprise in observation, so that students do not prepare a 'special performance'. However, such an approach does not allow for the development of a consensual, negotiated partnership which they consider to be fundamental to good mentoring.

Many writers (for example, Acton, Kirkham and Smith, 1992; Fish, 1995b; Brooks and Sikes, 1997). suggest that the mentor should meet the student before any observation takes place so that they can agree the following:

(i) the aims and purposes of the observation;

(ii) the student's intentions for the lesson and the way the objectives relate to the overall unit of work;

(iii) arrangements whereby the student can provide the mentor with relevant information about the lesson plan before the observation takes place;

(iv) any specific focus for the observation. The mentor and student may decide to relate the observation to one or more of the standards which are appropriate to the student's current stage of development. Secondary mentors commenting on observation of students' lesson in the survey conducted by Arthur, Davison and Moss (1997) felt that having a focus was a valuable exercise, especially in the early stages of school experience. On the other hand,, it was noted that "most students also appreciate feedback on the whole lesson as well" (p. 93).

Where a specific focus has been agreed, it is important that the mentor does not lose sight of this. If he/she has stated that it will be 'differentiating their teaching to meet the needs of pupils', then feedback should deal effectively with this, though it may be necessary to address any other major issues which have arisen in the lesson in which the student requires help.

(v) the duration and mode of the observation, for example, having the mentor sit at the back of the class, participate in agreed sections of the lesson or help small groups.

(vi) the sequence of activities which will be adopted, for example, observation, reflection, feedback, planning for future lessons and target setting;

(vii) the appropriate observation procedures and strategies to be utilised, for example, the forms to be completed and the reporting style to be adopted;

(viii) the balance to be struck between observation and recording during the lesson;

(ix) the data to be checked and the ways in which any records will be used;

(x) the time and place for discussion of the lesson after the observation;

(xi) the terms in which the lesson will be discussed, for example, questioning the student, pointing out specific issues, etc.

Fish (1995b) also refers to mentors' mindset. Are they willing to accept different ways of working from their own?

(b) **Observation of the Lesson:** The following are important considerations to be made in planning the observation of students' lessons:

(i) *the recording format used:* Techniques which are frequently used include:

- the CHECK-LIST approach where the items to be observed are listed down the page, for example, *efficient organisation of pupils for a specific task*, and the mentor records the number of occasions this item has been observed across the page;

- RATING SCALES where a list of competences derived from the standards is recorded and students are graded on a scale, for example, 1-4 with respect to such skills as ability to motivate pupils. Where this system is used, it is common practice to set out an explanation of each grade. Thus, scale 1 may indicate that a student has, in the mentor's judgement, fully achieved a standard throughout the whole lesson, scale 2 indicates a satisfactory grasp of the standard for the greater part of the lesson, scale 3 shows that the student has begun to develop the knowledge, understanding and skills associated with the standard, and scale 4 suggests that no such development has, as yet, been exhibited.

- COMMENT BANKS where key aspects of a lesson are listed, for example, preparation, planning and teaching skills, and comments are entered by the mentor. It is possible to use:

  - *closed banks* where the comments are printed on the form and the mentor underlines or circles the comments felt to be relevant to the lesson, for example:

    organisation of pupils' work: systematic and methodical; orderly; some evidence of planning; haphazard; unreliable; chaotic; poor clearing away; faulty timing.

  - *open banks* where mentors are free to enter their own comments as they wish. For example, the heading *organisation of work* is written on the observation sheet and the mentor enters an appropriate comment.

A combination of the two approaches can be employed.

- the DIARY APPROACH. The essence of this approach, which is described by Fish (1995b), is to record only what happens in the lesson without inserting any value-judgements, and to use the record as the basis for discussion with students in which the mentor's role is to encourage them to reflect upon their actions during the lesson. The mentor, therefore, will:

  - write just a summary of the events of the lesson without any comments on what he/she thought were the strong points and areas for improvement;

  - consider at the same time different possible explanations for what is happening by, for example, asking pupils questions, examining their work and scrutinising lesson notes in greater depth;

  - in the light of these considerations set out a list of questions which will be used with the student to encourage him/her to analyse performance. (Fish, 1995b, p. 123).

In any recording system it is important that at the end of the process the student has an understanding of:

- the strengths in the lesson;

- the ways in which improvements can be made;

- the evidence which has been offered for the judgements reached;

- appropriate targets which have to be met.

(ii) *use of duplicate/triplicate forms* so that the student receives a copy of the mentor's comments. In many partnerships, carbon copies of lesson observation sheets are used. One is then retained by the student, a second by the mentor, a third by the ITET co-ordinator and a fourth by the HEI tutor. It is beneficial if these forms contain a summary of the QTS standards.

(iii) *ensuring that the mentor can concentrate upon the task at hand:* It is important to ensure that other staff do not interrupt the lesson, for example, looking for the mentor in connection with other aspects of school business. This is especially important where mentors have a wide range of administrative responsibilities.

(iv) *following the procedures agreed with the student before the lesson:* It is necessary to adhere to the focus and objectives which have been set for the observation and to strike a balance between studying the lesson and writing the report. Mentors should resist the temptation to intervene in a lesson where they feel that they could teach some aspect more effectively, unless it has been decided beforehand that they will play an active role or the student asks for their help.

(v) *concluding the observation* by offering the student the opportunity to explain her/his perceptions of the lesson and thanking the student at the end.

Debriefing, in which the mentor provides the student with feedback on the lesson, is the topic of chapter nine. It should be organised as soon as possible after the lesson. Mentors quoted by Brooks and Sikes (1997) note that, with the pressure of other duties, it is not always feasible for them to hold a debriefing session immediately after a lesson. Ideally, it should be held within two days of the observation, while details of the events are still fresh in the minds of both mentor and student.

❯ Issues for consideration

1. Read section I *(research into students' experiences)* and state the extent to which you consider the findings of the studies quoted to be true of your experience with students. Organise your comments under the headings:

(a) *class management;*
(b) *teaching strategies;*
(c) *students' assessment of pupils' achievements.*

2. Next, discuss with your students any problems which they have experienced with respect to achieving the QTS standards.

3. List the principal strategies you employ to help your students meet these standards. Organise your comments under the headings:

(a) *providing a suitable framework for students' experience;*
(b) *modelling good practice;*
(c) *coaching;*
(d) *taking into account students' level of skills.*

4. Read section II (*helping students to meet the standards*) and report any changes you would make to your response to the items listed in question 3 (a) – (d).

5. Recount your own practice with reference to:

(a) *being sensitive to the student's situation:;*
(b) *prompting/reminding the student to carry out planned activities;*
(c) *ensuring that a supportive mentor figure is present during the lesson;*
(d) *monitoring progress and diagnosing any necessary interventions;*
(e) *providing the student with specific information;*
(f) *offering advice and suggestions for tactics;*
(g) *reviewing lessons/parts of lessons with the use of audio-recording equipment;*
(h) *giving encouragement and positive feedback;*
(i) *gradually increasing the scope and difficulty of the teaching activities.*

6. In the light of your reading list any changes you may make to the support with which you provide students during their teaching.

7. With reference to any pre-lesson discussion you have had with a trainee teacher record the advice you gave and the reasons why you gave that advice with respect to:

(a) *the student's ideas and intentions;*
(b) *the quality of the lesson plan;*
(c) *the student's anticipation of problems and consideration of potential solutions;*

8. List any skills you used in this pre-lesson discussion to which reference is made in the text, e.g. alerting, explaining, challenging, negotiating, suggesting and informing.

9. Explain the meaning of Tomlinson's concept of 'top-down' advice on lesson planning and state the extent to which you consider this approach to be helpful.

10. Read section III (*observation of students' lessons*) and recount your practice with respect to the following:

(a) *pre-lesson discussion of aims, objectives, etc.;*
(b) *establishing a focus for observation;*
(c) *deciding when to enter the lesson;*
(d) *deciding where to sit;*
(e) *willingness to accept different practices;*
(f) *intervention in the lesson;*
(g) *balance of observation and recording;*
(h) *the data to be checked.*

11. Brooks and Sikes refer to the view of some teachers that an element of surprise is needed in the observation of students by mentors. State with reasons your views on this proposition.

12. Reference is made in section III to different approaches which can be employed in recording comments on students' lessons (e.g. check-lists, rating scales, comment banks, diary approach). State with reasons your views on the optimum mode for recording lesson observations.

13. The following list of questions is based upon a framework for reflection devised by Fish (1995b). Think of any lessons given by students which you have observed recently and answer the questions, considering whether you would make any changes to your style of lesson observation:

- What exactly was the purpose of your observation?

- Did you make this intention clear to the student?

- On what exactly did you intend to focus in the lesson in order to achieve that purpose? Did you in fact focus upon it?

- Did you examine the student's lesson notes and preparation?

- If so, did you look at these notes and preparation before, during or after the lesson?

- What did you set out to watch and why?

- How did you organise your comments? Did you use a chronological approach or did you follow the order of the standards?

- What were the main judgements you reached?

- Did you make reference to the standards?

- What evidence did you have for the judgements you reached? Were these judgements made clear in your commentary on the lesson?

- Did you list the strengths in the student's lesson?

- Did you show the extent to which the student has made progress since the last lesson observation?

- Did you draw attention to areas for improvement?

- Did you provide evidence for the judgements you reached?

- Did you set targets for discussion with the student?

- What opportunities did you plan to allow the student to bring her/his views to bear upon the lesson?

- What issues did you decide to use in debriefing? Did you think of opportunities for discursive as opposed to pragmatic dialogue?

- Did you distinguish between what the student intended to do and what you yourself would have done in this situation?

- Did you consider *actual achivement* or *potential* or both?

- What allowance did you make for the effect of your presence on the proceedings?

- Did you consider that you were over-influenced by any incident or aspect of the lesson?

- What theories/beliefs/philosophies/ideas/values/views on 'good practice' influenced the student in planning and teaching the lesson?

- What theories/beliefs/philosophies/ideas/values/views on 'good practice' influenced your observation of the lesson?

- How would you rate the quality of your observation. Give reasons for your judgement.

- What (if anything) will you do differently another time?

14. "The students concerned eventually came to me and said that they didn't think that their [subject] mentor was very helpful and that everything they said or did was criticised out of hand, but there weren't any concrete suggestions made for how to improve. The only thing that was acceptable was to do it exactly like the mentor did it - and then it wasn't good enough either" (ITET co-ordinator quoted in Brooks and Sikes, p. 102). If you were this co-ordinator, what action would you take?

6 Developing students' knowledge of educational and professional issues

I: Changing views of the 'knowledge base' of teaching

(a) **The Requirements of the QTS Standards:** *Qualifying to Teach: Professional Standards for Qualified Teacher Status and Requirements for Initial Teacher Training* (DFES-TTA, 2002) and Welsh Office Circular 13/98 (Welsh Office, 1998) outline the knowledge and understanding of educational issues which all trainees must possess in order to be awarded qualified teacher status. As well as referring to planning, teaching, class management, and assessment, the standards include such other themes as the statutory frameworks relating to teachers' responsibilities, liaison with parents and carers, personal, social and health education, equal opportunities issues and policies for challenging bullying. Many of these topics are covered in schools and HEIs in courses which have traditionally been known as 'educational' or 'professional' studies.

(b) **The 'Disciplines' of Educational and Professional Studies:** In 1963 the Robbins Report (Committee on Higher Education, 1963) introduced the one-year BEd degree scheme to colleges of education, in which educational and professional studies was a major component. At that time it was the common practice for courses of this type to revolve around the 'four disciplines' of psychology, history, sociology and philosophy of education. A typical defence of this approach is given in the book *The Study of Education*, which was edited in 1966 by Professor J.W. Tibble, Emeritus Professor of Education at the University of Leicester. This work charts the development of 'educational theory', advocates the study of the four disciplines and devotes one chapter to each in turn. In the section on philosophy of education, for example, Richard S. Peters, Professor of the Philosophy of Education at the Institute of Education of the University of London, argues that a study should be undertaken of:

- education and philosophical psychology, including: the meaning of 'education'; aims of education; the differences between 'education' and 'training'; the justification of subjects in the curriculum; and 'child-centred' education and its assumptions about learning;

- ethical issues in education, including: problems relating to the authority of the teacher; the ethics of discipline and punishment; issues of freedom with respect to the child, the teacher and the parent; equality in education; and moral education;

- epistemology, or theories concerning the nature of knowledge.

The aim was to produce a generation of teachers who would be equipped to think critically about the state of education and who would act as *agents provocateurs*, bringing about desirable change in the curriculum and teaching methods (Hopkins and Reid, 1985). As Bell (1981) observes, these courses were often designed for the "education of the scholar who happened to want to be a teacher" (p. 13). In the 1960s, therefore, government hoped to create newly qualified teachers who would examine the existing system of education and put forward constructive ideas for improving it. By the early 1980s the four disciplines still tended to dominate courses in educational and professional studies (Patrick, Bernbaum and Reid, 1982; Furlong, Barton, Miles, Whiting and Whitty, 2000).

(c) **Changing Perceptions of Educational and Professional Studies:** In the past two decades, as Fitz, Davies and Evans (2001) show, these traditional disciplines have been replaced by the more pragmatic approach to ITET prevalent in such documents as DFEE Circular 4/98 (DFEE, 1998b). This has been the result of the following factors:

(i) *'Theory' and 'Practice':* It was realised that a dichotomy existed of educational *theory,* which was taught in college, and *practice,* which was confined to the schools. The college-based programme did not always relate very closely to students' classroom experience and the 'real' world of schools. It tended to be generalised and abstract. The topics cited by Peters provide a good example. His assumption was that HEIs should produce professional teachers who would be reflective, analytic thinkers, but the critical thought which characterised the type of course he favoured was directed towards wider educational issues rather than immediate classroom activities. Consequently, in 1975 a newly qualified teacher complained in an article published in *The British Journal of Teacher Education* (Jeffreys, 1975) that the educational studies offered to students of that era was of very limited value in terms of the actual task of teaching. This criticism was reiterated in the James Report (DES, 1972) which concluded that:

> *Much of the theoretical study of education is irrelevant to students who have had, as yet, too little practical experience of children or teaching, and the inclusion of this theoretical study is often at the expense of adequate practical preparation for their first teaching assignments* (p. 67).

Other writers (e.g. HMI, 1979; McIntyre, 1988) also noted the tendency of students during this period to fail to appreciate the value of the 'educational theory' taught during their ITET course, and similar criticisms have been made about the preparation of teachers in Canada in more recent times (Clifton, Madzuk and Roberts, 1994).

Nor were teachers always aware of the content of the courses run in the colleges of education or universities. They were rarely involved in helping students to apply concepts acquired in the college to everyday classroom practice and did not usually receive much information from the HEI about the nature of the educational and professional studies programmes offered by them. This regime ended with the creation of partnership under DFE Circular 9/92 and Welsh Office Circular 35/92, as college tutors were required to share responsibility for ITET with mentors in the school.

(ii) *Changes in the philosophy of government:* In the immediate post-war period government stressed that it wanted teachers to contribute to the development of the school system. Thus, in a report in1950 the Minister of Education, George Tomlinson, stated that education in the UK was a partnership "between the Central Department, the local education authorities and the teachers" (Ministry of Education, 1951, p. 1). In subsequent years teachers were regularly consulted by government about proposals for change. When, for instance, in 1964-65 Harold Wilson's Labour administration was planning to dispatch a circular to LEAs, requesting them to reorganise their schools on comprehensive lines, the Secretary of State for Education and Science, Anthony Crosland, discussed its contents with the teachers' unions before the final draft was completed.

During the 1980s, however, any consensus between government and teachers broke down in acrimonious disputes concerning pay and working conditions, and many commentators concluded that the governments of the 1990s did not want to listen to a teaching profession which was critical in its policies. Whereas the *raison d'etre* of educational studies courses which incorporated sociological and philosophical perspectives had been to produce what Rosaen and Schram (1998) call 'transformative intellectuals' capable of acting as change agents, the government now wanted teachers who would deliver a nationally prescribed curriculum. Thus, Carr and Hartnett (1996) have argued that the "utterly philistine Teacher Training Agency did all it could to render teachers compliant, exhausted, always under threat of surveillance and afraid". Similarly, Price (1994), writing of the 1994 Education Act, contends that ministers no longer wish ITET to involve the type of critical thinking which was encouraged thirty years before. The Act, he feels, is "directed to the cultural control of the hearts and minds of the young". Politicians, he continues, having identified the educational system as a potential threat to people's acceptance of their aims and have sought to control "the culture of teacher training ... to return the teachers to the task of technical instruction and to leave the promotion of ideology to the government" (p. 19). Bottery and Wright (2000) agree with these judgements, noting that government is not interested in producing teachers who have an understanding of what they call the 'ecological' areas of ITET, that is to say, influences on children outside the classroom. Helsby (1996) also feels that recent changes imposed by politicians have produced "a strategically planned programme of technical training" (p. 135).

(iii) *Attacks from the 'New Right':* Critics of initial teacher education such as Anthony O'Hear, Professor of Philosophy at the University of Bradford (1988), the Hillgate Group (1989) and Sheila Lawlor of the Centre for Policy Studies (1990) have accused ITET institutions of being wedded to three pernicious ideologies: progressive education; liberal education; and social reconstructionism. Hence, they advocate a move back to school-based, classroom-focused *training* rather than the wider *education* which was deemed to be desirable by the Robbins Committee. They also urge government to break the power of teacher training establishments, which according to O'Hear organise courses to suit their own needs rather than the needs of the consumer. In his view HEIs see education "in terms of its potential for social engineering rather than as an initiation of pupils into proven and worthwhile forms of knowledge" (O'Hear, 1988, p. 22);

(iv) *The Growth of Post-Modernist Thought:* A further change has been the growth of post-modernist thinking. Wilkin (1994) draws the distinction between:

- modernism, which stresses rationality, order and a belief in universal laws and values. In this philosophy, science is seen as an important subject likely to result in discoveries which may solve many of the problems experienced by mankind; and

- post-modernism, the adherents of which believe that no universal solutions can be found to the problems of mankind. Science, it is argued, has in practice failed to provide the answers which its advocates once claimed it could produce. Post-modernism places greater stress upon *efficiency* than upon exact knowledge as the key to success.

Wilkin contends that, under the regime of modernism, providers of ITET would stress the traditional 'disciplines' of education on the grounds that they provide valuable insights into the process of education. In the post-modern world, this claim would be discounted, and the emphasis would be more upon an individual's own personal theory, anyone's view being as valid as the next man's.

(d) **Values in Courses in Educational and Professional Studies:** Many writers on ITET have written in defence of the role of Educational and Professional Studies courses, where it can be shown that they help students to think constructively about their experience. Indeed, HMI in 1993 found that some three-quarters of students involved in a survey of ITET in England and Wales viewed such courses favourably, while research conducted by Powney, Edwards, Holroyd and Martin. (1993) found little evidence that students' professional performance improved when they spent less time on educational studies and more time in the classroom. Moreover, in a survey of the views of students in the last year of a four-year BEd course, O'Holligan (1997) writes: "Our results suggest that involvement with educational studies is very positive for students; they do not become 'distracted' from school realities as 'New Right' mythology claims" (p. 548).

Some of the key arguments for the teaching of courses of this type are offered by Eraut (1989), Furlong (1990), Smith (1992) and O'Holligan (1997):

(i) They challenge personal beliefs about many important issues, for example, ways in which children learn.

(ii) They provide students with alternative viewpoints. Thus, one student in O'Holligan's survey commented that he "was always quite frightened of how to deal with somebody in my class who was difficult. ... The course made me aware of the choices you have to deal with in a situation, and the child's point of view as well as how your own teaching methods might create problems" (p. 540).

(iii) They promote education as opposed to training, and help students formulate their own educational philosophy. As Furlong notes, educational and professional studies courses help them "sort out their fundamental values".

(iv) They encourage intellectual curiosity.

(v) They stimulate understanding that educational issues are often controversial, and they can promote tolerance of the plurality of viewpoints.

(vi) They offer students a vocabulary and sense of community, which enables them to converse with experienced practitioners.

(vii) Discussion organised at an HEI within courses of this type encourages trainees to share experience. Another student in O'Holligan's research commented that: "the special educational needs course was particularly helpful because we had the opportunity to discuss different kinds of educational difficulties which we'd come across in schools. You gain a far greater insight by discussing them with other people" (p. 542).

(viii) They can promote understanding of issues relevant to classroom practice. In one case a video about street children in Brazil helped a group to realise the problems facing 'travelling children' whom they met during their school placement.

(ix) They offer a perspective, which is missing in much of the post-modernist personal theory, derived from reflective practitioner models of ITET. Wilkin brands this type of theory as *pastiche*, and points to the danger that reflection is not undertaken in any disciplined manner. It may well be unstructured, indiscriminate and superficial. She therefore argues for the use of educational disciplines as a tool for reflection.

Halliday (1996) agrees with her argument, and feels that reference to established educational disciplines could complement the reflective practitioner model. He writes that:

In order to even begin to have any idea of whether one is a good practitioner it is necessary to appeal to the authority that comes from membership of a community with an established tradition of distinguishing good from bad practice. ... Hence we may favour those programmes of teacher education in which there is a partnership between teachers working across a range of practices including the theoretical practices of history, philosophy, psychology and sociology (p. 56).

Again, Paul Hirst (1996) expresses the view that, unless young people entering the teaching profession have a clear grasp of theoretical concepts, they are at the mercy of prejudice and badly conceived ideology. In a book written with Furlong, Pocklington and Miles (1988) he advocates a system of ITET based upon four levels of professional practice:

LEVEL 1: DIRECT PRACTICE, involving practical training through experience in schools and classrooms.

LEVEL 2: INDIRECT PRACTICE, or training in practical matters, which is usually conducted in classes or workshops within training institutions, for example, through books, videos, visits and talks.

LEVEL 3: PRACTICAL PRINCIPLES, or a critical study of the principles of practice and their use. At this level students are encouraged to question their teaching in the light of established professional principles.

LEVEL 4: DISCIPLINARY THEORY, which involves a critical study of practice and its principles in the light of fundamental theory and research. At this level students can subject themselves to questioning derived from disciplinary theory.

In this model formal theory, incorporating the traditional disciplines of education, is seen as a tool for critical questioning rather than as something to be 'applied'.

II: A programme for educational and professional studies

Programmes of Educational and Professional Studies are most likely to be delivered by both mentors and HEI tutors. An outline is offered below.

(a) **Aims:** Important aims are:

- To develop in students a knowledge and understanding of whole-school and professional issues in the field of primary or secondary education. In the view of Eraut (1989) theoretical knowledge of this type empowers them to participate in educational discourse with qualified teachers.

- To provide a context for students to reflect upon their school experience and the attitudes, values and assumptions they bring to the profession. As McLaughlin (1994) has observed, the notions of Schon and other advocates of the 'reflective practitioner' model of ITET do not provide any clear framework for students to pursue. If reflection is to have any value, it must be located within a specific context. A course in educational and professional studies can provide just such a context for critical reflection.

- To enable students to develop informed views on key educational topics through observation, through dialogue with practitioners and peers and through structured reading.

- To permit students to relate knowledge of their specialist curriculum subject to the wider contexts of educational purposes and practices.

(b) **Content:** In the following list of topics, which could be used as the basis for a course in educational and professional studies, it is possible for mentors and others to make reference to certain of the traditional disciplines. For example, in the topic on the authority of the teacher, it is possible to use the techniques of analytic philosophy to clarify the meanings of epistemic and institutional authority and to discuss with reference to sociology the difference between traditional, charismatic and legal-rational authority. Areas such as 'discipline' and 'sanctions' can be explored in much the same way, for example, theories for the justification of punishment – retribution, deterrence and rehabilitation. Other topics, such as equal opportunities and the educational philosophies of the 'New Right' (Demaine, 1999) and the 'Third Way' (Francis, 2001), can also be studied in the contexts of the disciplines, and students can then be set the task of debating their own views concerning the aims of education. The desirability of allowing students to reflect upon crucial issues and to make use of the educational disciplines within this reflection is stressed by Halliday (1996), Hirst (1996), Arthur, Davison and Moss (1997) and, in the United States of America, by Roth (1999).

(i) *ISSUES OF CLASS MANAGEMENT*

Catt and Sweeney (1995) describe the programme of the four-year BA/BSc course with QTS at Brunel University, and note that 'survival' is seen to be a priority with most students. Consequently, they suggest that an educational and professional studies course should commence with class management. Possible themes are:

1. *The Teacher as an Authority: Class Rules*

Current issues relating to the teacher's authority; epistemic and institutional authority; the nature of school rules and their justification; the enforcement of rules in the classroom; current legislation on whole-school behaviour policy - the Education Act of 1997 and the School Standards and Framework Act of 1998; the role of school governors, the headteachers and staff; the role of the LEA; expectations of parents.

2. *Discipline*

The meaning of 'discipline' and types of discipline; strategies for the maintenance of discipline in classes and schools; the use of positive strategies (e.g. 'Catch them being good' and positive cognitive intervention); recommendations of the Elton report and other DFES publications; recent research studies in this field; guidelines on class management; schemes such as assertive discipline (Canter and Canter, 1977); the role of parents, governors and LEA support services; home-school agreements.

3. Rewards and Sanctions

Types of rewards utilised in the school; the use of 'contingency contracting'; school sanctions and punishments; the justification of rewards and sanctions; the legal position on such sanctions as detention, physical restraint, the confiscation of property and fixed-term and permanent exclusion; the Education Act of 1996; the Education Act of 1997; the School Standards and Framework Act of 1998, guidelines on physical restraint in DFEE circular 10/98.

(ii) CURRICULAR AND TEACHING ISSUES

1. The National Curriculum

Origins of the National Curriculum; the Education Reform Act of 1988 and subsequent review of the National Curriculum by Sir Ron Dearing; Curriculum 2000 in England and Wales; current requirements at Key Stages 1 to 4; programmes of study, attainment targets and level descriptions; disapplication of the National Curriculum at Key Stage 4 to allow for work-related education; thinking skills and other aspects of the school curriculum in England; common requirements in Wales; role of the QCA and ACCAC.

2. Key Skills

Communication; application of number; ICT; problem solving; working with others; improving one's own learning and performance; language and literacy, including the National Literacy and Numeracy Strategy; cross-curricular policies for promoting key skills.

3. Learning and Teaching

The nature of learning and teaching; studies by Piaget, Bruner and Vygotsky; teaching strategies: instruction; the management of practical activity; modes of heuristic learning; investigation and learning from experience; discussion; creative activity; negotiated learning; group work; the Hay McBer report (2000) and other research into effective teaching; ways in which learning can be affected by pupils' physical, intellectual, linguistic, social, cultural and emotional development.

4. The Planning of Lessons

Criteria for the planning of lessons; aims and objectives in lesson planning; continuity and progression in learning; strategies for gaining motivation; questioning techniques; the organisation of discussion and group work; the reinforcement of learning; the use of ICT; involving pupils in planning and evaluating their own learning; criteria for lesson evaluation.

5. Special Educational Needs:

Definitions of special educational needs; changes since the Education Act of 1944; the Warnock Report; the Education Act of 1981 and its impact; the Education Act of 1993 and the Code of Practice for the Identification and Assessment of Special Educational Needs; government initiatives since the publication of the 1997 Green Paper Excellence for All Children: Meeting SEN (DFEE, 1997a); role of the SENCO; the Special Educational Needs and Disability Act of 2001; ways in which the class teacher can help pupils with various disabilities.

(iii) *ASSESSMENT ISSUES*

1. *The Nature of Assessment*

The nature of educational assessment; purposes of assessment; limitations in assessment procedures; whole-school policy on assessment; formative and summative assessment; norm-referenced and criterion-referenced assessment; ipsative assessment; synoptic assessment; differentiation; techniques of assessment; moderation; record keeping; current research into assessment and learning (e.g. Black and Wiliam, 1998).

2. *Assessment under the National Curriculum*

Assessment arrangements from the time of the Education Reform Act of 1988; current requirements under the Education Act of 1996; teacher assessment and national tests; the use of level descriptions; assessment at key stage 4; statutory regulations for GCSE examinations; the assessment of pupils with learning difficulties; the use of P-scales and entry level qualifications; uses of assessment: league tables, value added, baseline assessment and target setting.

3. *Educational Provision 16-19*

A and AS level examinations; vocational qualifications; the 1996 Dearing Report and subsequent developments: the National Framework of Awards; the structure of qualifications for the 16-19 age range: advanced subsidiaries and A level examinations from 2000; key skills; vocational and occupational pathways; the Learning and Skills Act of 2000; quangos with responsibility for educational provision 16-19 (the respective roles of the Learning and Skills Council in England and the National Council for Education and Training in Wales); qualifications in Wales.

4. *Reporting Pupils' Achievements*

Current government policy on annual assessment reports and the School Leavers' Progress File (Achievement Planner); good practice in writing reports; the use of Records of Achievement (RoA); forms of RoA and techniques of profiling.

5. *Target Setting, School Improvement and School Effectiveness*

Target setting legislation under the 1997 Education Act and the School Standards and Framework Act of 1998; setting targets within schools; STAMP (setting targets and monitoring progress); school improvement (e.g. audits, PEST and SWOT analysis, development planning, identifying criteria for success); school effectiveness (e.g. recent surveys by OFSTED and Estyn); research into school effectiveness, (e.g. the work of Sammons, Hillman and Mortimore [1995] and of Harris [1999]).

(iii) *PASTORAL ISSUES*

1. *Pastoral Care and Guidance*

The need for a pastoral care system in a school; aims in the provision of pastoral care; the 1989 Children Act; the organisation of pastoral care; research into the provision of pastoral care, strategies for developing pastoral care in schools; the pastoral role of the teacher; the respective roles of the school counsellor and home-school liaison teacher; the concept of peer counselling.

2. *Bullying*

Definitions of bullying; the extent of the problem; the legal position; strategies for combating bullying in primary and secondary schools: whole-school policies; curricular issues; working with pupils in a bullying situation; the school environment.

3. *Truancy*

Legal requirements relating to pupils' attendance at school; the duties of parents; school attendance orders; authorised and unauthorised absences; the problem of truancy; strategies for improving attendance; current initiatives.

4. *Personal, Social and Health Education (PSHE) and Work-Related Education*

Legal requirements relating to the spiritual, moral, social and cultural development of pupils; the non-statutory framework for PSHE and the statutory Order for citizenship in England; personal and social education (PSE) in Wales; examples of learning strategies and approaches; sex education; drugs education; careers education; education for citizenship; environmental education; approaches to the organisation of PSHE in the curriculum; work-related education: ACCAC's *Framework for Work-Related Education;* work experience; enterprise activities; mentoring on the part of employers; vocationally related courses; inputs from employers into the curriculum and coursework assignments; work-related education in specific subjects; careers guidance; co-ordinating school-industry links.

5. *The Transition from Primary to Secondary Education*

Differences between primary and secondary education; research into problems encountered by pupils in the transition from primary to secondary education; pastoral problems; the problem of liaison in the curriculum; the transfer of records from primary to secondary schools; strategies for easing the transition from one sector to the other.

6. *Equal Opportunities*

Provisions of the Sex Discrimination Act of 1975; the Race Relations Act of 1976 and subsequent amendments; the Special Educational Needs and Disability Act of 2001; the concepts of justice, equality and equality of opportunity; issues in education relating to gender and race; strategies for promoting equality of opportunity with reference to curriculum choice, multi-cultural education and the underachievement of boys.

(v) *LEGAL AND PROFESSIONAL ISSUES*

1. *The Educational System*

The educational system which emerged under the Education Act of 1944; important changes since 1988; the philosophies of the 'New Right' and of the 'Third Way'; Conservative and New Labour policies on education; powers of the Secretary of State for Education and Skills; LEAs and new systems of local government; financial delegation to schools; categories of school (e.g. community, voluntary and foundation schools); the issue of selection in secondary education (e.g. specialist schools); admissions arrangements; the role of the private sector in educational provision; education in Wales (e.g. powers of the National Assembly for Wales).

2. *School Governors*

The constitution of governors under current legislation; powers and responsibilities of governors (e.g. deciding the status of the school and its aims, conduct and values; development planning; target setting; home-school agreements; the curriculum; the school budget; charges for school activities; health and safety legislation; the annual report and annual parents' meeting; action plans; and complaints procedures); support and training for governors.

3. *Professional Issues in Education*

The appointment of teachers; the induction period in England and Wales; salary structure; the School Teachers' Pay and Conditions document; the career structure and national professional qualifications; staff development; dismissal of staff; the role of the General Teaching Councils for England and for Wales.

4. *Performance Management*

The development of systems of appraisal under the Education (No. 2) Act of 1986 and the Regulations of 1991; research studies into the effectiveness of school teacher appraisal under this legislation; current regulations governing the stages of performance management; the rationale underlying performance management; role and responsibilities; current discussion and opinions on the operation of performance management.

5. *School Inspection*

Origins of school inspection; recent legislation on school inspection (e.g. the 1992 Education [Schools] Act, the 1993 Education Act, the 1996 School Inspections Act, the Education Act of 1997, the School Standards and Framework Act of 1998, the Education Act 2002); OFSTED and Estyn; inspection teams and their training; the process of school inspection; the framework for inspection; school action plans; the treatment of various categories of failing school (e.g. Labour's 'Fresh Start' policy).

6. *Legal Issues in Education*

Health and safety (e.g. the Health and Safety at Work Act of 1974); the teacher's duty of care; the law of negligence; implications of the Human Rights Act of 1998; risk assessment; the Children Act of 1989; off-site visits and activity centres; the Misuse of Drugs Act 1971; assault and physical restraint; taking care of pupils' property; discrimination; the law of copyright.

7. *Parents' Rights*

Relationships between schools and parents; recent legislation on the rights of parents; parental preference for schools; government policy on school admissions; the Greenwich and Rotherham judgements; the School Standards and Framework Act of 1998; the provision of information to parents; parents' involvement in school activities; parental ballots; the rights of parents who sit on education committees; parents' evenings and other forms of contact; parents' associations.

III: Developing educational and professional knowledge: the role of co-ordinators, mentors and tutors

Any programme offered by ITET co-ordinators and mentors should be well planned with clear links to the work covered at the HEI. Ways in which relationships can be established between HEIs and schools are listed below.

(a) **Involvement of Co-ordinators and Mentors in the HEI Courses:** Both co-ordinators and mentors can be involved in lead lectures and seminar classes at the HEI. They are able to describe policy at their schools in relation to such topics as discipline, assessment, pastoral care, multi-cultural education and financial provision. This adds a fresh dimension to students' thinking and shows them the impact that government policies can have upon schools.

(b) **The Provision of Information to Students on Whole-School Policies:** OHMCI (1998b) argues that "good mentoring ensures that trainees have the necessary, relevant information about the school, including documentation on policies and organisation" (p. 4). In most partnerships it is expected that students receive copies of whole-school policies relating to the areas covered in the college programme, for example, procedures relating to discipline, safety, school visits, assessment, SEN and equal opportunities. These can then be used in seminars in school and college, where, as McIntyre, Hagger and Burn (1994) note, they are helpful in developing understanding and recognition of "why policies are as they are" (p. 68).

In many partnerships students are set tasks by HEIs tutors which require them to make reference to these whole-school policies. They are encouraged to take a critical stance (e.g. How could whole-school policy on bullying at the school be further developed?) and to compare and contrast the strategies adopted at different schools. The opportunity to share experiences of a variety of practice is one reason why UWIC students favour school-based as opposed to school-centred ITET.

(c) **Structured Observation:** It is a common practice for students to undertake observation of aspects of the work of the school outside the teaching of their subject. This allows them to note at first hand many of the aspects of school life they have studied at the HEI. A typical list of items for observation may include:

- aspects of school administration and organisation;

- curriculum planning meetings;

- welfare and pastoral arrangements;

- the everyday responsibilities of a member of the school staff outside specialist subject teaching;

- the tutorial programme devised for classes within a system of pastoral care;

- provision for SEN;

- the teaching of PSHE;

- INSET provision;

- decision making at staff meetings.

(d) **Seminars in Schools:** ITET co-ordinators usually hold regular seminars in their schools, each dealing with a topic covered at the HEI. This enables students to undertake a detailed study of school practice in the light of their reading and discussion. Concepts acquired in the HEI's reading programme can then be applied to the 'real' world of the school.

In the planning of their programmes, it is often helpful to co-ordinators if staff at the HEI inform them of the order of the topics covered in their courses and provide them with copies of the reading lists supplied to their students.

(e) **Seminar Papers:** Many schools and universities make use of student-led seminars. In planning these it is not uncommon for trainees to consult their mentors in order to acquire factual information about school policy and advice on presentation. Seminars are delivered to students' peers and may be conducted in the school or at the HEI. A typical format is for students to:

- prepare for the seminar by reading course material and other relevant sources and assembling overhead projector transparencies and 'handouts' for the other students. They undertake research with respect to policies and practices at their school, using documentation provided them by ITET co-ordinators or mentors, information gathered in interviews with teachers or questionnaire returns from pupils. This approach offers opportunities for investigative learning.

- lead the seminar session by speaking about the topic for fifteen minutes or so, summarising the key points and describing school experience.

- setting topics for sub-groups to discuss and to report their conclusions to the whole class. This allows all students to draw on their own school experience, to compare the policies operated at the different schools and to think critically about the optimum strategies which could be adopted.

- allowing the leader of each sub-group to sum up the overall points raised.

- drawing the ideas together and reaching an overall conclusion.

Other techniques for organising student debate include:

- pyramiding, where pairs initially discuss an issue, after which two pairs are brought together. Next a group of eight is formed and this process of combining groups continues until the whole class is involved in a plenary debate;

- individual responses, where students are given five or ten minutes to record their ideas individually before they contribute to a general discussion;

- advocacy, where one group prepares a case in favour of some proposition (for example, that the National Curriculum should not be changed within the next ten years), while a second group assembles opposing arguments;

- brainstorming as a prelude to general discussion.

Seminars of this type can be helpful in encouraging students to reflect critically on whole-school issues by:

- comparing and contrasting experience at the different schools represented by members of the seminar class;

- relating practices they have met in schools to the policies described in such texts as: Petty (1995); Dean (1996); Capel, Leask and Turner (1999); Cowley (1999); Nicholls (1999); Bartlett, Buton and Peim (2001); and Geen (2001b).

- discussing aspects of good practice in the light of their experience and reading;

- interviewing mentors and other school staff to gain an insight into the informed opinion of experienced practitioners;

- issuing short questionnaires to selected pupils, which allows them to gain an understanding of the perceptions of their 'clients';

- comparing the viewpoints of students teaching a variety of disciplines.

Student-led seminars also have the merit that they give participants a greater sense of ownership of the course, since they make a major contribution to its teaching.

A useful policy at UWIC has been for the student who is leading a topic to set specific tasks to the other members of the group a week in advance, for example, to bring in a piece of work they have assessed against the National Curriculum level descriptions or to complete a questionnaire on the management structure of their school. This ensures that all students are fully prepared to discuss the topic with reference to their school experience.

(f) **Use of Videos:** These can be of great value when used by mentors in seminars with students.

They fall into two categories:

- videos of lessons given by students at the school in previous years. It is sound policy to select a specific focus, for example, managing the class, organising group work, motivating pupils or consolidating learning. Videos of this type present an excellent opportunity for students to think critically about classroom performance. In a study by Geen, Bassett and Douglas (1998) of the role of the ITET co-ordinator, this technique was especially welcomed by students in the early stages of a placement.

- commercial videos, for example, *Developing Teaching Skills* (Local Education Authorities in Association with Higher Education Institutions, 1993a and 1993b).

(g) **Role play:** This is a technique which can be employed in seminars organised by mentors. McIntyre, Hagger and Burn (1994) suggest the use of role play in the following contexts:

(i) *looking in concrete terms at complex issues to which access might be difficult*, for example, students playing the role of school governors and debating problems which governors may face;

(ii) *providing simulated practice*, for example, mock interviews for a teaching post or role-playing a parents' evening in which students can practise the skills of reporting to and listening to the views of others.

(iii) *opening up debate on potentially heated issues*, for example, political issues in education such as the expansion of specialist schools in England.

Students gain most from these sessions when they have time to prepare their ideas and then, once they have completed the role play, to stand back and consider what they have learned from the experience.

(h) **The Use of Discursive Discourse in Debriefing Sessions:** In the first chapter the distinction was drawn between *pragmatic* discourse, where mentors' feedback centres on issues of immediate relevance to a given lesson, and *discursive* dialogue, where wider educational issues are explored. Hence, a debriefing which starts with an evaluation of a student's assessment techniques in a lesson could lead to debate about the whole issue of assessment in education and the purposes to which it is put. Mentors may lead students to reflect upon assessment under the National Curriculum, the use of 'league tables', the provision of information to parents to help them decide the school they wish their child to attend, and the whole 'market forces' philosophy of education.

(i) **First Hand Experience:** OMHCI (1998b) stresses that appropriate opportunities should be provided for trainees to play a full and active part in the life and work of the school. In many secondary partnerships they have the opportunity to work with a form tutor. McIntyre, Hagger and Burn (1994) recommend that, because of the nature of pastoral care, students should spend a substantial amount of time with one tutor, while observing the work of a number of others and talking to them about their responsibilities. They should have direct experience of taking a tutor group by being involved in the delivery of the pastoral programme, working with individual pupils, completing the register, checking homework diaries, giving out notices, helping with class assemblies and completing records of achievement. They should be observed by the tutor as they fulfil these functions and receive appropriate feedback. They may also attend meetings of the tutorial team and talk to parents and representatives of external agencies, for example, educational psychologists. In many schools they begin with observation, then work with the teacher and, finally, take on a more substantial pastoral role.

Attending parents' evenings is another important activity. In a study by Davies and Ferguson (1997) eighty per cent of qualified teachers felt that their initial training had not equipped them to fulfil this function.

(j) **Involvement of Expert Speakers:** Students benefit from contact with expert speakers, for example, representatives from the QCA and awarding bodies to talk about curricular and assessment issues, from OFSTED and Estyn to provide a further perspective on school inspection, from the police to inform them about drugs education and from the GTCs, TTA or teachers' unions to discuss the teacher's career structure. They may meet these people in classes conducted at the HEI, in schools as part of in-service provision, or in seminars planned by the ITET co-ordinator.

(k) **The Setting of Whole-School Policy Assignments:** It is common policy for students, as well as leading and participating in seminars, to extend their study of the seminar topic into a written assignment, the precise title of which is negotiated with the co-ordinator, mentor or tutor. A possible format which encourages reflection is for them to:

- review relevant literature on the topic of their choice;

- relate the topic to policy in their school, highlighting what they consider to be its main strengths and areas for improvement;

- reach some personal judgement on the issue, perhaps indicating how school procedures may be further developed in the light of their reading, reflection and discussion with students attending other schools.

(l) **Journals:** In some partnerships, students keep a journal of daily events on their ITET course covering seminars, school observation and experiences with a tutorial group, together with a personal response. Where this is the practice, they can be encouraged to relate school experience to studies undertaken at the HEI.

(m) **Briefing Sheets:** Some mentors use briefing sheets which set students specific activities, for example, to investigate a different school policy each week over a number of weeks and to keep a record of their findings with relevant notes and documentation. Briefing sheets can be set out under the headings of:

	Students' notes
TOPIC	
RELATION TO THE STANDARDS	
SUMMARY OF SCHOOL POLICY (in bullet point format)	
REFLECTION ON THE ISSUE (as the result of school and college seminars, investigations, etc.)	
OVERALL CONCLUSIONS	

(n) **Out of School Activities:** Educational trips such as a tour of the catchment area and visits to 'linked' schools to discuss primary-secondary transition are usually appreciated by trainees.

(o) **Partnership Meetings:** It is important that regular meetings are held between ITET co-ordinators and HEI tutors. This provides the opportunity for discussion of any problems in the liaison between the school and the higher education institution in the teaching of educational and professional studies.

IV: Research into the effectiveness of liaison between schools and HEIs

An attempt has been made at UWIC over a number of years to assess the effectiveness of the strategies employed to help students extend their knowledge of educational and professional issues and to use the findings of these surveys to improve the quality of mentoring. It has been observed that the introduction of partnership and the delineation of the responsibilities of co-ordinators, mentors and tutors have been highly beneficial in developing this aspect of an ITET course.

(a) **The Initial Impact of Partnership:** Partnership under the terms of DFE Circular 9/92 and Welsh Office Circular 35/92 was introduced to UWIC's secondary ITET courses in September 1994. Responding to a detailed questionnaire issued in the late summer of 1996, seventeen students in their last term of a four year undergraduate course pointed to a considerable improvement in their school experience when they compared the academic years 1992-93 and 1995-1996 (Geen, Bassett, Davies and Douglas, 1998). The main points they raised were:

(i) In the pre-partnership regime they had little opportunity to observe the work of the school outside their subject specialism and few ever met senior staff. One student saw the deputy headteacher once a fortnight and another once a month. Less than half received information on key school policies, and only two shadowed a class. None was offered an overview of the school's organisation; nor were any seminars organised within these school which had immediate relevance to the educational and professional studies courses held at UWIC. Hence, typical comments were:

> *Very little contact with senior teachers.*

> *What seminars? There were none !*

> *A brief welcome and introductory meeting were arranged, but no seminars took place and therefore no professional relationship was established.*

> *The deputy head was always very busy. Hence, there were no regular meetings.*

(ii) Under the partnership regime the position changed considerably. Most of the fourth year students felt that during the academic year 1995-96 they had received an effective introduction to the work of the school beyond the teaching of their subject. Six of them attended weekly sessions with the ITET co-ordinator, and two others had meetings at least once a fortnight. All considered that these seminars were well structured and informative, though only four considered that there was a clear link with the programme offered at the HEI.

Of the twenty first year students recruited to the course during the school year 1995-96, twelve had regular seminars in educational and professionals studies with the ITET co-ordinator - eight at least once a week. Two expressed the opinion that they had a strong relationship with the college course, while the others could identify a partial relationship. In every case these classes were deemed to have been valuable in offering perspectives on educational issues within the context of the school. Only one never met the co-ordinator at all. Seventeen obtained copies of policy documents, twelve were given full information about the school's management structure and eleven shadowed a form tutor.

(b) **Partnership by 1996-97:** A further study which examined the perceptions of 160 PGCE students concerning the role of the ITET co-ordinator during the period 1996-97 (Geen, Bassett and Douglas, 1998) found many examples of good practice with respect to the provision made for educational and professional studies:

(i) Most students received basic information on the organisation of the school, for example,

- Eighty-seven per cent obtained a school handbook and eighty-four per cent a statement of policy on discipline.

- Policy on curriculum and assessment was made available to seventy-four per cent and fifty-eight per cent respectively.

(ii) One student reported that her ITET co-ordinator, as well as providing all the necessary documentation, had organised a tour of the catchment area, which had enabled her to understand many of the problems facing the school.

(iii) Seventy-two per cent had been able to participate in extra-curricular activities and to work closely with a form tutor, sixty-three per cent were involved in in-service sessions and sixty-two per cent learned about the school's management structure.

(iv) Specific examples of good practice were identified, including the following:

- At one school the ITET co-ordinator did not take every seminar class himself. Rather, he superintended the overall organisation of the programme and regularly involved specialist staff, for example, colleagues with extensive experience in SEN, PSHE, pastoral care and assessment policy. This meant that trainees had access to staff with first hand expertise and a thorough knowledge of the topic under consideration. It also spread the workload for the co-ordinator, contributed to the professional development of the school staff and helped create a whole-school commitment to ITET.

- Some mentors encouraged students to chair school-based seminars, guided them to suitable texts and permitted them to conduct interviews with pertinent staff and pupils.

- In some cases students attended sessions organised for newly qualified teachers, which they found to be relevant and informative.

- In a few cases their lessons were videotaped and used for subsequent discussion with mentors and the ITET co-ordinator. Where a student was dissatisfied with a lesson, it was shown to other trainees in the cohort only with her/his permission.

- Students were encouraged to attend in-service sessions which dealt with new examination specifications, target setting and school improvement.

(v) Most ITET co-ordinators felt that contact between their schools and the HEI was satisfactory. Eighty per cent found the dispatch of students' reading material in educational and professional studies to be advantageous, though at least one admitted that he could not always find time to read as much of the literature as he would have liked. Seventy per cent felt that the guidelines provided by the HEI on co-ordinators' responsibilities with respect to educational and professional studies were clear.

In some schools, however, opportunities for students to extend their understanding of educational and professional issues were more limited.

(i) The opportunities for observation outside the department were restricted in certain schools. Thus, only forty-nine per cent of the PGCE students had the opportunity to observe the work of their school's SEN unit and only forty-five per cent were able to attend lessons in PSHE. Just forty-two per cent shadowed teachers of disciplines other than their own and a mere thirty-two per cent attended curriculum planning meetings.

(ii) In a minority of schools students did not receive all the requisite whole-school policies. In some instances they were provided with school handbooks which were lacking in detail. One PGCE student felt that her inability to secure a copy of the school's disciplinary code had adversely affected her classroom experience. Three other students stated that information had been attained only after frequent requests on their part.

(iii) Some ITET co-ordinators were too busy to work with the students on educational and professional issues. Hence, the comment was received:

> *The ITET co-ordinator said that he always had time to*
> *speak to us, but, whenever we asked, he was too*
> *busy and make it obvious that it was a struggle for*
> *him to fit us in.*

Only fifteen per cent of ITET co-ordinators could find time to offer advice and guidance to students in the preparation of their seminar paper and twenty-three per cent in the writing of their educational and professional studies assignments. Students reported that:

> *It is hard to know what the ITET co-ordinator's role is,*
> *as I haven't met her at all.*

> *They should be made aware of what the job entails.*
> *Mine never even knew my name.*

(iv) Problems were identified with the seminar classes held by some co-ordinators.

- Although they were asked to organise one class each week and to ensure that, as far as was possible, the content correlated with the topic being studied at the HEI, in practice only half the students were able to attend sessions along these lines once a week, ten per cent once a fortnight, four per cent once a month and ten per cent less than this. Three students alleged that over their entire period at the school only one seminar had been held, and a quarter of all respondents had no opportunity at all to meet the ITET co-ordinator for this purpose. Students stated that:

> *We did not have a single session with the ITET co-ordinator when college expected him to see us once a week.*

> *It would have been nice if we had had a meeting.*

- Where students did participate in these seminars, only forty per cent felt that they related to the topics covered in the college course. These classes were thought to have "introduced real life issues and problems", "prompted discussion of relevant case studies" and "offered useful, practical advice". A further thirty-six per cent of students expressed general satisfaction with the seminars, but just under a quarter criticised them on the grounds that they consisted of little more than "a general chat", were "unstructured and ill-co-ordinated" or dealt with themes which did not feature within the HEI's programme.

(c) **Partnership by 2001:** It is pleasing to report that in the most recent survey of PGCE students' experiences covering the academic sessions 2000-2001, a higher proportion judged that the provision made for educational and professional studies had been highly satisfactory. To a large extent, this has been the result of mentor training and an emphasis in communications with partnership schools upon the responsibilities of co-ordinators. Eighty-nine per cent of a sample of sixty students reported that they had been provided with a staff/student handbook which contained the information they needed, eighty-five per cent with the school's policy on discipline and eighty per cent with documentation concerning the curriculum. Seventy-one per cent studied the management structure of the school, observed the work of a form tutor and extended their knowledge of special educational needs through contact with the appropriate co-ordinator. Fifty-one per cent attended lessons in personal and social education, half had been invited to relevant in-service sessions and just over sixty-five per cent received a weekly seminar with the senior mentor. Two typical observations on the role of the senior mentor were:

> *There was frequent contact time and an enriching programme of seminars where various whole school issues were covered.*

> *The EPS programme offered in the school linked in nicely with what we had studied at the university. It was good to see policies on SEN and PSHE in practice. I could understand more vividly some of the things we covered in the seminars at UWIC.*

The main problems identified in 2001 by ITET co-ordinators were:

- *lack of time*, a problem which has been discussed in previous chapters;

- *coping with students from up to six different HEIs, each of which adopts its own syllabus in educational and professional studies.* Time does not allow for the organisation of separate seminars for students from each university, and, as the courses offered by these institutions are so diverse, it is impossible to plan a single set of classes which deal adequately with all the themes and topics they seek to cover. Consequently, most co-ordinators decide to follow the scheme of work devised by staff at one HEI only, although they are fully aware that this can be unfair to students from the other colleges.

  This problem has been noted in other schemes of ITET. For example, McIntyre, Hagger and Burn (1994) state that "working with different partnerships reduces the possibility of planning coherent programmes. ... For the professional tutor [i.e. ITET co-ordinator] working with several HEIs each sending student teachers to the school at different times and for relatively short periods, coherence of any kind will be very difficult to attain" (pp. 60-61).

- *coping with students who are pursuing different types of ITET course*, for example, PGCE, four year BA(Ed) and two year BA(Ed). Periods of school experience within these courses varied from four to fourteen weeks, while one-day visits were also organised. To add to the complexity of this situation, one institution sent PGCE students specialising in different disciplines into the schools at different times. This made it impossible for the co-ordinator to offer one coherent course in educational and professional studies.

- *costs*, especially those involved in photocopying policy documents and other information for students. In some schools up to twenty copies were required at any one time, and, since PGCE students are expected by central government to attend at least two schools, mentors had to cater annually for at least two separate cohorts.

(d) **Future Developments:** Some ideas for improving the quality of mentoring with respect to educational and professional studies are:

(i) *the provision of more time for mentors to fulfil their role:* Suggestions to achieve this end have been listed in the second chapter.

(ii) *the creation of a national policy (or local agreements) to define:*

- the periods of time students spend in HEIs and schools. This would allow ITET co-ordinators to plan seminars for all their students at the same time over the year;

- the content and order of input of ITET courses in educational and professional studies;

- a minimum student entitlement in terms of the provision of documentation, seminars with ITET co-ordinators and activities within the school to promote knowledge and understanding.

(iii) *delegation of responsibility:* In schools where the ITET co-ordinator is the deputy headteacher or another member of the senior management team with a heavy workload, it may be possible to delegate the role wholly or partly to colleagues who have more time. In planning activities relating to educational and professional studies, the co-ordinator could involve a team of staff. This would reduce the amount of time required of each person, and the students could benefit from meeting teachers with expertise in various fields. It may also be possible to organise several smaller seminar classes, the activities of each being supervised by a different member of staff. If this policy is adopted, it is, of course, important that the function of each teacher is carefully recorded to avoid overlap and unnecessary duplication.

(iv) *the organisation of a continuous cycle of training for mentors* so that they are fully aware of the demands of their role. This is especially important in schools when ITET co-ordinators retire or move to other posts and their successors are less sure of their responsibilities.

> Issues for consideration

1. Read sections I and II (*changing views of the 'knowledge base' of teaching* and *a programme for educational and professional studies*). As is noted in the text, some of the topics listed are relevant to seminars offered by both the ITET co-ordinator and mentors. Give four examples of such topics and suggest ways in which both types of mentor could handle them in discussion with students in such a way that the treatment is complementary but not repetitive.

2. Read section III (*developing educational and professional knowledge: the role of ITET co-ordinators, mentors and tutors*). List the items of information which are provided to students at your school with respect to whole-school issues.

3. Describe the provision made at your school for students to undertake structured observation in the following contexts:

   (a) *the management structure of the school;*

   (b) *the functions of senior members of staff;*

   (c) *pastoral and welfare duties;*

   (d) *the everyday responsibilities of a member of the school staff outside specialist subject teaching;*

   (e) *tutorial programmes of study;*

   (f) *working with pupils with SEN;*

   (g) *the teaching of PSHE;*

   (h) *INSET provision;*

   (i) *attending curriculum planning meetings;*

   (j) *attending appropriate staff meetings.*

4. Describe the system of seminars for ITET students. What strategies are adopted to secure liaison between these seminars and the course provided at the students' HEI?

5. What opportunities are available to students to experience the welfare and pastoral duties of the class teacher/form tutor (including meetings with representatives of external agencies)?

6. Distinguish *pragmatic* and *discursive* dialogue in the context of mentoring. Give examples of ways in which you could employ discursive dialogue in debriefing with students.

7. Students are often expected to complete journals, assignments and debriefing sheets. Describe any help which they are given in this process by the ITET co-ordinator and/or other members of the school staff.

8. List any activities which are organised by mentors at your school for ITET students beyond seminars and observation of school staff (for example, tours of the catchment area, visits to 'feeder' primary or 'receiving' secondary schools, links to FE colleges).

9. Read section IV (*research into the effectiveness of liaison between schools and HEIs*) and discuss the main issues with any students who are currently at your school. Ascertain their views on the effectiveness of the partnership between school and HEI in providing a coherent induction to educational and professional studies. List the principal strengths and any areas in which improvements could be made.

10. As a result of your analysis of current practice for promoting students' professional knowledge, devise an action plan for the future development of this aspect of ITET at your school.

7 Skills in mentoring 1

I: Mentoring skills

Previous chapters have dealt with mentoring roles, the organisation of ITET in schools and important aspects of student teachers' experience. We now concentrate upon the principal skills which mentors need in order to help students both in their classroom experience and in their study of the wider aspects of education. Several studies have been undertaken of the qualities trainees expect of their mentors. PGCE students at Cambridge have described successful mentoring in terms of accessibility and the provision of sympathetic and positive support. Key phrases include: 'encouraged me'; 'highly approachable'; 'supported me fully'; 'tact and sympathy'; 'made me feel welcome and useful' (Booth, 1995). Similarly, Anderson and Shannon (1995), Elliott and Calderhead (1995) and Maynard (2000) observe that student teachers desire a 'friendly' relationship with their mentors.

Many of these skills are self-evident, and in a study of students' perceptions of the qualities exhibited by their mentors (Geen, Bassett and Douglas, 1999b) the majority of respondents rated highly the teachers with whom they worked with respect to communication, challenging thinking without damaging confidence, listening to problems, counselling and helping with time management.

Nonetheless, problems can arise where:

(a) **mentors are coerced into the role and work with students without the necessary support and training.** An example can be given with reference to the comments received from one student in a survey undertaken at UWIC during the school year 2001-2002. She had previously embarked upon the registered teacher programme in England. The member of staff with responsibility for monitoring her progress - a specialist in design and technology rather than her subject area of music - complained that he had been compelled to take on the role with no allocation of time to carry out his duties and no preparation. Consequently, he failed to observe the student's teaching, and she was expected to compile a portfolio of evidence to indicate how she had met the seventy-six QTS standards of DFEE Circular 4/98 (DFEE, 1998b) with minimal assistance from the music department. As a result of these factors, she had withdrawn from the programme.

(b) **school staff do not really want to have students in their classroom.** This issue was raised in the second and fourth chapters where certain trainees reported that collaborative teaching had not been very successful since they had been made to feel like intruders in the classroom.

(c) **mentors feel vulnerable:** Some mentors do not consider that their lessons are of a sufficiently high standard for newcomers to the classroom to observe; others experience insecurity as the result of their lack of reading about educational issues.

(d) **mentors seek to establish a friendly relationship with a student, and are then reluctant to offer critical feedback.** As Back and Booth (1992) note, there can sometimes be a clash between the demands of 'friendship' and 'providing challenge'. Jones (2001) also observes that "the role of the assessor can generate tension in the trainee-mentor relationship, particularly when assessment is closely related to pre-determined outcomes" (p. 81).

(e) **mentors have unrealistic expectations of what students can achieve:** This problem has been identified in a study based upon the experiences of ITET students registered at the School of Education at Anglia Polytechnic University (Turner and Bash, 1999, p.21).

(f) **professional development fails to focus upon valuable mentoring skills.** The importance of professional development which promotes skills pertinent to the role of mentor has been stressed by Corbett and Wright (1994), Devlin (1995) and Moyles, Suschitzky and Chapman (1998), and in courses operated by many HEIs special attention is paid to such skills as communicating, counselling, listening and time management (Booth, 2001).

In a survey of the training received by mentors in schools in South-East Wales (Geen, 2000c), over half the respondents reported that they had been able to develop a number of skills, especially communicating with students, assisting them to anticipate and cope with classroom problems, and offering critical comments. Less time, however, had been devoted to helping students who experienced problems, negotiating targets and encouraging them to adopt a broader perspective when they had hit a plateau and were relying upon a limited number of teaching methods with which they felt comfortable.

In this same survey, students were asked to point to areas in which they believed their mentors would benefit from further professional development. At the top of their list were:

- stimulating them to experiment with alternative pedagogic strategies when they had settled into a routine;

- ensuring that they received regular feedback which would enable them to improve their teaching.

Suggestions for professional development for mentors have been listed in the second chapter. To enhance activities of this nature, some excellent packs have been produced which focus upon important skills (for example, Acton, Kirkham and Smith, 1992). In this and the next chapter some ideas are presented with the aim of helping mentors develop further their thinking about the skills they need, notably, the motivation of students, effective listening and communicating, negotiation, problem-solving, time management and target setting.

II: Motivation

(a) **Definition:** Motivation may be defined as the psychological force which drives a person to follow a course of action. It may be represented in diagrammatic form:

DRIVE DETERMINANTS (attitudes, emotions, interests, needs, wants) > DRIVE STATE > GOAL SEEKING BEHAVIOUR > GOAL ATTAINMENT > SATISFACTION/ DRIVE REDUCTION

In the context of mentoring, it can be argued that motivation is a powerful force for 'getting the best' out of the trainee. It lies at the heart of the process of ITET, and the task of securing self-motivation in students is an important function of co-ordinators and mentors.

(b) **Types of Motivation:** Three types of motivation are:

(i) *intrinsic motivation*, where a person participates in some activity for its own sake because it matches a need or relates to an interest;

(ii) *extrinsic motivation* where a person engages in an activity in order to achieve some goal which is rewarding but which is external to the activity itself, for example, a qualification which will lead to a better paid post;

(iii) *expectation of success*, where the person feels that he/she is likely to succeed at a particular activity.

Mentors need to take especial note of this third factor and set a sequence of activities in which students can achieve a sense of satisfaction through successfully accomplishing tasks and feel that they are making progress.

(c) **Studies of Motivation:** A number of psychologists and management theorists have sought to analyse the nature of human motivation. Some of the most famous studies are quoted below.

(i) *Abraham Maslow* (1954) examines human needs and argues that they are arranged in a hierarchy, ranging from primary physiological needs at the base, for example, the need for food, clothing and shelter, to self-actualisation - the development of inner talents and abilities - at the top. He believes that lower needs have to be satisfied before the higher ones come into play. Humans, he contends, are always striving towards the fulfilment of more positive growth.

Maslow's theory has been subjected to criticism over the years (for example, Argyris, 1972), but the argument that such needs as self-esteem and self-actualisation are helpful in understanding certain types of human behaviour is a recurring theme in the works of many social scientists and psychologists (for example, Lewin, 1935; Fromm, 1955).

(ii) *Frederick Herzberg* (1966) asked two hundred respondents - mainly engineers and accountants in industrial concerns in Pittsburgh - to recall times when they felt particularly positive about their jobs, and their reasons were recorded. They were then required to describe occasions when they had negative feelings about their work.

Herzberg's major finding was that the events which led to satisfaction were of a different kind from those which created dissatisfaction. Thus, he found that:

- *job satisfaction* generally stemmed from a person's need to realise his/her potential, for example, ACHIEVEMENT, RECOGNITION, ENJOYMENT OF THE WORK ITSELF, RESPONSIBILITY and ADVANCEMENT. These factors Herzberg called 'job satisfiers'.

- *job dissatisfaction* generally stemmed from the environment and work conditions, for example, POLICY AND ADMINISTRATION, SUPERVISION, SALARY, INTER-PERSONAL RELATION, STATUS, JOB SECURITY and WORKING CONDITIONS. These factors he called 'job dissatisfiers'.

Herzberg concluded that:

- The two feelings of satisfaction and dissatisfaction are not opposites. Rather, they relate to two different ranges of human needs. Factors associated with satisfaction stem from the need to realise potential, while factors associated with job dissatisfaction link to our need to avoid physical and social deprivation.

- Removal of the dissatisfiers will not necessarily result in satisfaction. Herzberg calls the dissatisfiers *hygiene* factors, arguing that, whereas lack of hygiene will cause disease, its presence will not necessarily result in good health. Similarly, the presence of dissatisfiers prevents job satisfaction, but their removal does not in itself promote job satisfaction.

- People should be placed in an environment where everything possible is done to increase the number of job satisfiers. There should be 'vertical job loading', where opportunities are provided for achievement, responsibility, growth and learning.

(iii) *T.J. Sergiovanni:* (1969) reached similar conclusions in a survey of teachers. The significant satisfiers were: ACHIEVEMENT, RECOGNITION (for example, from pupils, parents, colleagues and superiors), and RESPONSIBILITY. The most significant dissatisfiers were: INTERPERSONAL RELATIONS with other teachers and pupils, SCHOOL POLICY AND ADMINISTRATION, and SUPERVISION.

He found that satisfaction was most likely to be derived from a situation where teachers:

- exercised a high degree of autonomy in decision making;

- had increased responsibility in developing and implementing teaching programmes;

- were encouraged to develop personal skills.

Herzberg's research is discussed in greater detail by Luthans (1989, pp. 244-255) and Bush and West-Burnham, (1994, pp. 232-233).

(iv) *E.A. Locke* and *G.P. Latham* (1990) develop a 'high performance cycle' model which is based upon the assumption that satisfaction in the workplace depends upon a person's appraisal of the job matched to his/her system of values. In this model they highlight:

- *demands*, in terms of the tasks to be performed by the individual. These must be seen by him/her to be challenging and meaningful;

- *performance* which is influenced by such factors as ability, commitment, feedback, expectancy and the complexity of the task;

- *rewards* which may be internal, for example, seeing the task completed successfully, or external, for example, incentive payments;

- *satisfaction* derived from the rewards;

- *consequences* derived from satisfaction, such as commitment to the organisation and willingness to accept future challenges.

The implications of the model are that:

- Effective organisations should have high expectations of their employees. Low expectations can be demotivating.

- Superordinates must ensure that a sense of satisfaction is gained in return for effort.

- Satisfaction is derived from:

  - tasks which are seen to be meangingful and within the capacity of the employee to accomplish;

  - rewards received from successful performance.

- Superordinates need to understand what influences each individual and what promotes satisfaction for that person.

- They should encourage staff to set specific, challenging but realistic targets for themselves.

- Feedback on work performance should, where appropriate, help staff to identify effective strategies for improving future performance in the light of these targets.

(v) *James Belasco* and *Joseph Alutto* (1975) made a study in the USA of teacher satisfaction in relation to their ability to participate in decision making. They grouped the teachers involved into three categories characterised by:

- decisional deprivation, where the current level of participation was less than desired;

- decisional equilibrium, where the current participation was equal to the desired level of participation;

- decisional saturation, where current participation was greater than desired.

The results of the survey showed that "those teachers with lower satisfaction levels ... also possess the highest level of decisional deprivation" (p. 228).

(d) **Implications for the Mentor:** The findings of these studies suggest that:

(i) Trainees will not necessarily be happier and better motivated simply by the removal of dissatisfiers. Satisfaction tends to be related to achievement, responsibility, recognition, interest in the tasks they perform and personal growth.

(ii) Mentors should seek to remove as many potential dissatisfiers as they can. Some examples are given in research into students' perceptions of their ITET experiences in primary and secondary schools in partnership with the University of Nottingham (Robinson, 1994; Adey, 1997):

- contact with staffroom cynics who greet newcomers to the profession with comments such as: "What on earth do you want to come into teaching for?" or "What a crass decision to change careers !" A study of ITET in Australia has also shown that students' commitment to teaching can be weakened upon finding "a lack of ... enthusiasm from older staff" and the presence of teachers who manifestly despise their job (Field, 1994b, p. 59).

- expecting students to take classes with insufficient information about the pupils and the units of work they have been following;

- omitting to introduce students to staff with the result that they feel awkward when they enter the staffroom. Students in Adey's survey commented that dissatisfiers included not knowing where to sit, being unfamiliar with the names of staff members and being unsure what to say to teachers in the common room.

- failing to make clear to students that pupils were expected to behave in their lessons as they would in classes taken by their regular teachers.

(iii) Mentors should, as far as is feasible, seek to understand what influences students and promotes their satisfaction. This points to such issues as securing timetable alterations, changing working conditions and considering carefully the nature of the targets set. The way they address students may also vary. For some a sense of humour may be valuable; for others it may be less appropriate.

(iv) The tasks set the mentee should be challenging and meaningful. It is important to avoid decisional saturation in which the student is inundated with information about the school and expected to accomplish too many standards at once. If he/she is exposed to too many new skills at the outset, then that student is likely to lose confidence and feel that he/she is not coping

(v) Feedback should be positive and should help establish clear targets for future action. Recognition and credit should be given for achievement.

(vi) Mentors should understand that students lose motivation through exhaustion and that their development rarely proceeds in a direct line. Sometimes they make strides and then go into a period of stagnation before moving on again. Consequently, feedback should take account of their stage of development.

(vii) Mentees should be involved in planning their own targets and goals. There should be a high degree of participation in the planning process.

(viii) Senior management should try to ensure that the environment in which students are based is as pleasant as possible. The presence of posters and displays of pupils' work on the wall can all help to create the right type of atmosphere. Providing a cup of coffee or tea in the staffroom at break time is also a way of enhancing working conditions. At one school in partnership with UWIC, a room has been allocated solely for the use of students. It is bright, quiet and near the ITET co-ordinator's office. Housed within it is a collection of school policy documents and useful books on educational and professional issues. These facilities have been much appreciated by trainees, as they provide a tranquil location for lesson preparation and reflection.

III: Communication skills

(a) **Communication and Problems in Communication:** Communication is defined by Rogers (1997) as the process by which an idea is transferred from a source to a receiver with the intention of changing his or her behaviour. Such behaviour may encompass a change in knowledge and attitudes. Communications between mentors and students in schools can be of various types: oral; written; non-verbal (for example, body language); and electronic.

Problems in communications may be the result of:

- *semantic difficulties* such as ambiguities, for example, the road sign advertising a combined diner and gasoline station: "Eat here and get gas", or the sign in a university cafeteria: "Shoes are required to eat in the cafeteria", under which a student had added: "Socks can eat wherever they want" (Schermerhorn, Hunt and Osborn, 1991). In the context of mentoring, the use of terminology with which the trainee is not familiar can be confusing, for example, the language of the National Curriculum and examination specifications. Again, mentors may not always make clear their expectations. In a survey by Hayes (2001) students recounted the following experience:

  > *When we arrived, no-one knew exactly what we were supposed to be doing. There also needs to be more communication between the school and the class teacher as they also need to know.* (p. 11)

  In some cases students accidentally crossed invisible boundaries because they had not been adequately briefed about school protocol. On occasions, they were unsure about important aspects of their teaching:

  > *It would have been useful to have a set time with the class teacher to tell us what strategies are used in the room, which would have given us a basis for our lesson planning.*

- *distortion*, where the initial message is expressed in a lucid manner, but becomes distorted for a number of reasons. One of these is *selective perception* on the part of the receiver (Mondy, Sharplin and Flippo, 1988; Robbins, 2001). This occurs when he/she sees reality from a different viewpoint from the sender of the message. Distortion can also occur when the receiver is pre-occupied and does not listen properly to the message. A further cause is *inference*, where body language conveys a different message from the words used. Distortion can be a problem for mentors when they engage in debriefing, especially where their time is limited.

- *personality and relationships:* There is lack of trust between the two people and this prevents the flow of communications. Maynard (2000) reports cases where the mentor-student relationship has completely broken down. The consequences for the student, she writes, are dire. Some have commented that "they had 'gone home and cried every night'. Indeed, several students wept as they told me about what they described as their 'appalling' experiences in school" (p. 27). Some students, Maynard adds, feel that they have to 'manage' their mentor. In these cases, communications have been limited or non-existent.

- *overloading:* A person is unable to cope with the vast number of communications received and suffers from 'information overloading'. Mentors need to be careful that they do not bombard students with too many suggestions and ideas when they offer feedback, especially in the early stages of school experience.

- *organisational structure:* Typical problems are:

- SPLIT SITE SCHOOLS: A school is located on more than one campus, and a message from the ITET co-ordinator to the mentor is not received in time for action to be taken. This problem has occurred in some schools in partnership with UWIC. Again, difficulties arise when mentors have to travel from one building to another in heavy traffic to conduct a debriefing or weekly review with a student.

- POOR COMMUNICATIONS BETWEEN THE HEI AND SCHOOLS: This can lead to confusions over such requirements as the format for lesson notes. In the study by Hayes (2001) some students were unhappy that their mentors had not liaised sufficiently with college tutors and were themselves uncertain about partnership policy. The importance of communication of this type is again stressed by Glenny and Hickling (1995). In the early days of partnership between UWIC and schools in South Wales, some mentors were unclear about the procedures they should adopt, and imposed their own rules about the number of lessons which should be taught each day and the forms which should be used for evaluation. In some instances (Geen, Bassett and Douglas, 1998), UWIC students received feedback on their teaching which had been recorded on sheets designed by tutors at another university.

- INADEQUATE ACCOMMODATION FOR MENTORING: In some schools there is no suitable venue for debriefing and reflection.

Some of the ways mentors can communicate effectively with students are by listening carefully, structuring language clearly, establishing a good working relationship and ensuring that discussion takes place in a suitable venue.

(b) **Listening:** Part of the mentor's task is to listen to the student's views and opinions. Consequently, Acton, Kirkham and Smith (p. 15) urge that in discussing lesson planning with students or in conducting debriefing mentors should:

- be active and purposeful;

- be focused;

- pay full attention to the speaker.

They argue that communication is most effective when listeners stop:

- thinking about what they want to say and concentrate on the speaker;

- evaluating what they hear until the speaker has finished making the point. Rogers and Roethlisberger (1952) establish the rule that no-one should form a judgement on a communication received from another person until he/she can summarise accurately the sender's message *in toto*. Forming a judgement on a communication should be suspended until the very end of the message.

- filtering the information so that they hear only what they want to hear;

- contemplating other issues which are on their mind;

- looking around or being distracted.

The effective listener, they maintain, is able to ask questions relating to the speaker's words in order to seek:

- clarification;

- rectification;

- comprehension: he/she has understood what has been said and has an opportunity to delve further.

The effective listener does not take over, judge, divert or begin reminiscing, although he/she may sympathise with the comments being raised.

(c) **Structuring Communications:** Efficient communicators pay attention to:

(i) *the avoidance of ambiguity:* Effective responses - especially those which are written - should be organised so that a clear structure emerges. Examples of structures are:

- the CHRONOLOGICAL, where the main points in a lesson are recounted in order of occurrence. This structure can be employed where mentors wish to adopt a 'diary' approach and offer a value-free description of the events to stimulate students to diagnose the strengths and areas for development within their teaching.

- the INDUCTIVE-DEDUCTIVE, where the main points develop from the specific to the general (inductive) or from the general to the specific (deductive). In reviewing a lesson, the inductive is more likely to be relevant, since specific incidents are used to lead to discussion of performance in the light of the standards.

- the PROBLEM-SOLVING structure where the problem is first outlined and then ideas for solutions are listed. This can be useful where students have experienced serious problems in their lesson.

- the CAUSAL structure where the causes and the effects of a problem are outlined.

(ii) *terminology:* It is important to keep in mind the level of knowledge of the student and not to indulge in 'jargon' which is unlikely to be understood. In written reports it is often beneficial to keep sentences short, to use lists and bullet points and to remember that simplicity is the keynote to clarity.

(iii) *feedback:* It can be helpful to ask the student to summarise what has been agreed at the end of a debriefing or target-setting session so that the mentor can be sure that the communication has been understood.

(d) **Fostering Positive Relationships:**

(i) *discussion with students:* Acton, Kirkham and Smith point to the need for non-confrontational positioning in seating. Discussion, they maintain, should afford opportunities for sharing perceptions, and, consequently, physical barriers should be avoided. They recommend the following:

* Eye contact should be regular but non-threatening.

* Nodding is a positive response.

* Murmured 'hmms' signify understanding but not necessarily agreement.

* Discussion should end with the listener's thanking the speaker. In some contexts they may arrange a more formal meeting at another time.

(ii) *body-language:* Writers like Mehrabian (1971) and Pease (1991) show the importance of body language, of which examples are:

* HANDS: Danger signals could be: finger pointing; finger wagging; the clenched fist (with or without raised arm); and the raised arm (with open or closed palm).

* FEET: A wagging foot can sometimes be a sign of irritation.

* TONE OF VOICE: This can underline or contradict the words of the message being given.

(iii) *frankness and honesty:* In a study of mentoring newly qualified teachers (Wall and Smith, 1993), respondents made it clear that they wanted their mentors to be "honest and frank, tempered by sensitivity" (p. 59).

(e) **Establishing a Suitable Venue:** It is important that a venue is found which guarantees that there are no interruptions. The idea of setting aside a room exclusively for the use of students has already been mentioned. This does offer a suitable location for discussion concerning lesson planning, debriefing and target setting. It is highly advantageous if the room can also house all necessary documentation on school policy, perhaps on CD-Rom, and contain copies of the standards to which mentors can refer in their sessions with trainees.

IV: Problem solving

(a) **Contexts:** Problems can be of many types. They may face the mentor, for example, dealing with a student who is failing to make adequate progress, or they may be problems experienced by the trainee, for example, dealing with another person in collaborative teaching who is not making a sustained effort.

(b) **Definition:** A problem can be defined as any factor which prevents an individual or wider system from achieving set objectives. Resolution of a problem requires decision making, which is "a rational process leading to a conscious choice between alternatives" (Gore, Murray and Richardson, 1992).

(c) **Stages in Problem-Solving:** There are many volumes on problem-solving which offer the reader different advice. The following stages are adapted from the models constructed by Thompson (1965), Scott (1967), Francis (1990) and Robbins (2001).

(i) *recognising that a problem exists and analysing its nature* by developing a clear overall appreciation of the issues and the challenges. This involves identifying the problem and considering its root causes, its fundamental nature and the people who are in a position to alter the *status quo*.

(ii) *deciding priorities:* The problem-solver clarifies exactly what he/she wishes to achieve. Objectives or priorities are established at this stage.

(iii) *deciding criteria for judging the success of any solution which is adopted.* In the previous stage the problem-solver has decided what he/she wishes to achieve. At this stage it is necessary to determine criteria for judging whether the solution which is finally adopted does actually solve the problem and result in the achievement of the priorities identified.

(iv) *searching for possible solutions.* A list of potential solutions is drawn up.

(v) *selecting the solution most likely to match the priorities identified at stage (ii) above and defining a plan of action:* This stage involves judgement, which can cause difficulties since different people tend to hold different sets of values (Vickers, 1967; Brown, 1970; Harris, 1975). As a result, there is not always consensus on the 'correctness' of a judgement.

(vi) *adopting the solution chosen and reviewing future developments to ascertain the extent to which it has solved the problem and meets the criteria set out in stage (iii).* It is important to monitor future developments to check that the solution adopted does not create other problems which were not anticipated.

(d) **Strategies of Decision Making:** To help decision makers reach the 'right' choice, the following strategies have been advocated by such writers as March and Simon (1958), Snyder and Paige (1958), Vickers(1967), Braybrooke and. Lindblom (1970), and Allison (1971).

(i) *Optimising:* In this strategy, which is also known as the classical, synoptic, maximising and root model of decision making, the problem solver:
  • collects all the information relating to the problem;

- sets out every possible solution which could be implemented;

- calculates the consequences likely to arise from putting each of these potential solutions into practice;

- ranks these potential solutions in order by matching their anticipated consequences against the desired results (i.e. the objectives or priorities identified by the decision maker for the resolution of the problem);

- adopts the solution which heads the list. This solution is the optimum choice (March and Simon, 1958).

In practice, this model is often difficult to implement (Lindblom, 1968). Collecting all the relevant information and trying to predict the consequences of every possible solution can be very time-consuming and expensive. Nor is it possible always to calculate with any degree of precision the likely consequences of a course of action.

(ii) *Satisficing:* The term 'satisficing', as a tool to problem solving, was coined by Herbert Simon (1947). His thesis is that the problem solver, realising the drawbacks of the optimising model, does not seek to find the perfect solution. Rather, he/she selects the first solution which is thought to be 'good enough'. This is then adopted as the satisficing rather than the optimising solution.

In making decisions about setting up a structure of mentoring in a school for the first time, an ITET co-ordinator and her/his colleagues may utilise aspects of the rational model, considering carefully the costs associated with a range of options, for example, the number of students to be accommodated at the school and the number of mentors to be selected. Other issues which need to be taken into account include the time to be allocated to mentoring, the financial implications and training needs. However, because of the many variables involved, it is likely that, at the end of the day, they will adopt a system which will serve 'well enough' and follow Herbert Simon's precepts.

(iii) *Using interim solutions:* In this model a likely solution is adopted and put into practice on an experimental basis. The results are monitored, and then a decision is taken whether it has actually solved the problem. If it has not, a second solution can be devised and adopted - again on a trial basis. This strategy, which is frequently used in industry (Luthans, 1989, p. 540), has considerable value in ITET. For example, a team of mentors may decide to introduce a new system of profiling students. The first draft they compile can be implemented for a limited period to check whether it meets the desired objectives. If it is successful, it can be used on a permanent basis; if not, a second profile can be devised and employed to monitor students' progress, again as a trial run.

(iv) *Disjointed Incrementalism:* Braybrooke and Lindblom (1970) advocate 'disjointed incrementalism' as a means for helping problem-solvers make a choice among different possible solutions. In their system, the decision maker selects a course of action which usually involves only minor change to the *status quo*. If it does not solve the problem, another, similar solution can be tried. This process is repeated until the problem is resolved. As the solutions chosen differ only marginally from each other and involve minimal change, it is a simple matter to reverse any one which does not prove to be beneficial. A series of small changes, according to Braybrooke and Lindblom, avoids many of the pitfalls familiar to people who have embarked upon one far-reaching innovation which has proved to be disastrous.

Once a mentoring programme is up and running, most mentors, especially in times of constant change when there are many demands on their time, are likely to follow the policy of incrementalism and make only the necessary changes to a system which otherwise is functioning well. Responses to changes imposed by government, for example, establishing new standards and extending the period of time students spend in schools are usually of an incremental nature.

(v) *Distinguishing 'programmed' and 'non-programmed' decisions:* It is helpful for mentors to understand the difference between *programmed* and *non-programmed* decisions (Robbins, 2001). Programmed decisions are repetitive and routine. They are decisions which have been taken before, and do not require enormous amounts of time devoted to them because they have been solved before, for example, decisions about periods in the year when ITET co-ordinators should start moderating mentors' judgements about students' progress. Non-programmed decisions relate to problems which have not arisen before, and require fresh solutions and original thought, for example, moving from a school-based system of ITET to a school-centred system in which HEIs play a much smaller role.

Mentors should try to reduce as many decisions as possible to the level of programmed decisions. By routinising decisions they practise economies in terms of time and effort. It would, for example, be tedious to devote a substantial number of hours each year to making decisions about the documentation to be provided to students. To treat non-programmed decisions as though they were programmed is to waste precious time and energy.

(vi) *Basing decisions making upon the perceived wishes of the client:* This is frequently attempted in service industries, where questionnaires are given to customers to ascertain their expectations of the organisation. Managers are then, to a large extent, freed from the task of making value judgements, as the opportunity has been given to clients to state the services they desire.

The use of questionnaires to students along the lines suggested in the second chapter helps reduce the time spent debating different approaches based upon the value-judgements of staff. The users of the system can put forward their views, and analysis of their responses can be employed to inform the decision making process.

(vii) *Moulding one solution to fit the circumstances:* The problem solver does not brainstorm a large number of potential remedies, but concentrates from the outset upon one possible solution and shapes this initial idea until it meets the criteria adopted at stages (ii) and (iii) of the decision making system. Snyder and Paige (1958) show how this model was used by the United States government in 1950 when it was announced that North Korean forces had invaded the South. It was immediately agreed that action would have to be taken, and attention was turned to details of the size of the force which would be dispatched and the tactics which would be adopted. This approach is most commonly employed in crisis management. It would be relevant in ITET where a student was encountering especial difficulties and the mentoring team needed to formulate a suitable response.

IV: Negotiation

(a) **Contexts:** Negotation is often practised by mentors. Examples are:

- negotiating with senior management the allocation of limited resources in support of student development;

- negotiating with colleagues the range of a student's classroom/learning experience;

- negotiating the focus of an observation session with a student;

- helping a student to develop negotiating skills for use in the classroom and with colleagues;

- negotiating the appropriate time and place for review sessions;

- negotiating targets with the student.

Sixsmith and Simco (1997) argue for a model of ITET in which the mentor:

- observes the student teach;

- helps him/her to reflect on the lesson;

- reflects upon the student's performance;

- negotiates an evaluation with the student; and, finally:

- acts as a 'reflective agent' in negotiating with the student his/her next teaching experience.

They write that "negotiation in our model is a necessary aspect of the process" (p. 12).

(b) **The Concept of 'Negotiation':** Negotiation has been defined as "a way of reconciling interests and reducing conflict in situations where people have to interact with one another but where no side is powerful enough to impose its will. All human relationships have an element of co-operation and competition, and negotiation is lubrication between these two tendencies" (Lowe and Pollard, 1989, p. 120). In essence it is concerned with:

(i) *analysing the current situation* and realising that some change is necessary which will involve other people;

(ii) *entering into dialogue* with these people to decide a future action plan which will incorporate the desired change;

(iii) *reaching a conclusion* concerning the course of action to be adopted with the aim of producing mutual gains for both parties (a 'win-win' rather than a 'win-lose' situation);

(iv) *improving relationships* between the people involved in the negotiation process.

(c) **The Process of Negotiation:** Pennington and Gooderham (1987) produce a model of the process of negotiation:

(i) *Establishing the facts* and distinguishing between matters of fact, belief, opinion and value;

(ii) *Deciding objectives* and identifying general and specific objectives for the short and longer term;

(iii) *Preparing the case* where the negotiator maps out the position taken by the various people involved in the process of negotiation;

(iv) *Making claims:* At this stage there is a skilful presentation of one's own case, critical examination of opposing cases and, where necessary, transition to a pre-planned fall-back position;

(v) *Establishing agreements:* This entails clarifying and recording decisions and generating a commitment to be bound by them;

(vi) *Deciding implementation:* Decisions are made to clarify the action to be taken by each party, the nature of that action and the date by which it must be put into practice. It is also necessary to determine procedures for evaluating the consequences of the action taken.

Negotiation clearly calls for the application of many skills. Some of those listed by Mulholland (1991, p. 186) include the ability to:

- call for agreement;
- explain why there should be agreement;
- compare and contrast options;
- judge or evaluate ideas and options;
- clarify and test the views expressed;
- assess the strength of feelings;
- establish and reiterate goals.

In negotiation it is important to concentrate upon the problem and the evidence rather than personalities, to follow rational approaches to decision making, to decide issues and solutions on their merits rather than in accordance with the desires and wishes of either side and to avoid provocation. The quality of empathy - being able to understand how the other person is feeling - is an important dimension of negotiation. Mentors also need the ability to listen carefully in order to understand the other person's point of view, to communicate effectively and to clarify the issues at stake.

V: Time management

(a) **The Problem of Time:** Many ITET co-ordinators and subject mentors agree that time is one of the greatest constraints they face in fulfilling their role. Where co-ordinators are deputy headteachers, they have other crucial responsibilities besides mentoring students. Similarly, in secondary schools many subject mentors are busy heads of department. One co-ordinator in a South Wales school compared his role to a juggler who has to "keep lots of plates spinning at one time". Many research studies have shown that this is a key problem in schools. (Barber, 1995; Cross, 1999; Jones, 2000; Hayes, 2000; and Williams and Soares, 2000).

Students are also often under pressure. They find planning and evaluating lessons to be very time-consuming. Those who participated in Furlong and Maynard's research (1995) frequently made reference to the time factor. One spoke of her frustration in spending hours upon the preparation of worksheets for a primary school class which "the children would whiz through in five minutes" (p. 86). In much the same vein, a student commented in the survey by Hayes (2001) that "the first couple of weeks were busy, hectic and frustrating" (p. 12).

(b) **Strategies for Time Management:** Basing their recommendations on the ideas of such management theorists as John Adair (1983) and Peter Drucker (1968), Acton, Kirkham and Smith (1992, pp. 73-76) suggest the following strategies:

(i) *to record the use of time* by keeping a time log and diary.

(ii) *to analyse one's use of time*, by asking should questions as:

- What tasks actually need to be tackled?

- What am I currently doing with my time?

- Do I establish priorities?

- If so, do I devote sufficient time to those priority areas?

- Once priorities have been dealt with, how do I use the rest of my time?

- Are activities too fragmented? Could small parcels of time be consolidated into larger, more useful units of time?

- Do unplanned activities tend to take over from planned intentions?

- Can I use any of my time to better advantage?

(iii) *to improve time management:* Examples of standard techniques are:

- to CLARIFY OBJECTIVES: Pertinent questions would be:

  - What are the main objectives I am trying to achieve in my capacity as mentor?

  - What duties do I have to fulfil in meeting the needs of ITET students?

- to PLAN THE USE OF TIME: Useful strategies include establishing a daily list of tasks which have to be accomplished during the school day and/or using a long-term planner in which priorities can be entered for each week of the school year.

- to PRIORITISE activities into the categories of:

- imperative: tasks which have to be completed, for example, weekly reviews with students, ensuring that targets are set for them, updating their profiles and sending reports to the HEI by the deadlines agreed;

- highly desirable: tasks such as meeting each student individually to engage in a 'strands of reflection' review which will cover a half term's school experience;

- desirable: participating with the ITET co-ordinator in a seminar for students concerning relationships with parents.

- to DELEGATE tasks and responsibilities to other colleagues. The question can be asked whether it is possible to delegate upwards as well as down.

Thus, a time management action planner could consist of the headings:

TASKS	IMPERATIVE	HIGHLY DESIRABLE	DESIRABLE	COMPLETION DATE	DELEGATION
1					
2					
3 etc					

- to BE ASSERTIVE AND SAY 'NO'. Four steps suggested by Acton, Kirkham and Smith for mentors who are asked to take on further responsibilities are:

- to listen;

- to decide whether to agree to take on the additional duty or not;

- to give reasons if they refuse to undertake some function;

- to suggest alternatives, where possible.

- to DEAL WITH PAPER WORK ON A REGULAR BASIS, for example, to scan documents speedily, to decide on priorities for answering, to have an effective system of classifying and storing information and to use ICT.

- to ELIMINATE TIME WASTERS such as unplanned activities. It is necessary to practise self-discipline and not to devote time to non-essential activities, for example, spending too long in conversation in the staffroom when important work has to be attended to elsewhere.

- to MANAGE AND PARTICIPATE IN EFFECTIVE MEETINGS. It is important to decide, first, if a meeting needs to be held, and, then, if it is to be held, to decide the format it will assume, for example, informal, problem-solving or informational. It is also necessary to decide upon a starting and finishing time, to keep to these times and to ensure that the meeting is effectively chaired. Participants should confine their comments to what is relevant.

(c) **Guidelines for Students:**

(i) At the University of Warwick students are given guidelines during their induction about managing their time, including:

- planning their time so that all documentation such as lesson files and evaluations is kept up to date;

- planning their time for periods when they are not teaching classes;

- managing their time during lessons;

- planning their time when at home (Brooks and Sikes, 1997, p. 87).

(ii) At one school in partnership with UWIC the ITET co-ordinator holds a tutorial on time management and asks students to analyse their use of time. Sometimes, he reports, too many hours are devoted to non-essential tasks. In one instance the students were busy preparing elaborate teaching aids which merely duplicated materials already available in the school and in the pupils' texts. Once this analysis had been completed, he was able to direct them to reflect upon the tasks they performed and to decide where a short, sharp effort would be more productive. Sometimes, he has advised students to take a weekend off, as endless work and preparation can be counter-productive.

› Issues for consideration

1. Read sections I and II (*mentoring skills and motivation*) and record any guidelines which mentors may derive from a study of the writings of Maslow, Herzberg, Sergiovanni, Locke and Latham, and Belasco and Alutto with respect to the motivation of trainee teachers.

2. In the light of your reading state any strategies you employ:

(a) *to remove 'dissatisfiers' which students may experience at the school;*

(b) *to promote students' satisfaction;*

3. Read section III (*communication skills*) and state what you consider to be good practice in communicating with students.

4. Consider your last debriefing session with a student teacher. List what you consider to be your strengths in relation to good practice in communication and suggest any ways in which you can improve your skills of communication.

5. Identify any communication problems which have arisen at your school in the context of mentoring, for example, semantic difficulties, distortion, overloading and problems arising from the structure of the organisation. Suggest ways in which these problems could be resolved.

6. Read section IV (*problem solving*) and summarise the six main stages in the process of problem solving. Then, briefly explain the meaning of:

(a) *optimising solution;*

(b) *satisficing solution;*

(c) *use of interim solutions;*

(d) *disjointed incrementalism;*

(e) *programmed and non-programmed decisions.*

7. Reflect upon a problem you have encountered in your role as mentor.

(a) Write down the problem and the solution which was adopted.

(b) If the solution was successful, write down the strategy used and the reason why you believe it proved to be successful.

(c) Categorise the solution adopted in terms of the strategies discussed in the text (for example, satisficing, conducting a trial run of some innovation, incrementalism).

(d) If the problem still exists, explain the strategy used and consider why the attempted solution did not succeed.

8. Read section V (*negotiation*). What do you understand to be the essence of negotiation?

9. Think of a situation in your role of mentor in which you have had to negotiate agreement. Explain:

(a) *your goals and the other person's goals;*

(b) *your perceptions about the issue and those of the other person;*

(c) *the solution you adopted;*

(d) *the reasons why that solution was adopted;*

(e) *the ways in which it led to a 'win-win' situation;*

(f) *the negotiation skills which were employed.*

10. The following scenario is devised by Acton, Kirkham and Smith. Read it through and decide what action you would take.

"As the senior mentor with responsibility for a number of students, you are informed by two students of their dissatisfaction with the room in which your debriefing sessions take place. It is not seen as an area that is conducive to relaxed review and target setting sessions. The headteacher suggests that you allocate a more suitable room for this important aspect of your role.

There is a small room next to the staffroom which is vacant but which is used by the smokers on the staff. This could be ideal as it has armchairs and a carpet and is in a quiet area of the school. The other possible location is a marking room which is not used often by staff who seem to prefer to mark in their classrooms or at home.

The staff have heard on the grapevine about the possibility of losing their smoking and marking room and are not very happy about this 'decision by senior management'. A representative group of staff has asked to see you to sort out the problem." (p. 51)

11. Read section V (*time management*) and with reference to your experience as a mentor:

(a) State what you consider to be the main constraints upon your time.

(b) Identify any time wasting factors and consider how their impact could be reduced.

(c) Answer the questions set in section V(b)(ii).

(d) Record any of the time management strategies described in the text which you feel could be of value in your role as mentor.

12. What advice would you give students at your school to help them utilise their time to best effect?

8

Skills
in mentoring 2

In this chapter the skills to be discussed are: reviewing students' progress; setting targets; critically discussing trainees' ideas; setting boundaries; challenging; and counselling.

I: Reviewing students progress

(a) **The Importance of Regular, Organised Reviews:** It cannot be stressed too much that students need regular meetings with their mentors in which their progress can be reviewed. Where this is not the case, major difficulties can arise. The following are problems which have been reported in research studies into mentoring:

(i) *Failure to conduct regular reviews:* Although UWIC partnership literature clearly states that weekly reviews should be held, one undergraduate, participating in a survey of mentoring arrangements during the session 2000-2001, reported that she had been nearly a full term in her school and had in that time received not one review with the mentor. In the very last week of her school placement she was given a written report which was severely critical of her progress in terms of a number of the QTS standards. By this stage, she observed, there was little she could do to remedy the situation.

(ii) *Reviewing without a clear structure or framework:* In some cases the review is poorly conduced, does not take full account of past performance and does not result in the recording of a clear action plan for the student.

(iii) *Reviewing which moves too quickly and does not foster the important stages of analysis and synthesis:* Watkins and Whalley (1993) show that review can proceed through four stages: the *knowledge* phase, where students recall events from past experience; the *analysis and understanding* phase, where they seek to understand why things happened the way they did; the *evaluation* phase, in which they make judgements about the learning situation and evaluate what has been learned; and the *synthesis* phase, where they fit learning into an overall context and decide future objectives . In some cases review is conducted so quickly that analysis and synthesis are ignored.

(iv) *reviewing without any record of past activities so that it is difficult to chart objectives and the progress made in attaining them.* Unless some record is kept of the student's activities, it is difficult to maintain a clear record of progress.

(b) **A Framework for Weekly Review:** The following headings can be valuable in designing a weekly review format:

(i) *a record of the date of the meeting between the student and the mentor;*

(ii) *a summary of the main elements in the student's programme during the week*, for example, lessons observed, classes taught in collaboration with the mentor, aspects of the work of the school observed and any extra-curricular activities undertaken;

(iii) *a list of the main successes:* The mentor and student need to list the main successes achieved at this stage of the course and to ensure that the comments entered relate to the QTS standards. Particular attention must be paid to targets set in previous meetings which have now been accomplished. This section of the review is essentially affirmative and should help to secure motivation. It also provides the opportunity for reflection.

(iv) *a list of key points for consideration:* These will be areas for development in terms of the standards or activities which can be undertaken by the student to help him/her at this stage of development, for example, further observation of the work of the SEN unit or discussion with the assessment co-ordinator.

Where students are encountering specific difficulties, it is beneficial for the ITET co-ordinator and HEI tutor to join the mentor during the review, and for very precise targets to be set. Targets are discussed in greater depth in the next section.

(c) **Involving Students in Evaluating their Own Progress.** Popular ways of involving students in discussion about their progress are:

(i) *encouraging them to review their successes by asking open-ended questions*, for example,

> *"Name some of the ways in which you have found things to be different this term."*

> *"Recount the areas of your school experience about which you have felt better during the last month."*

> *"In which elements of your course do you feel most motivated?"*

> *"State those factors which make you feel really satisfied in your teaching."*

(ii) *using a review sheet* in which key aspects of the course are listed and students are expected to record comments on their progress. Most writers on ITET agree that self-evaluation on the part of students is vital, as it encourages reflection and critical thought. It puts into practice the ideals of the reflective practitioner philosophy. However, mentors who participated in the survey of Arthur, Davison and Moss (1997, p.94) noted that certain students found self-evaluation difficult and needed guidance. Consequently, it is suggested that for self-evaluation to be effective students need:

- specific criteria for judging pupils' learning and their own teaching;

- a clearcut model for evaluation.

The question has also been raised (Jones, 2000) of the number of lessons students should be expected to review each day. Jones compares the experiences and perceptions of a sample of students in England and Germany. The English students were required to analyse every lesson they taught, which, in the view of the German group, was a bureaucratic task resulting in superficial description rather than depth of thought.

In the light of these considerations a model for students' evaluation of their teaching over an ITET course is suggested, in which they evaluate lessons in varying degrees of breadth and depth at different points in their school experience. This model can be divided into three distinct phases.

(A) **FIRST PHASE:** In the early stages, for example, the first term of a PGCE course, trainees can be expected to evaluate their lessons in general terms with reference to criteria derived from the QTS standards. A list of 'prompt' questions can be provided. The following list was used by the author when he was PGCE Course Director at University College, Cardiff and on some ITET courses at UWIC. It is not intended that every single question should be answered for each lesson. Students are given discretion to select only those relevant to the lesson they are reviewing. They are required to use relevant questions to record:

- the strengths perceived in the lesson;

- any modifications which could be made to the lesson if it were to be taught again; and:

- in the light of this analysis an action plan which highlights the strategies to be adopted in future lessons.

In undertaking this mode of evaluation they are expected to begin with the *pupils' learning* and then to focus upon the process of *teaching*. It is suggested that detailed analysis of *one* lesson chosen by the student each day is preferable to evaluation of every single class taken.

The outcomes of these evaluations can be used in seminars with groups of students. In one case at Cardiff University a student was experiencing many problems with a certain class. She presented a thorough analysis of one lesson, and other members of the group discussed with her ways in which she might tackle the difficulties identified. Ultimately, an action plan was formulated which proved to be highly beneficial.

The list of prompt questions is printed below:

A: *PUPILS' LEARNING: OBJECTIVES/TARGETS:*

1. How did the lesson objectives relate to the programmes of study for the subject within the National Curriculum?

2. How did the objectives contribute to the progression of the learning process outlined in the course aims?

3. Did you set targets for (i) the whole class (ii) groups of pupils (iii) individuals?

4. Did the objectives set high expectations for all pupils?

5. Did all the pupils achieve the objectives/targets set? If not, why not?

6. How far did the work develop as planned?

B: *QUALITY OF LEARNING:*

1. What progress did the pupils make in the development of knowledge, skills and understanding contained within the National Curriculum Order(s) relevant to the content of the lesson?

2. What key skills were developed in the lesson, for example, communicating information, using ICT, solving problems, working co-operatively with others, and improving learning?

3. What thinking skills did pupils need to complete the tasks set, for example, seeking information, enquiring, reasoning and evaluating outcomes?

4. What opportunities were provided to enable pupils to plan their own learning?

5. What opportunities were exploited to promote pupils' wider educational development, including their personal, spiritual, moral, social and cultural development?

C: *PREPARATION:*

1. Were you sufficiently well-prepared?

2. What provision did you make for differentiation?

3. Did the tasks set match the pupils' capabilities?

4. Did the children respond to the tasks as expected?

5. Did you have ready all the necessary materials and equipment?

6. Did you arrive in your classroom in advance of the class?

7. Did you select and make good use of textbooks, ICT and other learning resources to enable your objectives to be met?

D: *CONTENT:*

1. Was the content suited to the age, ability and level of attainment of the pupils?

2. Did it build on prior attainment?

3. Did you over-estimate or under-estimate the pupils' ability? Boredom and inattention are useful criteria here.

4. Did you relate the content to previous relevant lessons?

E: *BOARD WORK AND VISUAL MATERIALS:*

1. Was your board work legible?

2. Did you remove extraneous matter from the board?

3. What was the quality and clarity of your handouts, worksheets, charts, OHTs etc.?

4. Were aids positioned so that they were clearly visible to the class?

5. Were teaching aids effectively used?

6. In the case of demonstration was it clearly visible to all pupils?

F: *ORGANISATION OF CLASS ACTIVITIES:*

1. How satisfactory do you judge the organisation of the lesson to have been?

2. Was the seating arrangement of the room suitable for the purposes of the lesson?

3. Did you employ suitable learning strategies?

4. Did you judge when to change from one activity to another?

5. Were you able to direct all pupil activities in an effective and efficient manner?

6. Were the pupils clear about the activities they were to undertake? Were they confused? Did they repeatedly ask questions about what they were to do next?

7. Did you endeavour to encourage the pupils to be self-reliant?

8. Could you gain the class's attention when you needed it?

9. Did you ensure that there was orderly movement within the room?

10. Was your introduction suitable?

11. Did you effect a smooth transition from one section of the lesson to the next?

12. Did you employ appropriate closure techniques, for example, questions, summary of main points, signposting, review of the achievement of targets, setting of homework, and pre-viewing the work of future sessions?

G: *TIMING:*

1. Was timing satisfactory?

2. Was enough time allowed to cover each stage of the lesson adequately?

3. Did you allow sufficient time for a proper conclusion to your lesson?

H: *CLARITY OF EXPOSITION:*

1. Were there any discontinuities of theme and inexplicable jumps from one aspect of the work to another?

2. Were there self-interruptions?

3. Were there unfinished sentences?

4. Did you go back to some earlier point to rectify omissions?

5. Were there frequent pauses while you thought of what to say next?

6. How effectively did you use visual material and support your explanations?

7. Did you use unnecessary or unexplained technical terms?

8. Was your vocabulary too complex for the class?

9. Did you explain technical terminology?

10. Were your sentences grammatically correct?

11. Did you use sufficient examples and illustrations?

12. Did you reinforce the main points in the lesson?

I: *SUPERVISION OF PUPILS' WORK:*

1. Were pupils able to work safely?

2. Did you supervise adequately?

3. How well did you divide your attention between pupils?

4. Did you give sufficient help to those pupils who needed assistance?

5. Were the pupils aware of your presence throughout?

6. Were you in control of events?

7. Were your directions audible and did the pupils act upon them?

8. Did the children work independently and efficiently?

9. Were you able to supervise the work of individuals without 'losing sight' of the rest of the class?

10. Were you able to scan the class effectively?

J: *QUESTIONING TECHNIQUES:*

1. How effectively did you use questions to:

   • stimulate motivation?

   • consolidate learning?

   • uncover incorrect ideas and assumptions?

- promote cognitive skills?

- acquire feedback?

- maintain order?

- promote relationships with the class?

- provide a variety of activity?

2. Were sufficient questions asked?

3. Did you have a mixture of higher and lower order questions, i.e.

- recall?

- comprehension?

- application?

- analysis?

- synthesis?

- evaluation?

4. Did you allow sufficient time for pupils to answer?

5. Did you tend to provide answers yourself?

6. Did you adequately prompt the pupils to answer correctly?

7. Did you pause effectively?

8. Did you redirect any questions?

9. Did you involve as many pupils as possible, including non-volunteers?

10. Did you use pupils' answers effectively in order to advance their learning?

11. What questions did pupils put to you? Did you deal with them adequately?

12. Did you pay attention to pupils' errors and misconceptions and help them to correct these errors?

K: *DISCUSSION AND GROUP WORK:*

1. What types of discussion/group work did you utilise, for example, single task group work, buzz groups? Why did you use these techniques?

2. What criteria did you set for forming the groups (for example, ability, friendship)?

3. Did you appoint specific roles within the groups?

4. What rules did you set for the discussion/group work? Were they followed?

5. Did the pupils have sufficient knowledge to be able to discuss the issues sensibly?

6. Did everyone contribute to the discussion?

7. Were the pupils' answers sufficiently clear?

8. Did you summarise the key conclusions?

L: *DISCIPLINE AND RELATIONS WITH THE CLASS:*

1. Did you succeed in enforcing the main classroom rules?

2. Did you constantly have to interrupt your teaching in order to reprimand individuals?

3. Were you clear about the rewards and sanctions available to you?

4. Did you use sanctions sparingly?

5. Did you make idle threats?

6. Did you make effective use of praise and encouragement?

7. Did you use non-verbal cueing to encourage responses?

8. How well did you know the pupils' names?

9. Was the arrival and dismissal of the class orderly?

10. Did you encounter any especial difficulties of control in your lesson?

11. If so, what could you suggest to rectify them?

M: *STIMULUS VARIATION:*

1. Was sufficient variety of stimulus provided?

2. Did you change your speech pattern, for example, variation of rate, volume, expressiveness?

3. Did you utilise a variety of sensory channels of communications, for example, use of the board, diagrams, objects, pictures, the OHP, powerpoint etc.?

4. Were there sufficient changes of interaction, for example, teacher-centred, teacher-pupil, pupil-pupil interaction, individual work?

5. Did you move *purposefully* about the teaching space?

6. Did you focus behaviour by verbal emphasis, for example, "watch", "look", "listen", or

by effective gesture?

7. Was your behaviour in any way distracting, for example, unnecessary gestures, inappropriate movement, voice too loud or too quiet or too monotonous?

8. Have you noticed in yourself any annoying mannerisms?

N: *MOTIVATION AND ACHIEVEMENT:*

1. What provision was made for intrinsic motivation, extrinsic motivation and expectation of success?

2. Were the pupils interested and enthusiastic? What indicators were there of this?

3. Did the pupils remain on task throughout?

4. Did they perform as you expected?

5. Did they complete the tasks? If not, why not?

6. Was outstandingly good/bad work produced?

7. How do you account for this?

8. Were there aspects of the work in which the pupils showed little interest?

9. Were there any behavioural difficulties as the result of poor motivation?

10. Was the pacing of the lesson satisfactory?

11. Were the pupils pleased with what they achieved?

12. Did you challenge pupils' thinking?

13. Were there any examples of 'jerkiness' in the lesson?

14. Were pupils involved in decisions relating to their own learning?

O: *REINFORCING LEARNING:*

1. Did you provide opportunities for pupils to consolidate their learning?

2. Did you set homework?

3. If so, was it well-focused to reinforce and develop what had been learned?

P: *ASSESSMENT:*

1. Were you able to identify the level of the pupils' achievements in accordance with relevant level descriptions in the National Curriculum?

2. Did you use your assessment of pupils' achievements in planning your teaching?

3. Did you establish and make clear to the pupils the criteria which would be used in assessing their achievements?

4. Did you involve the pupils in their own assessment?

5. Did you provide constructive feedback to pupils on their achievements?

6. On the basis of your assessment did you set your pupils suitable targets?

7. Did you record pupils' achievements?

8. Did you use your records to check that pupils had understood and completed the work set?

9. Did you check that pupils were continuing to make demonstrable progress in their acquisition of the knowledge, skills and understanding pertinent to the subject?

10. Where applicable, were you able to implement the assessment requirements of examination specifications?

Q: *PERSONAL QUALITIES:*

1. Do you feel that your voice was fully audible to all pupils?

2. Were you suitably dressed for the lesson?

3. Did you feel that you communicated enthusiasm for your subject?

4. Did you exhibit a confident, business-like manner?

(B) **SECOND PHASE**, for example, the second term of a PGCE course: Here students are required to focus in greater depth upon a range of specific teaching competences. Again, they are asked to evaluate one lesson a day, but now they concentrate upon a single focus area. A different focus area is set each week. The aim is to have them analyse performance in greater depth than they did during the first phase.

Examples of possible topics are given below. In each of these areas students' self-evaluation should emphasise the positive aspects of their lessons together with issues that need to be addressed in future planning. After answering the questions, they should consider:

- an evaluation of pupils' achievement and learning;

- an evaluation of their teaching;

- the main implications for the next lesson.

AIMS AND OBJECTIVES

With reference to a lesson you gave today:

(1) list the aims that are appropriate to the unit of work;

(2) list the objectives which you selected for your lesson;

(3) show the relationship of (2) to (1), demonstrating how you intend to ensure progression in the learning process;

(4) examine each objective carefully and show the ways in which it was translated into a pupil activity (i.e. "How did I try to ensure that the pupils accomplished this objective?");

(5) state the extent to which you consider each objective to have been realistic. Did you record objectives which were not actually carried out, for example, 'discuss' when no opportunity was given for the pupils to speak?;

(6) examine the objectives set and consider:

  (a) the criteria you selected to ascertain whether or not they had been achieved;

  (b) the extent to which they were in fact achieved;

(7) if any objectives were not accomplished,

  (a) suggest reasons for this;

  (b) suggest strategies which could be utilised to ensure the accomplishment of these objectives in future lessons.

CLASSROOM CONTROL AND MANAGEMENT

With reference to a lesson you taught during the day:

(1) list the rules you required the class to follow;

(2) provide a rational justification for each rule;

(3) list the techniques you employed to ensure the enforcement of these rules;

(4) state the degree of success you consider you achieved in controlling your classes and directing learning activities;

(5) (a) describe any particularly difficult situations you encountered;

MOTIVATION

(b) suggest reasons for the difficulties experienced;

(c) suggest strategies which could be utilised to resolve the problem.
With reference to a lesson taught today answer the following questions:

(1) What strategies did you utilise to arouse interest and motivation in the introduction? Refer to such considerations as:

- the selection, creation and use of visual aids and exemplar materials;

- reference to current issues of interest;

- problem-posing stratgies;

- linking the lesson to the work of previous sessions;

- focusing on specific objectives.

(2) How did you endeavour to maintain motivation during the lesson? Refer to such issues as:

- the logical sequencing of lesson material;

- the transition from one section of the lesson to another;

- clarity of exposition: What steps did you take to:

  (i) ensure that language would be at the level appropriate to the age and ability of the class?

  (ii) anticipate difficulties in exposition?

  (iii) illustrate concepts clearly?

  (iv) cite relevant examples?

  (v) question the class/individuals to check understanding?

  (vi) provide easy ways for pupils to recall concepts?

  (vii) demonstrate relationships/techniques of working?

- pacing;

- avoiding 'jerkiness';

- setting a standard;

- fostering self-esteem;

- monitoring pupils' progress;

- allowing pupils a degree of control over their own learning;

- providing a variety of stimulus, for example,

  - a variety of activities;

  - a variety of sensory stimulus/speech pattern etc.;

  - variation in the teacher-pupil interaction.

QUESTIONING

With reference to a lesson you gave today:

(1) list the questions you used;

(2) explain the purposes of your questions (for example, as an aid to motivation, to consolidate learning, to promote cognitive skills, to clarify the learning achieved, as a tool for management/discipline, to promote teacher-pupil relations);

(3) categorise your questions under the headings:

  (a) recall;
  (b) comprehension;
  (c) application;
  (d) analysis;
  (e) synthesis;
  (f) evaluation.

(4) consider the quality of the answers you received. How successful was your questioning in promoting pupils' learning?

(5) give examples of any occasions when you used:

  (a) short, rapid-fire questions;
  (b) prompting;
  (c) redirection;
  (d) pausing.

(6) explain why you used these strategies and show the extent to which their use was effective.

(7) refer to good and less satisfactory practices associated with questioning (Geen, 2001b) and consider your performance in accordance with each of these factors.

THE REINFORCEMENT OF LEARNING

With reference to a lesson taught today answer the following questions:

(1) What steps did you take to reinforce learning? Make reference to:

(i) any recall strategies you employed;

(ii) strategies by which theory was *applied* to practice.

(2) What closure techniques were employed? Make reference to:

- consolidation and the summarising of key concepts:

  - throughout the lesson;

  - at the conclusion of the lesson;

- signposting;

- the use of praise and encouragement;

- the setting of homework: When did you return it? What criteria were used in marking? What comments did you make on the pupils' work?

- setting future targets.

CRITERIA FOR SUCCESSFUL TEACHING

Describe the lesson which you consider to have been your *most* successful today, and state the *reasons* why you consider it to have been successful. Make reference to the following criteria where appropriate:

(1) course aims, lesson objectives and the relationship between the two; progression in the learning process;

(2) preparation and differentiation;

(3) visual material: charts, aids, worksheets, information sheets, the use of ICT;

(4) organisation of classroom activities and teaching strategies;

(5) timing;

(6) clarity of exposition;

(7) supervision;

(8) questioning;

(9) management of discussion and group work;

(10) discipline and relationship with the pupils;

(11) stimulus variation;

(12) motivation and achievement;

(13) assessment of pupils' work and feedback on their achievements.

PROBLEMS AND SOLUTIONS

Consider:

(1) the main problems that you faced in your teaching today;

(2) the solutions you would adopt to alleviate these problems. Refer to the criteria for lesson evaluation offered in the previous stage of school experience.

(C) **THIRD PHASE:** This could be the final term of a PGCE course. Here students are allowed to use their own judgement in determining evaluation criteria. Such a strategy allows them to decide their own ideals and to develop their thoughts on criteria for assessing their effectiveness as teachers. In reaching decisions of this type they still need to focus upon:

- what they considered the strengths of a lesson to be;

- any perceived areas for improvement (with analysis of the reasons for this judgement);

- the action plan to be adopted and the success criteria they will employ to enable them to determine the extent to which the plan has been helpful.

The action plan would then be implemented in subsequent lessons and the degree of success attained monitored by the student. Where it was not successful, a different plan would be adopted for subsequent lessons.

Another system, used at Warwick University, is the GRASP model (Getting Results and Solving Problems) which has been adapted from an industrial setting. At regular intervals students in consultation with mentors answer a cycle of questions to help them:

- formulate precise objectives;

- construct a clear picture of the results which they seek to achieve so that they know what the end product will look like;

- explore alternative means of pursuing goals as a way of selecting the most appropriate;

- identify specific criteria by which performance may be judged;

- monitor progress on a regular basis and revise targets accordingly.

The mentor's principal role is to assist them with these questions and to ensure that realistic targets are set in the light of their self-evaluations. A full account is given by Brooks and Little (1995).

II: Target setting

(a) **Contexts:** Target setting is important within ITET, for example,

- clarifying aspects of a mentor's role which require development and identifying opportunities for further enhancement of her/his skills;

- establishing priorities for students' future teaching in debriefing sessions or formal progress reviews.

(b) **Definition:** A target is a clearly defined task which a person has agreed to undertake in negotiation and agreement with another. It is a priority for development over a given period, and usually contains procedures for establishing the degree of success achieved by the person in meeting her/his goals over a specific period of time. Many targets agreed between ITET students and mentors will relate to the QTS standards.

(c) **Stages in Target Setting:** Target setting is very similar to the process known as 'management by objectives', which was first advocated in the 1960s in an industrial and financial context by the Austrian management consultant Peter Drucker (1964 and 1966). The main stages are:

(i) *Deciding Targets:* The student and mentor review progress along the lines discussed in the previous section. On the basis of this discussion, they negotiate the priorities on which the student needs to work over the time period agreed. As it is desirable that students reflect upon their performance and make a full contribution to the process, they can be requested to produce a list of the targets which they consider to be important at that stage of their development. The mentor needs some time to consider this list, which is then used as the basis for discussion. He/she may also make reference to the views of other teachers who have supervised the trainee.

The most successful targets are those which are decided jointly by the mentor and student. Although each begins the process with her/his own individual priorities, the outcome is a single agreed list. Hence, as Trewthown (1983) notes, the process of target setting makes demands upon both parties.

Once a list has been compiled, the items can be arranged in order of priority. Each target should be unambiguously expressed and make challenging but realistic demands of the student. Many partnerships make reference to SMART targets which are short-term, measurable, achievable, realistic and time-bound (i.e. they can be achieved within an agreed time span). For each, it is necessary to record:

- the success criteria which will enable the student and mentor to judge the extent to which the target has been met when they hold their next review;

- the strategies the student will follow to attain these objectives;

- the time-scale for achieving each target with due consideration given to the student's total workload;

- the resources and support which the student will need;

- a date for review when they will meet to discuss the progress made.

The agreed targets are recorded on a specific form and are amended only by mutual agreement. A typical form could consist of the following headings:

AGREED TARGET STATEMENT

TARGET	STRATEGIES	SUCCESS CRITERIA	TIME-SCALE/ TARGET DATES	SUPPORT AND RESOURCES NEEDED

Signed ....…..............(*Student*) ...….............…..............(*Mentor*) Date ....

(ii) *implementation:* The student puts into practice the strategies listed in the above statement to achieve the targets.

(iii) *review:* The mentor and student meet on the agreed day to review progress, utilising the criteria they have negotiated to judge the degree of success the student has had in accomplishing the targets. Where he/she has been successful, discussion centres on the next set of targets, which may require the application of more ambitious pedagogic strategies or introduce the student to a wider ability range. This can be an effective method of stimulating trainees who have reached a good standard and need to be challenged.

Where difficulties have been encountered in meeting the agreed targets, the reasons are analysed and a new action plan is drawn up to resolve the problems which have been identified. Additional support and resources may be provided or alternative approaches adopted. In some cases the targets may be too ambitious and may need to be modified.

(d) **Target Setting for Students who Experience Problems;** Where weekly reviews reveal that students are encountering major problems, it can be beneficial for mentors, perhaps in association with HEI tutors, to engage in more frequent target setting to chart small steps in achievement. At UWIC weekly forms are employed with the following sections:

- targets set;

- progress made against the set targets;

- outcome of the review:

  - sufficient progress has been made in relation to the set targets;

  - insufficient progress has been made. Moderation procedures will be arranged.

(e) **Benefits of Target Setting:** Target setting has the merit that it establishes a clear framework for monitoring progress, which can assist the maintenance of student profiles, a topic for discussion in chapter eleven. Students are aware of their progress at all stages, and are required to reflect upon their teaching in accordance with the QTS standards. Motivation can be secured where they feel that they are gradually mastering these standards and that their achievement is being recognised. Target setting along these lines also prepares them to complete the career entry profile, and, when they are experienced teachers, to participate in the annual reviews which are integral to performance management.

III: Helping students to develop their ideas

Most student teachers bring with them to their ITET course ideas about learning and teaching which they have acquired through their own experience as pupils. Observation at the start of their school placement, together with ideas acquired at the HEI and in reading, also influence their thinking. Throughout their period of school experience they need to reflect about their teaching and to explore different strategies. It is important that they think critically about their work and constantly review their basic assumptions about teaching, learning and the role of education. In this process, the mentor can bring to bear a number of valuable skills. Some helpful techniques are:

(a) **Exploring Ideas about Teaching in General**, for example, the kind of relationship students believe teachers should have with their classes, the merits of various types of teaching strategy, and the overall aims and purposes of education. This could involve:

(i) *general discussion in the early stages of an ITET course:* Dialogue can be initiated in the early days of a placement before students begin teaching by themselves so that mentors can learn about the ideas they bring with them. Typical questions which could be raised by mentors include:

- What are your main reasons for wanting to join the teaching profession?

- Which of your teachers influenced you most when you were a pupil? For what reasons did they have this influence upon you?

- What did you like and dislike most about your own schooling? What have you learned from your own schooling? What practices employed during your schooling do you think you will adopt? What practices would you not want to follow as a teacher?

- What type of teacher do you hope to become? Do you see yourself as a subject specialist or a 'missionary' or someone committed to bringing about greater social justice?

- Do you have an particular interests in teaching which could influence your career development, for example, special educational needs?

- Why do you believe your subject to be important? How will you share your enthusiasm for your subject?

- How do you perceive your own role as a teacher? Is the teacher a leader, counsellor, facilitator or entertainer?

- What kind of teacher do you want to be? What type of relationship do you want with your pupils?

(ii) *ideas derived from literature*. Ideas may be drawn from students' reading in relation to their subject specialism or educational and professional studies courses. Many of the topics listed in the sixth chapter constitute a valuable focus for discussion, especially where students undertake pertinent observation. Thus, mentors may stimulate debate about such topics as the role of governors and the rights of parents. In some schools in partnership with UWIC which have established rooms for the use of trainees, recent publications have been stored for them to peruse during periods when they do not have responsibility for classes.

(iii) *ideas derived from general observation of lessons given by experienced teachers:* It has been suggested in earlier chapters that students should be encouraged to reflect upon pedagogic issues during their observation and collaborative teaching. Discussion can then take place with respect to a variety of issues, for example, the contexts in which instructional and heuristic teaching are most applicable and the quality of learning promoted in lessons they have seen.

(iv) *ideas acquired in college-based components of the ITET course:* An important source of ideas for stimulating students' thinking about their approach to teaching is the programme of subject studies and educational and professional studies operated by the HEI. It is important that all mentors are aware of the content of these programmes, so that reference can be made to issues which have been debated at the university or college, for example, the use of rewards and sanctions, equal opportunities policies and the planning of activities for children at the nursery and reception stage which develop their physical, intellectual, emotional and social abilities.

At all stages in the process of encouraging students to undertake self-evaluation, important skills which mentors need to employ are:

- helping students to analyse their experiences;

- enabling them to frame their questions in coherent manner;

- pointing out to them alternative perspectives, opinions and ideas, without suggesting that these are necessarily 'correct';

- challenging their thinking, where necessary, by asking them to provide justification for their conclusions and ensuring that they understand the implications of the judgements they reach. It is important that mentors challenge without damaging confidence;

- helping them synthesise and make sense of their experiences.

(b) **Focused Discussion Centring on Specific Lessons:** Debriefing is the topic of the next chapter. It is, nonetheless, relevant to note some of the skills which mentors can employ to stimulate students' thinking:

(i) In discussion they can help students clarify their thinking, for example, by questioning them about the strengths and limitations of the teaching strategies they have used. It is possible to elicit their views on the efficacy of a certain approach taken in a lesson they have just taught and to consider other topics in which the same methodology might with advantage be employed. Through questioning the mentor can also enable the student to be aware of different types of lesson where alternative techniques would be more suitable.

(ii) It is important that mentors set a good example of critical reflection by offering clear justification for the value judgements they reach. In a survey of the views of students of mentors' skills (Geen, Bassett and Douglas, 1999b) eighty-seven per cent of respondents felt that their mentors did explain the basis for their judgements and that this helped them to understand more clearly the practices they adopted.

(iii) Mentors need to be aware that they can do great harm by forcing their views upon a student in a dogmatic manner. One mentor, whom the author encountered, seemed to believe that there was only one way to teach any lesson. Comments to trainees therefore revolved around the extent to which their teaching accorded with her lesson plan. Invariably, minor deviations from the structure she favoured received harsh, critical comments, which merely demotivated and upset trainees.

(iv) Although occasions arise where it is necessary to challenge students' assumptions, this has to be done in such a way that confidence and self-esteem are not crushed. Usually, skilful questioning and focused observation can help resolve problems. In one interesting example given by Hagger, Burn and McIntyre (1993, p. 88), a geography mentor, who was reviewing a student's lesson plan, found that she had read a book on the value of role play in the subject and had accepted all its arguments uncritically. As a result, she was using this approach frequently without considering the needs of individual classes. In this case, the mentor put a number of constructive questions to help her understand that this strategy would not be effective with at least one of the classes she was going to teach ("How are you going to decide which pupil is in which group? Does everyone in the group have to record their decisions? When they are reporting back, how interested is everyone else in the class going to be in hearing what somebody else is saying?").

In another example from the same source, a student set out with the aims of being a friend to her pupils and courting popularity. Her mentor was concerned about the implications of this philosophy and the assumptions upon which it rested. Accordingly, to encourage the student to think critically, she recorded the comments addressed to that student by pupils in one lesson and made these the focus of discussion after the lesson. The student, reflecting upon these comments, began to question her beliefs and asked the teacher for advice on ways of creating a more appropriate relationship with her pupils (p. 87).

(v) Many students learn a great deal about learning and teaching when they are able to try out and test their own ideas. In the survey into students' ability to meet the QTS standards for assessment (Geen, Bassett and Douglas, 2001), it was noted that thirty-four per cent of the sample had been permitted to develop, put into practice and evaluate assessment techniques devised by themselves. This was a procedure which they found to be highly advantageous.

(vi) In cases where over-confident students will not accept that there is another point of view or that their methods do not constitute the only valid approach, an effective solution is to have them examine the work of several classes pursuing the same topic but taught by different means.

(vii) Mentors need to resist the temptation to dominate discussion about specific lessons. Some students want the teacher's opinion of a lesson they have taught the minute they have finished it, and mentors may rush in and offer their views, especially where they observe the need for substantial improvement or have noted some other problem. This denies the student the chance to reflect and to learn from self-analysis.

(viii) In some schools mentors do not regularly question students about their teaching or seek to develop their thinking about pedagogic and wider educational issues. This is usually because the students seem to be competent and their lessons appear to be progressing well. A further factor is that the mentors are fully occupied in teaching classes and cannot always find time to discuss with students all their ideas and views in the detail which might be desirable. This again points to the importance of the provision of regular contact time between mentors and trainees.

IV: Establishing boundaries

(a) **Potential Problems:** Watkins and Whalley (1993, p. 166) argue that mentors should not find themselves in a situation where a limit or boundary in terms of students' conduct has been reached and surpassed. Examples they give are :

(i) A student telephones the mentor at home late on a Friday evening to talk in general terms about non-urgent matters relating to school experience.

(ii) A student waits until a meeting is ending before raising crucial issues.

(iii) A student's demands upon the mentor's time are more than the mentor feels to be appropriate.

(b) **Strategies** for overcoming such problems include:

(i) *Establishing from the Outset the Mentor's Expectations:* Most HEIs do establish rules of conduct for their students, for example, dress code, punctuality and the nature of the comments which should be made after observation of lessons. Generally, these rules create a relationship with which both school staff and students feel comfortable. As with the establishment of class rules, it is desirable that the underlying reasons are made clear to all parties. Consequently, it is advantageous for ITET co-ordinators and mentors to explain:

- the expectations of the school, for example, times when trainees should be on the premises, the importance of their being fully involved in the life of the school, activities in which they should be engaged when they are not teaching classes, and contributions to after-school events;

- the structure of roles so that students are clear about the positions and responsibilities of people within their 'role map';

- channels of communication so that they know to whom they should turn if they have any questions or problem. They also need to be made aware of the time and venue of meetings with their co-ordinators and mentors, the preparation they should undertake for these meetings and ways of making contact with mentors outside periods set aside for formal discussion;

- targets students are expected to meet at all stages;

- rules governing meetings, for example, ensuring that minutes are readily available, keeping to the set agenda and allowing all people to contribute.

(ii) *If necessary, re-establishing these expectations and rules:* Where students ignore the boundaries set by the mentor, it is necessary for these to be re-established. At the same time, it may be desirable to set further rules to clarify 'grey' areas.

(iii) *Dealing with an issue in an assertive but not aggressive manner:* It is necessary to distinguish 'assertiveness' from 'aggression'. Typically assertive statements which may be made to students are:

> *Thank you for your telephone call. It is not convenient for me to talk to you now. Perhaps we could find some other time to talk. Could you see me about this on Monday?*

> *I find your views interesting, but I am afraid I do not agree with you because ...*

> *I am grateful for your contribution to our meetings, but I really would appreciate it if you could in future establish them on the agenda at the very start.*

V: Challenging and handling conflict

(a) **Challenging:** The term 'challenging' often suggests an activity alien to the context of helping a person. It may even conjure up images of abrasiveness and hostility. Some mentors are reluctant to challenge because they feel that they are intruding or they fear that their action will lead to conflict. Again, they may believe that any critical comments will cause distress. However, challenging can be used in a positive sense as a strategy for examining some aspects of classroom activity and for encouraging students to understand more fully the implications of their conduct. As Watkins and Whalley write, "the goals of challenging are to help a learner overcome a blind spot, develop a new perspective and thereby become able to act" (p. 164). Examples they give in the context of mentoring are challenging:

(i) *omissions,* for example, when a student has been told on more than one occasion that he/she needs to bring about some change and has failed to take the requisite action.

(ii) *discrepancies,* for example, between what people say and what they do and between their view of their performance and that of other people:

> **You seem to suggest that you've experienced a problem with communications with this class. Your subject mentor cannot see the evidence for this.**

(iii) *excuses,* where a learner is reluctant to recognise a problem and the opportunities for resolving that problem:

> **But you keep on mentioning all those other tasks as the reason for your not getting the planning done. Don't you have to prioritise?**

(iv) *distortions:* Some people cope with matters they find difficult to face by distorting them in various ways:

> **Do you really think it's the case that all these ideas are 'just theory'?**

(v) *oversimplifications:*

> **If you go on saying it's all the fault of other people, you run the risk of leaving yourself out of the picture completely.**

(vi) *blocks:*

> **We don't know that these pupils dislike this approach, and you may never know, unless you try something different.**

Watkins and Whalley suggest that mentors need to keep in mind their ultimate goal, which is to help the learner and earn the right to challenge by developing an effective working relationship, trying to see the issue from the student's point of view and being open to challenge themselves. They need the ability to be tactful without being insipid or apologetic.

At the same time, they can avoid situations of conflict by not expecting students to learn too much too quickly, and on some occasions they can phrase their questions in such a way that they invite learners to challenge themselves.

(b) **Handling Conflicts:** Although most people would prefer to avoid conflict situations, certain writers on management such as Mary Parker Follett (1941), Kornhauser, Dubin and Ross (1954), Kast and Rosenzweig (1985) and Daft (2001) note that it can have a constructive role in fostering creativity and innovation. In the literature on conflict management the following strategies have been expounded:

(i) *ignoring or suppressing conflict,* which is likely to perpetuate the *status quo* and ignore the possibility of finding a satisfactory solution;

(ii) *smoothing*, where some attempt is made to solve the problem, but the real issues are glossed over, differences are minimised, and, although agreement is reached on minor changes, the real sources of the problem remain;

(iii) *domination,* where one side wins a total victory over the other. Kast and Rosensweig (p. 595) illustrate this technique with the words of a company chairman calling for a vote: "All in favour, say 'aye'; all opposed, say 'I resign'." This strategy is not always successful in the long run; attitudes harden and the defeated party seeks ways of reversing the decision at a later stage;

(iv) *compromising*, where people on both sides agree to give up some of their objectives in order to end the controversy. This is a common technique. The main difficulty is that conflict may emerge again at a later date if neither party is really satisfied with the compromise;

(v) *finding integrative solutions*, where both parties in the conflict are satisfied and neither has to sacrifice anything. This is a 'win-win' rather than a 'win-lose' situation. Mary Parker Follett writes that "integration involves invention, and the clever thing is to recognise this, and not to let one's thinking stay within the boundaries of two alternatives which are mutually exclusive" (p. 33).

(vi) adopting the following steps in the management of conflict:

(c) **Conflict Management Skills:** The following strategies have been found to be useful:

(i) *to ensure that the real reason for the conflict is identified:* Mary Parker Follett (p. 40) urges the parties to a conflict to "find the significant rather than the dramatic features" so that time is not wasted in dealing with irrelevancies and trivialities.

(ii) *breaking the issue down into its constituent parts:* This involves analysis and discussion.

(iii) *detaching ideas and viewpoints from personalities.*

(iv) *encouraging the people involved in the dispute to talk openly to one another.*

(v) *encouraging them to listen carefully to the point of view expressed by others.* It is important that everyone has the opportunity to speak without interruption from other disputants.

(vi) *encouraging parties to state their aims, views and feelings openly but calmly.*

(vii) *trying to put the conflict into the context of the enterprise.* The prime aim is the development of the student so that he/she meets the QTS standards and acquires the attributes needed to become a member of the teaching profession.

(viii) *trying to build on each other's ideas.* This can often lead to an integrative solution.

(ix) *involving a third party:* Sometimes the ideas of a neutral third party can be helpful. As Schmuck (1985) observes, conflict can sometimes be resolved when the persons involved respond to the advice of someone who does not have a vested interest in the issue at stake.

(x) *employing humour:* Humour can provide a temporary respite from tension, displace aggression and serve as an appeal to the people involved to rise above the present difficulties to some more inclusive goal. Making oneself the butt of the humour has often achieved satisfactory results.

(xi) *focusing upon future action rather than past events.* A conflict episode should result in the setting of targets with which both mentor and student are happy. It should not dwell on past recriminations.

VI: Supporting and counselling students who have problems

(a) **Supporting and Counselling:** Brooks and Sikes (1997, p. 113) note that very few students have problems which are so severe that they are in danger of failing an ITET course completely. Nonetheless, it is vital for mentors to be on their guard for difficulties which may arise and to take action as soon as possible, since problems can occur if a student is failed and complains that he/she was not given any warning that this was likely to happen. Steps which can be taken to avoid this problem are listed below.

(i) Mentors maintain regular contact with their students, hold frequent debriefing sessions, review progress, discuss ideas, set targets and give honest appraisals of the lessons they observe. In this way, they are more likely to be aware of difficulties before they become too serious and not allow a trainee to remain in the school for a whole term before offering critical feedback.

(ii) Mentors can sometimes anticipate problems, for example, mature students who have to collect young children from school, by learning about the person's background from the *curriculum vitae*, which should be conveyed to the school at the outset of the ITET course.

(iii) During debriefing and other regularly organised meetings, students can be encouraged to reveal any problems they are facing so that these can be discussed at an early stage. They should be given the impression that by drawing attention to these difficulties they are not confessing to heinous sins. Where teachers adopt the reflective practitioner approach themselves and regularly analyse their own performance, students can be made aware that self-evaluation is a normal part of their role.

(iv) Students should be clear from the outset of the channels of communication which exist, so that they can approach the appropriate member of the school staff if they need help. In this way, they do not have to wait until the weekly review to raise some matter which is troubling them.

(v) Where problems arise of a personal nature (for example, family circumstances), it is important that all staff who need to be aware of this are in fact informed and that the respective tutor at the HEI is also contacted

(vi) Few mentors are trained counsellors. Nevertheless, they can use the listening skills described in the last chapter, and other interpersonal skills. In some cases counselling can be valuable in assisting students to think more clearly about the problem and to adopt for themselves the solutions they feel are most suitable (Nelson-Jones, 1993). Mentors can question students, guide them to understand the consequences likely to arise from choosing a course of action, and may point to further possible courses of action, but the ultimate choice and value-judgements are the responsibility of the student.

Hence, key questions in counselling are:

- What do you see as the problem?

- How do you feel about it?

- What do you see as your options?

- What consequences so you see arising from the implementation of each option?

- How do you feel about each of these?

- Have you considered such alternatives as ...?

- Which options are you going to choose?

- When, how and where are you going to put this into practice?

- How will you know whether the problem has been resolved?

Mentors and ITET co-ordinators can generally fulfil this role without great difficulty. Most HEIs also have trained counsellors to whom students may be referred.

(b) **Personality Clashes:** As Brooks and Sikes note, there can be clashes between mentors and students. The advice they give to mentors is to be analytical, separating issues from emotions and trying to help the student find realistic solutions to the problems he/she faces. The temptation to offer palliatives should be resisted. Where problems relate to progress in meeting the standards, some of the strategies discussed in earlier chapters can be adopted, for example, organising additional structured observation or collaborative teaching and providing constant feedback.

Brooks and Sikes are well justified in advising mentors always to be fair and not to decide after only a few days that the student is a 'total fail'. In one case observed by the author a student was based with a mentor who had a reputation for being an outstandingly able teacher. As a result, the trainee was in awe of this person, and, being very nervous, she performed in her first two lessons at a level which the mentor did not feel was satisfactory. From that moment the student was branded as a 'dud', and her confidence diminished day by day. Ultimately, she was failed and attended another school in order to retrieve her position on the ITET course. At this school, where she was based with a sympathetic mentor, who nonetheless expected high standards, she made substantial progress and completed the course successfully. Mentors do need to be aware of the danger of dismissing trainees too lightly and of the importance of checking whether poor progress is entirely the fault of the student. At all stages, performance rather than personality should be the issue at stake.

Where differences between mentors and students cannot be easily resolved, strategies which have proved to be advantageous are:

(i) to ensure that the student is observed by as many teachers as possible in order to obtain a range of views;

(ii) to have the ITET co-ordinator evaluate lessons more frequently than would normally be the case;

(iii) to inform and discuss the situation with staff at the HEI;

(iv) to arrange additional visits on the part of the HEI tutor;

(v) to pass the matter to the HEI, which can then organise its own moderation procedures;

(vi) to ensure that all formal procedures in the partnership agreement are followed;

(vii) in some cases to move the student to another school. Brooks and Sikes observe that this stage should be reached only when all other approaches have failed.

In some cases reported by Bridges, Elliott and McKee (1995) and by Jacques (1992) mentors have preferred not to take any action, hoping that the situation will improve. Such aspirations have not always been fulfilled.

❯ Issues for consideration

1. Read section I (*reviewing students' progress*), and describe the strategies you employ to review students' progress (e.g. open ended discussion, structured methods, use of formal review sheets).

2. Note any strategies which could be adopted to improve the reviewing of students' progress at your school.

3. Read section II (*target setting*), and describe the practice used in your school for target setting with student teachers. In the light of your reading highlight any changes which you feel should be made to the practice.

4. Write down five targets you may negotiate with students, and for each target state the criteria you would adopt to assess the extent to which the students actually achieve that target.

5. Read section III (*helping students to develop their ideas*), and recount any discussion which takes place at your school to help students explore ideas about teaching in general terms (for example, discussion at the outset of school experience, ideas derived from literature, ideas derived from lesson observation or ideas derived from

the HEI course).

6. Describe the ways in which you encourage students to think critically both about their ideas concerning teaching and about their lesson performance. Relate your comments to those aspects of the mentor's role discussed in the text.

7. A subject mentor in history is aware from discussions at an early stage that his student has a very 'traditional' view of teaching the subject, i.e. she stands at the front, enforces silence and transmits content to the class. How might the mentor challenge this student's thinking without destroying her confidence?

8. In the text reference is made to some of the constraints experienced by mentors when they try to encourage students to reflect critically. Show the extent to which any of these constraints may be true of your role as a mentor, and suggest ways in which their influence may be mitigated.

9. Read section IV (*establishing boundaries*), and state the rules which you think should be established with student teachers from the outset of their school experience. Consider role boundaries, time boundaries and limits upon the responsibilities of mentors.

10. Read section V (*challenging and handling conflict*). Write a short guide for mentors on strategies for handling conflict which may arise with students.

11. Consider the following case study and state the action you would take as the ITET co-ordinator in this situation.

A PGCE student has made poor progress during her school experience. It is the second term that she has been in the school and her notes are still very thin. She makes little effort to produce her own materials, preferring to rely heavily on teaching aids devised by the department. Her knowledge of subject matter is limited and she has not always acted upon advice from the subject mentor or college tutors on basic issues such as the selection of appropriate teaching strategies and questioning techniques. Her relationship with some classes has become strained; pupils regard her as 'boring' and 'abrasive'.

The student has received regular counselling from school and college staff and, although she has frequently said that she welcomes constructive criticism, no real improvement has been detected. She says that she is working on her lesson preparation until the early hours of the morning, but little evidence can be produced to substantiate this claim. The subject mentor has heard from another student that this person is a 'night-owl' who enjoys an active social life and does not normally start lesson preparation until after midnight.

By the middle of the second term this student seems to be blaming everyone else for her problems and is seeking to elicit support from one of the teachers' unions to 'sort out' the school mentors and college tutors. She asks her subject mentor for permission to be absent from school for an afternoon so that she can visit the dentist, but in fact she has made an appointment to see the senior representatives of one of the unions to complain about the school and the college. As the union representatives contact the college, both school and university staff know that the student lied about her whereabouts that afternoon. The subject mentor is appalled and sees the student's conduct as unprofessional and insulting to her department.

12. Read section VI (*supporting and counselling students who have problems*). If you were training a new mentor, what advice would you give that person about counselling students with problems?

13. The following case study is taken from *The Good Mentor Guide* by V. Brooks and P. Sikes. Explain the action you would take to resolve the problem.

> *"I did really well on my first practice and I thought that I'd got it sussed. The teachers were pleased with me, they agreed with how I was trying to do things and I felt really comfortable there. But when I moved to my second school it was the opposite. I did things the same, I thought I was getting on well with the kids, but it turned out that the teachers weren't at all impressed. And I couldn't understand it until my university tutor said, 'Look. It's not you. They have different values and ways of working there compared with at H.' But what got me was that I could have failed at that second place, doing what I was getting praised for at my first school"*
> (English student, p. 145).

14. A student has been based with a low ability class year 10 pursuing a course in catering. She has coped extremely well in terms of class management, and the pupils have produced work with which the mentor is very pleased. However, the student considers that she is a potential 'fail' because the standards of the pupils do not meet her high expectations. The following is her self evaluation of a lesson which both mentor and HEI tutor considered to be highly successful when judged by the QTS standards. What would you say to the student after reading her self-evaluation?

Self-Evaluation

OBJECTIVES: Most of these were achieved with all but two Swiss rolls on the presentation table by the end of the lesson. Time was short and pupils will complete their self-evaluations (obj. 5) at the beginning of the next lesson.

CONTENT: The pupils are getting into the routine of following a method of work, and the class coped well with the level of practical work. However, there are some pupils who are still not taking a pride in their work and others rely on answers from me.

PREPARATION: As usual, the lunch hour had to be used to ensure thorough preparation. Pupils are always asked to inform me prior to the lesson of any difficulties with ingredients, but, as always happens, no-one did so and three turned up without any ingredients. I do not know how I can get them to bring ingredients.

VISUAL AIDS: I think these were appropriate and positioned where all pupils could see them. They had had access to them in the previous demonstration lesson.

ORGANISATION: Too long was allowed at the start for the introduction because half the class arrived late. They knew what they had to achieve as the result of the demonstration in the last lesson.

TIMING: Since this is the last lesson of the day and the pupils must leave on the bell to catch buses, there was a rush at the end of the lesson. I was very disappointed that the ending was hurried and the pupils could not all be dismissed in the usual orderly manner after seeing and evaluating the finished products.

CLARITY: I think that the explanations and spot demonstrations were adequate.

SUPERVISION: I tried to ensure that I did not neglect the pupils who were completing theory. The lesson was generally under control with much circulation on my part. I hope that I noticed the errors and corrected them, for example, pupils collecting the sugar with a spoon but no plate, setting the wrong temperature and walking around with hot baking trays. I was aware of running short of time and would have liked more organisation at the end.

QUESTIONS: Mainly recall. Individual questions put to pupils doing the practical to consolidate learning.

DISCIPLINE: The pupils doing the theory work are a constant cause of concern, since they never bring ingredients and the handouts that I have prepared fail to motivate them. They do not file them as I have asked, but leave them lying around. On occasions, I have provided ingredients for them with disastrous results.

MOTIVATION: The nature of the lesson created some degree of motivation. I had previously shown them pictures of Swiss roll variations that we could do in the future once the basic recipe was mastered.

CONCLUSIONS: Even at this stage, I still have to mention jewellery and hair. I have asked them while in the corridor before the lesson to take off their jumpers and roll up their sleeves - this is still not being done spontaneously. Evaluations are done and completed in the next lesson since I have never received them when they are set for homework. There is no support on homework or discipline crises in this school. All the pupils took home an edible, and in most cases, attractive Swiss roll, but I doubt my ability to motivate this class and to have the pupils work to a satisfactory level.

15. Make a list of some of the more common problems which students have experienced in the course of their time at your school. How would you set about trying to help them?

16. Some writers on mentoring have referred to problems which can be experienced by mature students, for example, people in their forties who have perhaps been made redundant from other jobs. What difficulties might they face on school experience which are not shared with younger students entering teaching shortly after taking a first degree, and how could mentors provide the necessary support?

Debriefing and feedback

I: Aims in debriefing

The importance of "clear and objective feedback" is stressed by the Welsh Inspectorate in the publication *Mentoring in Initial Teacher Training: Secondary Phase: A Good Practice Document* (OHMCI 1998c, p. 4). Most mentors seek to combine the apprenticeship, competency and reflective practitioner models in meeting the following aims:

- informing students of the progress they are making;

- motivating them by stressing the standards in which they are strong;

- establishing procedures to enable them to improve their performance. Many such procedures have been described in earlier chapters, for example, offering advice, leading by example, observing and teaching collaboratively;

- building confidence in their own skills. Lazarus (2000) argues that the manner in which feedback is given can have a considerable impact upon a student's sense of progress;

- assisting them to reflect critically;

- encouraging them to elicit meaning from action. Techniques such as Ghaye and Ghaye's 'deconstruction' and Fish's strands of reflection can be helpful in attaining this goal;

- helping them to understand the professional role of the teacher. Discursive dialogue is one technique for promoting such understanding;

- leading them towards independent practice (Stengelhofen, 1993, p. 173).

II: Forms of debriefing

Four approaches to debriefing are:

(a) **Lesson Critiques:** The traditional 'lesson crit' relates very much to the apprenticeship philosophy of ITET and involves analysis of the salient points of the lesson - both positive and critical. The mentor offers professional judgement and assists the student with appropriate 'tips', 'hints' and advice derived from her/his superior experience. This is essentially 'feedback' about progress and allows mentors to present their views and opinions. The critique mode does not stress very much the ideals of reflection and self-evaluation.

(b) **Formal Asessment:** This consists of an official judgement about the lesson in terms of the QTS standards. It is rooted in the competency model of ITET. In most schools specific forms are used to record performance against the standards. Examples are:

(i) *Assessment forms for a review of a single lesson:* The UWIC lesson assessment form is built around the standards of Welsh Office Circular 13/98 (Welsh Office, 1998) and allows mentors to enter their comments on each of the following items:

- CONTEXT OF THE LESSON:

- PLANNING: Mentors are especially asked to scrutinise lesson plans.

- TEACHING AND CLASS MANAGEMENT:

- MONITORING, ASSESSMENT, RECORDING, REPORTING AND ACCOUNTABILITY:

- OTHER PROFESSIONAL REQUIREMENTS:

- KEY POINTS FOR CONSIDERATION INCLUDING COMMENTS ON PREVIOUSLY SET TARGETS.

Other types of evaluation sheet were discussed in chapter five. Shaw (1995) has devised a lesson assessment format which prompts the mentor by putting a series of questions in relation to each main heading. Although this form was compiled before the current standards were drawn up, it is, nonetheless, possible for mentors to use the overall approach and to make reference to appropriate standards as they enter comments under each of the headings:

- THE LEARNING ENVIRONMENT: Was the environment safe and all potential hazards explained? Was any work by pupils displayed in the room? Were tables and chairs arranged in a manner conducive to concentration and listening? Did pupils have a clear view of the board or screen?

- PREPARATION: Were all the materials and resources required for the lesson ready in the room? Had differentiated work been prepared in readiness for the lesson? Had previous work been marked? Were constructive comments used in marking?

- ORGANISATION: Was there a set procedure for entering and leaving the room? Were books, folders and worksheets, etc. ready for the pupils' use? If not, were these given out and later collected in a controlled and speedy fashion?

- CONTENT: Did the student relate the work to what had been previously achieved? Did the class understand the objectives of the lesson? Was there a good balance between teacher-centred and pupil-centred activity? Did the student appear to have control of the subject matter?

- PRESENTATION: Were overhead transparencies clearly printed and legible from all angles of the room? Was the board work clearly written so that it could be read by all members of the class?

- CLASS CONTROL/RELATIONSHIP WITH THE PUPILS: Did the student gain the pupils' attention before the commencement of the lesson? Did he/she insist on complete silence on the part of the class during the initial instructions? Did the student insist that pupils put up their hands to answer questions and to seek assistance? Were questions used to involve non-volunteers?

For each of the questions asked under these categories, mentors tick a YES/NO column and have the opportunity to write general comments. At the very end of the sheet they answer the following question:

How would you rate the following?

Item	Good	Satisfactory	Unsatisfactory
Class Control			
Teaching Technique			
Pupil Learning			
Pupil Activity			

(ii) *Assessment forms for review of a block of school experience:* Debriefing need not be confined to a single lesson. It can relate to a block of school experience and to the comments recorded by a mentor in a profile. A good example is the system of profiling utilised by the Leeds University Secondary School Partnership. Again, it was drawn up before the publication of the current standards, but the general method of recording progress can, with advantage, be adopted by ITET providers. It is described in full by Peter Tomlinson (1995, pp. 150-159) and consists of:

(1) a list of key COMPETENCES: In the profile described by Tomlinson these are:

- explicit knowledge base;

- planning and preparation;

- interactive teaching;

- wider professional roles; and

- professional self-development.

(2) a set of SUB-AREAS relating to each of the key competences. Thus, in the case of 'interactive teaching' the sub-areas are,

- intelligent and effective assistance for pupil learning, organisation and resource deployment;

- effective assessment and monitoring of pupil learning activities and progress;

- appropriate assessment relating to and influencing pupils, their behaviour, motivation and well being;

- effective assessment and monitoring of pupil behaviour, motivation and well-being.

(3) PROMPT MATERIAL for each sub-area. For example, in the sub-area 'effective assessment and monitoring of pupil learning activities and progress' mentors are to have regard for forms of immediate awareness and strategic elicitation, both direct and

indirect. Immediate forms of awareness include looking and listening, both generally (scanning) and with a particular focus. Strategic elicitation includes relatively direct forms, such as questioning and discussion, and indirect forms, such as inferences from classroom events and pupil products by way of class and homework.

(4) GRADING on a rating scale. For each of these sub-areas mentors tick the appropriate box:

Insufficient information	Seriously weak	Needs attention	Satisfactory	Strong	Outstanding

(5) the setting out of an ACTION PLAN for each sub-area.

Other modes of profiling are described in chapter eleven.

(c) **Reflective Practitioner Models of Debriefing:** As was shown in the first chapter, there are different practical approaches within the 'reflective practitioner' philosophy of ITET. The common thread running through them is that the observer and the observed explore what happened during the lesson, think about its significance, perhaps with reference to personal and more formal theory, and contemplate strategies for future development. The person observed has the opportunity to examine and refine her/his own professional judgements. Specific approaches to debriefing along these lines are:

(i) *Analysis of the lesson by the student*, using the framework given in the first chapter. The trainee considers the extent to which her/his lesson objectives were achieved and, together with the mentor, reviews performance in the light of agreed criteria. The debriefing concludes with the formulation of an action plan.

(ii) *Extending the debriefing to cover wider educational and professional issues:* This entails discursive as opposed to pragmatic dialogue. Examples have been given in chapter six of ways in which this can be accomplished. The prime aim is to extend the student's professional knowledge and understanding.

(iii) *Investigating moral and ethical principles underlying teaching:* Writers such as Zeichner and Liston (1987) and Van Manen (1990) urge mentors to encourage their students during debriefing to probe the fundamental moral and ethical principles underlying their educational practices. Zeichner and Liston, for example, refer to two aspects of the role of the teacher:

- the 'technician' who is concerned with the successful accomplishment of ends and the justification for classroom actions in terms of educational principles;

- the 'moral craftsperson' who pays attention to the ethical implications of institutional arrangements.

Reflective practitioners in their view are students who engage in systematic enquiry into the moral and ethical dimensions of their own teaching. These are able to "assume greater roles in determining the direction of classroom and school affairs according to purposes of which they are aware and which can be justified on moral and educational grounds as well as on instrumental grounds" (pp. 25-26).

Mentors who wish their students to become reflective practitioners in accordance with this analysis will stimulate them during debriefing to consider such issues as:

- the aims of education, the arguments with which they would justify their views on educational aims and the manner in which they would seek to promote these aims in the classroom.

- the type of person they feel the educational system should produce. Pring (1984) analyses the concept of a 'person' and highlights different forms of personal development which depend upon the inculcation of intellectual and moral virtues, social competencies, theoretical knowledge and personal values. Students can reflect upon the values and traits they feel should be fostered and ponder a range of questions, for example,

  - Should schooling concern itself primarily with the task of producing well balanced citizens?

  - Is its principal purpose to provide employees who will meet the needs of industry?

  - To what extent is it the role of education to help individuals to develop their potential?

  - Do we want an educational system which seeks to develop young people who are committed to ending social injustice?

- the manner in which the ethos of the school and the class can convey powerful messages to children and bring about different forms of personal and social development.

- ways of teaching moral and political issues without abdicating personal responsibility but also without indoctrinating young people.

- the right of the state to determine the content of education.

- the forms of knowledge and understanding which should underpin the curriculum.

- the ways in which children best acquire this knowledge and understanding.

- equality of opportunity for pupils within the educational system with reference to curriculum choices, the distribution of scarce resources and underachievement.

- the relationship which should be established between teachers and their pupils. Should it be based upon the philosophy that education is a 'banking' concept or should it involve problem-posing and dialogue (Freire, 1972)?

- the use of rewards in schools: Many schools use systems of rewards for pupils who follow their rules and/or achieve good results. Should these systems be viewed as a form of moral education, instilling the 'right' habits into children, or as a type of bribery which teaches young people the wrong values?

Discussion along these lines can be a valuable strategy for encouraging reflection of fundamental ethical issues and ensuring that a future generation of teachers will not consist of rational technicians passively delivering an education, the nature of which has been determined by politicians.

(iv) *Strands of reflection:* One approach to debriefing, which has been developed by Fish, Twinn and Purr (1991) on the basis of the earlier work of Zeichner and Liston in 1987, involves four interrelated strands for encouraging reflection on practice (Fish, 1995b, pp. 139-144). It incorporates several of the principles of the other reflective practitioner models and can be especially helpful in reviewing a series of lessons:

(1) the FACTUAL strand which is descriptive. This is where the trainee sets out a narrative of the events which took place in the lesson together with his or her comments upon them. The mentor may also compile a narrative. Fish outlines three aspects of the narrative:

- *Setting the Scene:* Here, the context of the lesson is described, for example, the aims, planning and preparation, the abilities of the pupils, the point they have reached in previous lessons and the physical organisation of the room.

- *Telling the Story:* A chronological reconstruction of the events of the lesson is given together with the thoughts of the student.

- *Pin-pointing the Critical Incidents:* This involves focusing upon the key moments of the lesson and considering them critically, for example, incidents which caused surprise, offered scope for learning or made the student think twice. At this stage the trainee is encouraged to say why the incident seems to be critical and to describe her/his resulting actions, thoughts and feelings.

(2) the RETROSPECTIVE strand, where the entire set of events which took place over a number of lessons is reviewed, and a search is undertaken to derive patterns and meanings from these events. At this stage the trainee endeavours to develop theory from practice. The mentor's role is to stimulate reflection, which may be achieved by offering alternative interpretations of events, by stimulating further critical reflection about the points raised by the student or by introducing perspectives which have not yet been considered. Examples of questions suggested by Fish are:

- What main patterns are visible as a whole in the school experience to date?

- What underlying logic drove the overall school experience?

- What were the overall aims and were they achieved?

- What comments might be made by such other people as teachers or pupils involved in this period of school experience?

- What new understanding about teaching has been achieved?

- How did the student judge her/his performance over the period of school experience?

- What patterns were there of critical incidents, failures, successes, emotions, frustrations, limitations, constraints, coercions, etc?

(3) the SUBSTRATUM strand, where it is intended that the trainee explores the assumptions, beliefs and value-judgements underlying the events and ideas which are identified in the strands above. The mentor is concerned to help him/her to articulate a personal theory, and, in doing so, to consider perspectives derived from the formal theory of books and from the personal experience and ideas of other professionals. From this interaction students are encouraged to see that a range of views can exist about procedures and that there are no hard and fast 'right' answers.

Questions suggested by Fish at this point are:

- What beliefs, values, assumptions and prejudices were endemic in or brought to the teaching?

- What was their origin?

- What basic assumptions, beliefs and values underlie the actions and decisions reported in the earlier strands?

- What beliefs are emerging about knowledge and the ways it is gained and used?

- What ideas about theory and practice are implicit in the practice and the reflections upon it?

- What moral and ethical decisions are embedded in the student's planning, actions and reactions to the lesson?

- What theories has the student acted upon?

(4) the CONNECTIVE strand, which is concerned with ways of applying the conclusions reached in the above stages to the student's thinking about future practice. Thus, the information and understanding gained in the previous strands are related to such contexts as:

- other practical situations and experiences;

- other conclusions drawn from reflection upon teaching, for example, those strategies described in the last chapter;

- the actions of other professionals;

- other theories which the student has developed from reflection upon practice and from reading. Arthur, Davison and Moss (1997) suggest that such theories could relate to:

- the 'traditional' educational disciplines of philosophy, psychology, sociology and history;

- to pedagogy;

- to the teaching of the student's subject;

- to the role of the subject within the curriculum;

- to the curriculum in general;

- to the classroom, for example, how the words and actions of the teacher and those of the pupils are manifestations of their culture, knowledge, learning, needs and interests, and how they interact;

- to methods by which teachers may become more effective.

In discussion of these issues the mentor encourages the student to outline a plan of action for future lessons.

Key issues suggested by Fish include:

- What has been learnt from this analysis and how will it relate to future experiences?

- What tentative further theories might be developed for future action?

- What implications do these reflections have for future practice?

She stresses that these strands are intended to offer a framework for reflection. They should not be treated as a rigid series of questions to be answered in a set order at specific points of a school placement. The framework is "a means of facilitating learning through practice via debriefing" (p. 143).

(v) *Using the views of pupils' to promote reflection:* Loughran and Northfield (1998) examine Schon's conception of 'reflection-on-action' and consider ways in which it can in practice be achieved by ITET students. They believe that self-analysis is important, but contend that it is very difficult for individuals to change their interpretations or 'frames of reference' as the outcome of *individual* reflection. They need to take into account the views of others. Consequently, Loughran and Northfield advocate a policy of reflective practice which involves:

- the keeping of a journal to record descriptions, reactions and interpretations associated with daily teaching and pupils' learning;

- comments received from pupils about their perceptions of learning;

- pupils' writing: This covers both class work and responses to classroom experiences.

In recounting the experience of a student who adopt this mode of reflection, they write that, as he began to understand the pupils' perspective, "their responses to the demands of schooling often made more sense than the learning attitudes and outcomes he was seeking" (p. 16).

(d) **The Self-assessment Mode** which provides a framework for the student to assess her/his own performance and to take responsibility for supporting her/his own professional development. Examples of techniques were given in the previous chapter in the section concerned with supporting students' self-evaluation. The maintenance of diaries and journals is also a common practice in many schemes of ITET to prompt self-analysis.

III: Students experiences of debriefing

(a) **Research Studies:** In a research study conducted at UWIC (Geen, 2001a) comments were received on debriefing procedures in schools in South-East Wales from 123 mentors and 237 students. Interviews were also conducted with thirty-four mentors over the academic year 1999-2000. Supplementary research was undertaken during the 2000-2001 session involving sixty postgraduate and thirty-six undergraduate students. A summary of the key points is offered and reference is also made to other surveys in this field.

(b) **Frequency of Debriefing:** All UWIC students received a good level of feedback on their teaching and progress. A third received comments on every lesson they taught and one-fifth were given feedback on at least one lesson each day. The remainder took part in a formal debriefing at least once a week. Usually, the sessions were of between five and fifteen minutes' duration and held immediately after the lesson. Just over half the students also attended a weekly review with their mentor. Eighty-six per cent received comments orally and in writing.

(c) **Lesson Critiques and the Apprenticeship Model:** This model was immediately familiar to mentors, as ninety-eight per cent offered students 'tips', 'hints' and general advice on ways of developing their classroom expertise. In about a fifth of the schools oral and written comments were supplemented with student observation of experienced teachers. Eighty-six per cent of students were satisfied with this degree of feedback received on their teaching, describing it as either 'highly satisfactory' or 'satisfactory'.

Some criticisms were, however, received:

(i) Certain comments from mentors tended to be unclear and not well structured. The lack of a logical order and inability to focus upon one theme at a time did not help students understand areas in which they could improve their teaching. This points to the need for mentors to develop their communication skills along the lines suggested in chapter seven.

(ii) Demonstration of teaching techniques was not always helpful unless it was accompanied by a clear account of the thinking and rationale underlying the teacher's actions. In the chapter on students' observation it was shown that, where mentors were unable to explain why they acted in a certain way, trainees were unlikely to learn very much.

(iii) About a tenth of the sample claimed that they had received contradictory advice from different teachers of the same subject.

(iv) Some mentors expected students to become 'clones' of themselves and feedback tended to contain recriminations where there had been any deviation from the way in which the mentor would have taught the lesson.

(d) **Formal Assessment and the Competency Model:** Although the importance of relating debriefing to the standards is emphasised very clearly in the literature provided by all the HEIs in partnership with the schools in the UWIC surveys, over a third of students claimed that their mentors made little or no reference to them in their lesson debriefing or in their weekly progress reviews. Where the standards did constitute the focus of discussion, the emphasis was placed upon teaching methodology and class management rather than upon monitoring and assessment. Clearly, mentors need to put into practice the strategies outlined in chapter five to ensure that their students acquire the necessary knowledge, understanding and skills pertinent to assessment and to ensure that their debriefings do not lose sight of these standards.

Other difficulties reported by students were:

(i) Less than a third of mentors examined their lesson preparation files and discussed the contents with them. In sixteen per cent of cases planning was not evaluated at any stage over the school placement.

(ii) In the early stages of school experience it would be helpful if mentors concentrated upon just a few of the standards, so that trainees could 'see the wood for the trees'.

(iii) Seven per cent of students were not provided with evidence to substantiate the judgements made by mentors about their progress in relation to the standards.

(iv) When some students reached a level which their mentors considered to be satisfactory, opportunities for debriefing were considerably reduced.

(e) **Reflective Practitioner Models:** Whereas some two-thirds of students in the survey of 2000-2001 reported that their mentors did encourage them to reflect upon their teaching, few of these mentors possessed much knowledge of the techniques devised by Schon, Fish, Arthur, Davison and Moss or Loughran and Northfield. Forty-three per cent of students engaged in some form of discursive dialogue, thirty-nine per cent experienced Schon's 'follow me' methodology and twenty-seven per cent participated in his 'hall of mirrors'. Fish's strands of reflection were familiar to about a third of the sample, and thirty per cent debated with their mentors ethical and moral values underlying their classroom performance.

Several reasons can be advanced to explain why these reflective practices are not more commonly adopted.

(i) The training available to mentors rarely deals in very much depth with this aspect of ITET. For example, in a survey of the in-service provision offered to thirty-nine senior and eighty-four subject mentors in schools in South-East Wales (Geen, 2001c) it was found that only one-fifth had been able to study the models promoted by such writers as Schon and Fish.

(ii) Finding time to practise certain of these modes of reflection is a problem in many schools. Where mentors teach subjects like physical education and have responsibility for extra-curricular duties, they encounter particular difficulties. Other studies (e.g. Stidder and Hayes, 1998) have reached similar conclusions.

(iii) McIntyre and Hagger (1996, p. 159) suggest that certain mentors are reluctant to engage in discussion of the wider range of educational issues with their students because they believe that 'theory' is the province of the HEI.

(iv) In some cases students are unwilling to challenge the fundamental beliefs and values of their mentors. Hence, they feel uncomfortable when opportunities are presented for them to be involved in reflective practitioner models of debriefing.

(v) Separating academic discourse from discussion of more practical matters can be a complex matter. In one example quoted by Dart and Drake (1996) a student teacher was prevented from raising these deeper issues because the mentor considered that they were not relevant to the scope of the lesson debriefing.

Other observations made by students in the UWIC research were:

(i) Nearly sixty per cent of them felt that their analysis of the lesson was taken into account when targets were set. Some forty per cent were able to put their views at the commencement of the debriefing.

(ii) Only two-fifths of mentors examined students' self-evaluations and used these as a starting point for discussion. Hence, the records which students kept with a summary of their reflections upon their classroom performance and their personal responses to school experience were not employed to stimulate the type of debate advocated in the last chapter.

(iii) A small number of students (seven per cent) claimed that their views were totally ignored in debriefing. Mentors had formed their own judgements on a lesson and were determined to impose these on the students.

(iv) Where discursive dialogue was employed, over half the students found that the concepts explored did not correlate with the content of their course at the HEI. Because of time constraints mentors rarely had the opportunity to explain all the issues they raised to the extent that students would have liked.

(f) **Constraints:** Further problems in debriefing have been described in other studies, notably those by Watkins (1992), Stengelhofen (1993), Tomlinson (1995), Dart and Drake (1996), McIntyre and Hagger (1996), Brooks and Sikes (1997) and Jones (2001).

(i) Some degree of conflict can be discerned among the aims of debriefing cited above. On the one hand the mentor is expected to assist the student to reflect critically upon practice and on the other to offer ideas and advice.

(ii) As Jones (2001) observes, the two functions of the mentor - acting as helper and assessing performance - can come into conflict (p. 81).

(iii) In models of reflection there is the problem that the student may merely go through the motions of self-evaluation simply to please the mentor and may not derive any genuinely new insight from the process.

(iv) Some students tend to remember only the negative points which may arise from a debriefing session. Hence, it is important for mentors to reinforce the positive aspects of a lesson as well.

(v) Some students' perceptions of what happened in the debriefing may differ from that of the mentor. Mentors should realise that trainees sometimes have selectivity of awareness. An immense amount of activity is generated in most teaching encounters and humans are selective in what they perceive. Hence, students may miss certain issues or assume that they did or did not occur to fit in with their perceptions. Similarly, there are limitations on students' memories and they may have difficulty in recalling events in lessons. As Tomlinson notes, "by the end of the lesson, much of what they did see earlier may be difficult to recall or already unconsciously reinterpreted to fit the main/preferred bits" (p. 192). As a consequence, it is possible that the student will not be ready to accept the mentor's advice.

(vi) In two studies (Wright and Bottery, 1997; Bottery and Wright, 2000) it is noted that some mentors do not see students' professional development as a priority. They conceive professional development only in terms of dress code and behaviour in the staffroom and ignore wider educational issues.

(vii) Problems can arise when mentors, being reluctant to undermine trainees' confidence, offer only praise, and refrain from providing the degree of critical commentary which is really needed if they are to make progress.

(viii) Where mentors force their views upon the learner, there is likely to be a bad atmosphere and the student may resist acting upon their advice.

(ix) Writers such as Gay and Stephenson (1998) and Hayes (2001) point to the importance of a good relationship between mentor and mentee. Mentors need to be sensitive, to understand the emotional state of the student and to be constructive in their comments. Their feedback should be direct but not threatening (Burgess and Butcher, 1999). In practice, some of them have been insensitive in their handling of students during debriefing, for example, frequently looking at their watch. Where no positive ideas for improvement emerge, students are likely to become demoralised.

(x) Students' confidence can also be damaged if mentors step in and take over a lesson or dominate discussion and then complain that the student has not contributed very much.

IV: Guidelines on debriefing

The following guidelines were developed at a conference of ITET co-ordinators held at UWIC in 1997 (OHMCI, 1998c, p.3).

(a) Feedback should be given as soon as possible after a lesson has been observed. Shaw (1995) suggests that no longer than two days should elapse between the lesson and the debriefing. If a student is emotionally upset as the result of some problem which has occurred with a class, it is probably better to leave the discussion until he/she is ready to receive comments in a calmer frame of mind

(b) There is a need to make the debriefing a genuine learning experience for the student. Hence, it is essential for the mentor to be clear about the focus of the debriefing and to ensure that the student also understands the purpose of the exercise.

(c) Ideally, feedback should be presented in both oral and written form.

(d) The format of the debriefing may vary with the mentor's aim and the needs of the situation. Where a reflective approach is adopted, it is often desirable for students to present their perceptions first, so that their interpretation of the situation can be the focus for the initial part of any discussion. It can sometimes be advantageous to require them to undertake an evaluation of the lesson, perhaps in writing, before the formal debriefing. In certain contexts their responses to the lesson review questions described in the last chapter can be employed for this purpose.

If, on the other hand, the mentor's purpose is to lead the student to discover some cardinal point, questioning would seem to be a more appropriate strategy. Again, if it is to demonstrate some specific skill, instruction or structured observation may be more valuable.

(e) For some sessions students' self-evaluations can be used as a starting point. In the research cited in the previous section it has been shown that not all mentors do in fact refer to students' analyses. One way of reminding them of this obligation is to have printed on the lesson observation and debriefing sheets used by the school the instruction: "Please check the student's lesson evaluation file."

(f) It is usually wise for mentors to deal with the positive points about the lesson before they concentrate upon areas for development. Trainees can be asked for their views on what was particularly successful before the mentor offers her/his thoughts. A similar approach can be adopted in identifying ways in which the lesson could have been improved. The mentor can then confirm students' judgements or question them further to help them reflect upon those aspects which might have been more efficiently handled. By the end of the debriefing, mentors need to ensure that trainees are aware of strategies by which their performance can be enhanced in the future and that the key points of the discussion are built into targets. Students should be able to contribute to the target setting process.

(g) In reviewing lessons mentors should try to take into account as many dimensions as possible, for example, the aims and objectives, the planning, the student's value-base and experience, and different interpretations which could be placed upon events within the lesson. However, they should avoid trying to tackle too many items at once in dialogue, especially where trainees have had only limited contact with a class. They should seek to foster a sense of progress, and this can often be accomplished by concentrating on groups of standards. In certain debriefing sessions it is helpful to agree a focus in advance. There should be a systematic and gradual increase in the level of complexity of what is expected of students both in terms of classroom performance and involvement in self-evaluation.

(h) In making value-judgements mentors should be concrete and specific. Vague or generalised comments ("I liked your delivery") are rarely very helpful. Evidence from the lesson should be used to justify judgements and this should be treated in as objective a manner as possible. An example is:

> *Your skills in communication were highly satisfactory. Your boardwork was tidily set out and clearly showed the difference between vertebrates and invertebrates. You illustrated the meaning of 'vertebrates' with examples this age range could understand and asked the class to contribute six examples before you proceeded to the meaning of 'invertebrates'.*

Evidence for the judgements made can be derived from examples of pupils' work undertaken during the lesson, the student's notes and specific incidents which took place during the lesson. The use of videos and tape-recordings has been suggested by Shaw as a further source of obtaining evidence. These techniques make it possible for mentors to pinpoint specific parts of the lesson.

Evidence can be used for different purposes, for example, written critiques provided for the student on a whole lesson, or comments which serve as the basis for discussion about the progress made in mastering specific standards during a block of school experience, for example, clarity of exposition or questioning techniques.

(i) Reference should be made to the QTS standards. It is valuable to have either a list of the standards themselves or a summary of them printed on the lesson evaluation sheet. Another possibility is to set out appropriate levels derived from the standards which students are expected to reach at each stage of their course. Examples are given in the next chapter on assessment.

In debriefing mentors should ensure that standards which are relevant to a lesson are not ignored. As has been evident from the surveys conducted at UWIC, the assessment of pupils' achievements has sometimes been a neglected area. Formative assessment has a role to play in most lessons, and its implications in promoting learning should be fully discussed.

(j) Mentors should also try, wherever possible, to practise discursive dialogue and to discuss with students the wider areas of educational 'theory'. They need to realise that the whole thrust of partnership is that they have a key role as teacher *educators* and that the days have long since gone when 'practice' was the province of schools and 'theory' was taught only in the HEIs.

(k) In some contexts it may be beneficial for the views of pupils to be utilised in the evaluation of a lesson. Nearly half the students in the UWIC survey of 1999-2000 saw merit in this system, although they were clear that any such scheme would need careful thought and planning. A project has been launched in selected schools in partnership with the University of Nottingham during the academic year 1998-1999 in which year 10 pupils have received training so that they can act as mentors to small groups of students. A report on the progress of this scheme by Youens, Hall and Bishop (2000) suggests that the trainees acquired a clearer understanding of pupils' thinking and motivation, gained greater confidence from the feedback they received and developed fresh ideas for teaching methodology.

(l) Debriefing requires a range of inter-personal skills. Positive, warm, non-verbal communications are important, for example, smiling and making eye-contact. Becoming excited, raising one's voice and adopting a confrontational stance ("You've got a nerve to say that, considering you've only been here five minutes.") are not likely to promote confidence or build up a positive relationship with a student. Again, mentors should seek to avoid praise and blame situations, suggesting in dogmatic terms that there is one correct way to teach a lesson and engaging in power struggles with newcomers to the classroom. They should also resist the temptation of being over-influenced by their own strong reactions to one particular section of a lesson and not let this colour their whole debriefing. They need to know when, how and why to use the skills discussed in the previous chapters, especially, listening attentively, motivating students, helping them to reflect upon and to learn from experience, enabling them to solve problems and negotiating targets.

(m) Where students are unhappy with a lesson and/or the debriefing, it is essential that they have the opportunity to express their views, and that negative feelings, for example, anxiety, fear, confusion and resentment are addressed. If a student counter-attacks, mentors should not become annoyed. They should try to understand the student's point of view, show that they take into account what is said, listen to the student's comments and illustrate their own position with evidence from their notes. They should try to show that they are neutral at the personal level, or even that they are positive about the student as a person.

(n) Where targets are set, mentors need to be sure that students fully understand the action they are expected to take. It can sometimes be beneficial to ask them at the conclusion of a debriefing session to state what they have learned from the discussion and what they will be doing in the next lesson to meet the targets which have been agreed.

(o) Where students are not succeeding and fail to recognise that a problem exists, it is necessary to be firm and:

- to provide them with very clear and unambiguous assessments together with precise (SMART) targets and success criteria;

- to provide evidence that this has been done and that the student understands the situation and recognises the deadlines set for meeting the success criteria;

- to keep careful notes of what has been said and written and the ways in which the mentor has sought to help, advise, counsel and offer opportunities for improvement;

- where necessary, to retain these as evidence that everything has been done to help the student. If the student constantly fails to meet the targets set, the mentor can show that he/she has made every endeavour to help that trainee to improve;

- in the case of students who are not making progress, to make their position clear to them, to ask the reasons why they are failing to respond to advice, to listen sympathetically and to indicate unambiguously the standards in which they are deficient.

(p) Records should be kept of the events being reviewed. Mentors therefore need to make a written note recording the outcomes of the student's teaching and the contents of their debriefing. In most schemes of ITET, lesson record sheets are used in conjunction with the QTS standards and copies are retained by the student, the mentor, the ITET co-ordinator and HEI tutors.

(q) The following helpful guidelines for students are provided by Acton, Kirkham and Smith (1992, p. 45):

(i) *Listen:* Do not jump to your own defence at once. Give yourself time to make sure you are clear about what is being said.

(ii) *Decide* whether the feedback is helpful. Criticism can be rejected, but it is helpful to understand how others see your behaviour.

(iii) *Respond:* Decide how to react as the result of feedback to aid your personal and professional development.

(iv) *Let Go:* Do not build up the criticism in your mind.

› Issues for consideration

1. Read sections I and II (*aims in debriefing* and *forms of debriefing*) and in your own words define the following modes:

(a) lesson critiques;

(b) formal assessment;

(c) reflective practitioner modes;

(d) self-assessment.

2. On the basis of your experience state what you consider to be the advantages and limitations of debriefing within the context of:

(a) the apprenticeship model of ITET;

(b) the competency model of ITET;

(c) the strands of reflection approach.

3. Consider a debriefing session which you have recently held with a student and state:

(a) the stage reached by the student in her/his course and the subject;

(b) the overall focus of the debriefing;

(c) the form(s) of debriefing;

(d) the pedagogic style employed (e.g. questioning, instruction);

(e) the format of the debriefing (e.g. whether you opened the debriefing or whether the student put her/his views first);

(f) the evidence you used in forming a judgement;

(g) the interpersonal skills you used;

(h) any targets which were set;

(i) ways in which you were sure that the student understood what he/she had to do to meet the targets;

(j) the relationship of the debriefing to the apprenticeship model;

- Were you clear in the advice you offered?

- Is there the danger at your school that students receive contradictory advice from mentors?

- Did you explain the rationale behind any observation you organised for the student?

- Is there any danger that you expect students to be 'clones' of yourself?

(k) the relationship of the debriefing to the competency model, especially the use of the standards.

- To how many standards did you refer?

- Did you concentrate only upon teaching and class management?

- Did you examine the student's lesson file so that you could discuss the standards associated with planning, expectations and targets?

(l) the relationship of the debriefing to the reflective practitioner model.

- Did you refer to the student's lesson evaluations?

- Did you encourage the student to reflect upon the lesson?

- Did you engage in discursive dialogue? If so, what themes were explored?

- Did you encourage the student to probe ethical and moral assumptions underlying teaching?

- Did you encourage the student to formulate theory from practice?

- If so, which strands were taken into account (e.g. formal theory from reading, theory expounded by other experienced practitioners or theory derived from previous experience and discussion)?

4. Read section III (*students' experiences of debriefing*). Analyse the debriefing sessions you have held this academic year and list:

(a) what you consider to be your strengths as a mentor in debriefing;

(b) any problems you encountered in the light of the comments put by the students in the research studies cited in this chapter.

5. Suggest strategies for the alleviation of the problems you have identified.

6. Consider the case for involving pupils in the debriefing of students at your school.

- What advantages might there be?

- What constraints would have to be taken into account?

- What age ranges might be involved?

- What preparation and training would these pupils need?

- Who would provide it?

- What are the views of students at your school on this issue?

7. Read section IV (*guidelines on debriefing*). If you were organising a training day for other mentors at your school on good practice in debriefing, what would be the key themes and messages which you would wish to include?

8. Suggest guidelines which could be given to students to help them gain the maximum benefit from debriefing sessions.

10 Assessment

I: Modes of assessment

Assessment of a student's achievements in ITET may be of three basic types.

(a) **Formative assessment** entails recording, reporting and commenting upon achievements in the classroom and in other activities. Personal qualities, professional attitude and social skills may also be taken into account. This assessment may be undertaken by the mentor, the student or both *as the student progresses* throughout the ITET course. Thus, assessment is undertaken *during* the learning process. Its aim is to help the student become aware of her/his strengths, to identify weaknesses and to plan ways of improving performance. In effect, formative assessment is part of the learning process.

Moreover, it can be:

(i) *corrective*, showing how and where the student 'went wrong' and how he/she may improve;

(ii) *confirmatory*, demonstrating that what the student has acquired in terms of skills and concepts is suitable for the tasks which lie ahead.

Formative assessment plays a major role in ITET courses and adheres very much to the model of the reflective practitioner. It is ubiquitous in many of the activities outlined in earlier chapters, especially discussing students' lesson notes, preparation and self-evaluations, conducting debriefing at the end of a lesson and undertaking weekly progress reviews. Other opportunities for formative assessment arise during sessions with the ITET co-ordinator, where attention can be paid to achievement in all areas of school experience, including written assignments and projects relating to whole-school issues.

(b) **Ipsative Assessment:** This is a type of assessment where a student's current performance is compared with her/his own past performance. Target setting often involves ipsative assessment, as the mentor and student begin by deciding the latter's current level of achievement, for example, in terms of teaching skills or relationship with pupils or members of the school's staff. Targets for future development are then set, based upon this analysis, and the student fully participates in the subsequent review of progress. The GRASP project, to which reference has been made in a previous chapter, is another example of this form of assessment.

(c) **Summative Assessment** takes place when a statement or report is prepared which consists of a summary of a student's level of achievement. Examples in ITET are:

- reports drawn up by mentors for transfer to the next school attended by that student;

- end of course reports, on the basis of which the decision is taken whether a student should be awarded QTS;

- profiles, the content of which is determined by the Teacher Training Agency in England and the National Assembly in Wales.

II: Current requirements for assessment in courses of ITET

(a) **The Role of ITET Co-ordinators and Mentors:** One of the key changes introduced by the then Department for Education in the early 1990s in DFE Circulars 9/92 and 14/93 (DFE, 1992 and 1993b) and Welsh Office Circulars 35/92 and 62/93 (Welsh Office, 1992 and 1993) was that schools should work in full partnership with HEIs not only in the *training* of teachers but also in their *assessment*. ITET co-ordinators and mentors therefore have an important responsibility for assessing trainee teachers. This requirement was reiterated in DFEE circular 4/98 (DFEE, 1998b) and Welsh Office circular 13/98 (Welsh Office, 1998), while the Welsh Inspectorate in *Mentoring in Initial Teacher Training: Secondary Phase: A Good Practice Document* (OHMCI, 1998c) referred to the need for "regular and sustained observation and rigorous assessment of the trainee's teaching" (p. 4). The current requirements for initial teacher training set out by the DFES and TTA (2002) again state that all providers "must work with schools and actively involve them in the assessment of trainee teachers for qualified teacher status" (p. 16). As Allsop (1994) notes, for some teachers this is a new experience, especially where they have only recently been appointed as mentors or co-ordinators.

(b) **Competence-Based Assessment:** The DFES in England and National Assembly in the Principality expect all student teachers to be formally assessed by means of competence testing with reference to the QTS standards. This is a form of criterion-referenced assessment in that performance is judged against a series of statements outlining the knowledge, understanding and skills a person must acquire if he/she is to be awarded the qualification sought.

This form of assessment, as Whitty and Willmott (1991, 1995) observe, has been popular in the USA since the 1970s. In the UK, it has been utilised since the late 1980s within National Vocational Qualification courses, where candidates are tested upon their ability to carry out specific tasks which are judged to be essential to a given occupation. It was subsequently argued by such academics as David Hargreaves (1990) that this approach could be applied to the assessment of student teachers. The first official requirement that competence-based assessment should be adopted in secondary ITET was contained in DFE Circular 9/92 and Welsh Office Circular 35/92, which defined a list of competences under the headings of:

- subject knowledge;
- subject application;
- class management;
- assessment and recording of pupils' progress;
- further professional development.

Similar arrangements were announced for primary ITET in DFE Circular 14/93 and Welsh Office Circular 62/93. In DFEE Circular 4/98 and Welsh Office Circular 13/98 the competences were replaced with a list of standards. Similar criteria were established for students' performance in the teaching of English, mathematics, science, Welsh and ICT. The revised standards which came into force in England in 2002 are set out in the appendix to chapter one.

(c) **Profiling:** Profiling is compulsory for all students taking a course of ITET. The Teacher Training Agency and Welsh Office have produced a Career Entry Profile For Newly Qualified Teachers, which they must take to the schools to which they have been appointed. Profiling will be described in greater detail in the next chapter.

(d) **Advantages Claimed for Competence-Based Assessment:** The system of competence-based assessment is a good example of what Carr and Kemmis (1986) have called the 'technical rationalist' approach to ITET, which implies that "the job of the teacher" can be "redefined along the lines of a technician" (Kydd and Weir, 1993, p. 409). Advantages claimed for it have been discussed by Hextall, Lawn, Menter, Sidgwick and Walker (1991), Chown and Last (1993), Bullough and Gitlin (1994), Garland (1994), McCulloch (1994), Whitty and Willmott (1995) and Geen (2001a). Some of the arguments which have been advanced are:

(i) It provides a clear statement of the criteria according to which student teachers are assessed. From the very outset of their course, they are aware of the standard they have to reach, and they can be involved in evaluating their progress in relation to these assessment criteria.

(ii) At the conclusion of their course, a profile is completed so that their level of competence can easily be judged by all parties concerned: mentors; students; HEI partners; and employers. In a study of the perceptions of England and German students on ITET (Jones, 2000), it was noted that the majority of students in schools in partnership with Edge Hill College of Higher Education favoured the standards for this reason, though they did find making reference to them in lesson evaluation rather repetitive. Students from both countries preferred assessment in accordance with pre-determined criteria to systems in which performance was judged by external examiners whose subjective standards would decide whether or not they passed the course.

(iii) Programmes of ITET can be constructed around the standards prescribed by the DFES and National Assembly for Wales. It is, of course, possible for ITET providers to add other themes and topics, but the requirement that all courses incorporate the standards acts as a quality control mechanism, since it helps to obviate the problem that different partnerships or schemes of school-centred ITET have radically different approaches. It ensures a minimum standard of provision.

(iv) A survey of the views of 237 ITET students (Geen, 2001a) shows that ninety-eight per cent of them welcomed the use of the standards in Welsh Office Circular 13/98 for the following reasons:

- They made clear what trainees are supposed to achieve during their course. It is a fundamental principle of assessment that students should be aware of the criteria on which they will be judged before they embark upon any activity or project (Geen, 2001b, p. 111), and the standards provide this information.

- It is possible to refer to them during the preparation of lessons, and this gives students confidence that their planning is based upon the criteria by which they will be assessed.

- They provide criteria for the evaluation of a lesson both by students individually and by students and mentors in debriefing.

- They offer a focus for critical reflection. As one student observed, reflection is important, but guidelines need to be at hand so that people know the issues about which they should be reflecting.

- They are valuable in feedback and target setting. There was much support for mentors who recorded their comments on a lesson under the headings of the standards.

- They enable students to gauge their progress over the period of the ITET course. Drever and Cope (1999) have found that the standards are well received by trainees for this reason, though, in practice, they tend to consider groups rather than single standards. One student participating in this research study stated that she rarely entered a lesson saying 'I'll develop my competence of using appropriate rewards and sanctions today'. (p. 104)

(v) It has been claimed that assessment is easier to carry out when performance is judged against specified performance criteria. The current system permits lesson evaluation to be undertaken in an objective manner. Thus Garland (1994) argues that a list of competences can "ensure the maintenance of objective, reified standards" (p. 17).

(vi) The standards can be used within formative assessment and student-centred learning, as mentors can refer to them as they help trainees master specific skills. A statement of achievement in terms of the standards can also serve as a useful form of summative assessment within the student's profile. Moreover, they relate to the induction standards which newly qualified teachers are expected to meet in their first year of full employment (DFES, 2001b) and serve as a foundation for future career development (TTA, 1998).

(e) **Limitations of Competence-Based Assessment:** On the other hand, mentors need to be aware of some of the main limitations of competence-based assessment:

(i) The approach advocated by the DFES and National Assembly for Wales assumes a universally accepted version of what constitutes good teaching, but agreement on this issue is not a straightforward matter. Teaching is not a low-skill craft which can be acquired through mastery of a series of atomised skills. As Hyland (1993) remarks, this model is clearly unsatisfactory for higher level activities involving strategic, organisational and management skills of the kind which typically characterise teacher education and professional development.

(ii) The application of a fixed set of standards assumes that they can be applied mechanistically in any situation. Norris (1991) wonders whether there is "a fundamental contradiction between the autonomy needed to act in the face of change and situational uncertainty and the predictability inherent in the specification of outcomes" (p. 335).

(iii) It is assumed that assessment is a simple, objective procedure of watching lessons and deciding whether or not a student can perform certain tasks, for example, "establish a purposeful learning atmosphere" (DFES-TTA, 2002, p. 11). Certain writers have criticised this view, e.g.

(1) McCullogh (1994) and Bridges, Elliott and McKee (1995) note that assessment involving profiles of specified competences or standards is based upon the false assumption that knowledge, skills and attitudes demonstrated in a given context can be "generalised as context-free abilities" (McCullogh, p. 230). In other words, it is assumed that the student will always be able to display this competence in any situation. In teaching it is possible for a student to achieve a given standard with certain classes, but he/she may fail to meet that standard with other pupils. This can be true of many experienced teachers. In such circumstances, can that student be said to have mastered the standard?

(2) Donald McIntyre (1989) questions certain of the assumptions about criterion-referenced assessment in ITET and asks whether teaching is to be seen as a set of personal characteristics, as a skilled craft, as a theory-based technology, or as a political activity.

(3) In a survey of the views of sixty PGCE students at UWIC during the session 2000-2001 eighty-five per cent agreed with the statement that each class encountered is a new challenge and requires the use of judgement rather than the automatic application of specified skills. McIntyre (1989) also points to the problems in applying pre-specified criteria to the uncertainties of human behaviour and interactions.

(4) Glass (1978) writes that it is difficult to decide absolute standards in assessment of this type, and feels that assessors should focus on judgement about improvement or deterioration in performance.

(iv) Chown and Last (1993) comment that the provision of a list of competences fails "to account for much of what teachers do and, more importantly, *why* they do it" (p. 15). Professional judgement is not always taken into account in assessment of this type.

(v) No guidance is given on the evidence for satisfactory performance in a standard. How often and in how many contexts should a student demonstrate a standard/ competence before he/she can be said to have mastered it? Nor, in the view of two thirds of the UWIC students, did assessment against the standards remove the subjective judgement of mentors. One student felt that during her first school placement the mentor's expectations in terms of preparation and class management were extremely high. During her next experience another mentor expressed total satisfaction with the lesson file, even though, as the student admitted, she had on some occasions forgotten to enter references to the National Curriculum programmes of study, attainment targets and key skills. This second mentor's own class management skills, it was alleged, left much to be desired, and few constructive comments were offered to the student about ways in which she could improve her relationships with the pupils.

(vi) Writing in *The Times Educational Supplement* in November 1999, Professor Colin Richards has argued that assessment of ITET students in accordance with the large number of standards imposed in DFEE circular 4/98 - both general and subject-specific standards for the core disciplines - is an impossible task. Indeed, in a ballot conducted by the National Primary Teacher Education Conference, over ninety per cent of respondents expressed the view that they were being forced to comply with the untenable belief that all these requirements could be met. It is, Richards maintains, hypocritical of schools and HEIs to claim that students emerge from their ITET courses proficient in every one of the standards (Richards, 1999 p. 15).

(vii) Assessment of performance does not always take into account the individual's personal interpretation of the context. For example, a student may judge that a certain standard does not have much relevance in a given situation. Does this mean that the student is seen to be 'failing' that standard? Similarly, other competences and skills may be deemed to be important with a specific class but lie outside the lists provided by the DFES and National Assembly for Wales.

(viii) The competence-based approach fails to identify the extent to which the student is actually learning as opposed merely to following guidelines. This argument can be related to the distinction between *training* and *education*. Trained people can perform skills without any depth of knowledge and understanding, whereas educated people have underlying knowledge on which to draw in deciding courses of action. Eight of the sixty students participating in the UWIC survey of 2000-2001 felt very strongly that they wanted to develop their own style of teaching and did not wish merely to respond to a set of competences defined by central government.

(ix) What assessment should be made of a student who can be said to 'pass' on all the standards individually but who cannot establish a long-term relationship with a class, has little rapport with pupils and who lacks imagination?

(x) Traditionally, as Whitty and Willmott (1991) stress, undergraduate ITET courses (for example, BEd, BA [Ed]) have sought to develop students' intellectual and imaginative powers, problem-solving skills and ability to see relationships within what they have learned and to perceive their field of study in a broader perspective. Little scope is available for the application of these deeper intellectual powers in a programme which is purely geared to the acquisition of competences.

(xi) Competence-based assessment ignores the moral dimensions of teaching, as it does not require students to think about the justification of their actions (for example, the reasons underlying the rules they expect their classes to follow), value systems (for example, aims in education) or important theories (for example, the nature of knowledge and the optimum format of the curriculum). Thus, James Arthur, Davison and Moss (1997) write that "many have criticised competences and their use in teacher education because of their instrumentalist emphasis which fails to respect the value-laden or moral quality of teaching" (p.41).

(xii) Mike Newby, Chair of the Universities Council for the Education of Teachers, feels that a distinction should be drawn between 'standards' and 'quality'. Although the latter is harder to quantify than the former, it is, in his view, of greater importance. He concludes that "quality cannot be so easily measured and presented in league tables, but an expression of quality will be of far greater worth than a profile of performance showing eight hundred tasks per newly qualified teacher" (Newby, 1999a, p. 16).

(xiii) The reduction of teaching to a series of mechanistic competences denies the importance of:

- professional knowledge, which is usually built up over a long period of time and involves socialisation into the values of the profession. The essence of these values is the priority of the client's interests, and they are often expressed in a code of practice.

- the need for professional discretion: The work of the professional is deemed to be complex. It requires the exercise of skills based upon professional knowledge. The practitioner exercises these skills and knowledge in contexts where judgement predominates over routine. Hence, professional people need freedom to make decisions based upon their knowledge and experience (Downie, 1990);

- the importance of personality to success in teaching;

- the activities of theorising, reflecting and learning during action.

Hence, Russell (1989), Winter (1989), Carr (1992), McLoughlin (1994), Fish (1995b) and Arthur, Davison and Moss (1997) advocate a model which takes into account the ideals of reflective practitioner philosophies as well as the acquisition of skills. They suggest that the standards imposed by the DFES and National Assembly for Wales should be regarded as a basic requirement for legal reasons, but they should be seen as only one aspect of assessment and should be supplemented with other areas of achievement. Assessment, they contend, should focus upon *professional artistry*, which involves:

- subject or content knowledge base and associated curriculum knowledge;

- a repertoire of teaching skills, some of which will be derived from the standards;

- educational and professional knowledge consisting of:

- learning and teaching strategies,

- the wider aspects of the teacher's professional role, for example, pastoral concerns and contractual issues outside classroom teaching,

- educational contexts, for example, the legal framework of primary and secondary education.

- professional understanding and judgement. This involves:

- pedagogical knowledge to enable the student to select the teaching and learning strategies appropriate to a given situation;

- the ability to 'read' a situation, to respond to it and to improvise;

- capacity for professional collegiality, that is to say, the ability to work with a wide range of fellow professionals;

- capacity for professional development, including:

- the ability regularly to reflect upon her/his own practice and to learn from this reflection;

- the ability to theorise in practice and to recognise theories underlying action.

- a personal repertoire, including qualities of character and disposition, a general knowledge base, self-knowledge, and the ability to extend this repertoire. Important aspects are: self-awareness; sensitivity to others; the ability to engage in balanced self-assessment; open-mindedness; empathy; enthusiasm; and imagination.

Fish argues that these aspects of professionalism should not be 'second level' activities to be learned after the basic skills/standards have been mastered. They should be "an integral part of what is learnt from the beginning of the course" (p. 159).

III: Forms of assessment in ITET

(a) **Aims of Assessment:** In the light of the discussion about the strengths and limitations of competence-based assessment and the importance of fostering professional artistry, mentors need to be clear about the purposes of assessment. If the arguments of the advocates of professional artistry are accepted, then it follows that assessment is concerned to form a holistic judgement about the student derived from a wide range of evidence rather than narrow judgements based solely upon measurable performance. In other words, assessment should include more than a set of competences or standards; reference should be made to students' written work, their contribution to discussion and extra-curricular activities, and their professional attitude.

(b) **Approaches to Assessment:** It is also assumed that continuous assessment will be the norm. The paper by Jones (2000) reporting the views of English and German ITET students shows that both groups prefer continuous to end-of-stage assessment. The following are forms of assessment usually undertaken within ITET.

(i) *lesson observation*, which, according to supporters of the professional artistry model, should be wider than that associated with competence-based assessment. The mentor's role is not so much to 'tick boxes' of standards as to assess the student on a wider range of criteria. In the formal assessment of lessons decisions have to be taken about:

- THE SCOPE OF THE OBSERVATION. As well as viewing the lesson, mentors should examine all the written materials, for example, students' lesson file, preparation and teaching aids. In the debriefing they may form of judgement about the trainee's ability to evaluate her/his own teaching, to diagnose learning needs and to formulate meaningful theory from experience and other relevant sources. Students should be aware of the criteria which will be used for formal assessment and they should be informed about those lessons in which they will be assessed and others in which they are free to experiment

- THE RANGE OF SITUATIONS IN WHICH THEY WILL BE FORMALLY OBSERVED. Brooks and Sikes (1997, pp. 130-131) suggest that it is valuable for formal observation to be carried out with discrete classes at different times of the day and that different types of lesson should be assessed. The focus for evaluation should also be decided, depending upon students' level of experience. Formal observation should involve the whole lesson, unless specific sections have been targeted for a good reason.

- THE NUMBER OF ASSESSORS TO BE EMPLOYED. As has been noted, the reliability of assessment is increased if several people are involved (Ebel and Frisbie, 1991; Freeman and Lewis, 1998). As Brooks and Sikes write, "involving a number of assessors ...

enhances the reliability of the assessment. The theory of assessment suggests that when judgements have to be made in areas which are subjective - as assessing teaching competence surely is - the reliability of the assessment can be improved by increasing the number of independent assessors who contribute to the assessment and the number and length of the occasions on which assessment is carried out" (p. 127). Hence, assessment could involve: the mentor who has specific knowledge of the class being taught; other teachers who regularly take those pupils; the ITET coordinator; other teachers who have a professional involvement with the students, for example, staff with a specialism in PSHE; HEI tutors; external examiners; students themselves through their self-assessment and contributions to debriefing; and other students, especially where pair teaching and team teaching are practised.

(ii) *assessment against the standards:* An account has been given of some of the main limitations which have been identified in assessment against the standards, especially the problem of subjectivity among mentors. Several practices have been adopted to resolve these difficulties:

- THE USE OF LEVEL DESCRIPTIONS: In some ITET courses, groups of standards are taken and a description is given of the stage the student should reach at specific points in the course. At some schools these 'pen portraits' have been designed by ITET co-ordinators; elsewhere the HEI has taken the lead in providing these descriptions. Within UWIC's primary BA(Ed) course three levels have been designated to describe the performance expected of students by the end of each year, and a similar system is used to pinpoint student progress at three points within the PGCE course. Separate descriptions have been compiled for: knowledge and understanding; planning; teaching methods; class management and organisational strategies; evaluating teaching; assessing; and further professional requirements.

According to the first level descriptors for 'teaching methods' a PGCE student, by the end of the first key stage 1 placement, should be able, among other items, to:

- *show enthusiasm for the subject being taught and generate pupils' interest and enthusiasm for learning in selected activities;*

- *ensure that pupils are aware of the substance and purpose of what they are asked to do;*

- *recognise a range of direct teaching techniques, for example, questioning, instructing, explaining and demonstrating, and begin to use these skills appropriately to communicate with pupils;*

- *recognise higher and lower order questions and use questioning to ensure that pupils take part;*

- *present content clearly, around a set of key ideas, and summarise key points to consolidate learning;*

- *listen carefully to pupils and note their errors and mistakes in the subject;*

- *be aware of a range of indirect teaching methods, for example, researching, problem solving and knowing the importance of using a variety and range of methods;*

- *make good use of suitable resources, including ICT, to support teaching sessions;*

- exploit opportunities to consolidate and improve pupils' basic skills in literacy, numeracy, ICT and study skills.

At the third level, they should, by the end of the course, be able to:

- use direct and indirect teaching methods, matched to the subject matter and pupils being taught, which keep pupils on task;

- communicate enthusiasm for the subject being taught and foster pupils' motivation;

- ensure that pupils are aware of the substance and purpose of what they are asked to do;

- present content clearly, around a set of key ideas, using appropriate subject-specific vocabulary and suitable illustrations and examples;

- structure information well, including outlining content and aims of learning at the beginning of sessions, signalling transitions and summarising key points to consolidate learning;

- use clear instructions and demonstration and accurate explanations;

- use questioning, including higher order questions to promote learning and to ensure that pupils take part;

- cope adequately with subject-related questions which pupils raise;

- take note of pupils' errors and misconceptions and attempt to remedy them;

- listen carefully to pupils and respond constructively;

- recognise when it is appropriate to intervene to re-focus or challenge pupils' thinking;

- further develop the ability to use an increasing range of resources, for example, textbooks, ICT and other materials, to support planned teaching;

- set high expectations for pupils' learning, motivation and presentation of work;

- where appropriate, assist in implementing individual education plans for pupils at stage 2 and beyond of the Code of Practice;

- provide opportunities for pupils to consolidate and revise knowledge and understanding and make efforts to reinforce and develop what has been learned;

- exploit opportunities to contribute to the quality of pupils' wider educational development, including their personal, spiritual, moral, social and cultural development;

- exploit opportunities to improve pupils' basic skills in literacy, numeracy, ICT and study skills.

● THE USE OF VIDEOTAPES to exemplify a level of performance which is deemed to meet the standards. During the academic year 1998-1999 funding was made available to HEIs in Wales for the production of a range of written materials and other aids which could be employed in accredited courses for mentors. These materials were completed and were duly distributed to all interested parties across the Principality in December 2000. Among the initiatives was a fifty-five minute videotape of extracts from lessons given by primary students designed to illustrate the QTS standards (HEFCW, 2000). This has been a useful resource in training mentors to understand more clearly classroom performance which accords with the standards and has, at least partially, helped to overcome the problem of subjectivity in assessment.

(iii) *student-led seminars:* In chapter six reference was made to the important role which student-led seminars can have within an ITET course. Performance in these seminars can constitute a valuable vehicle for the assessment of students' understanding of educational and professional issues.

At UWIC the assessment criteria for the secondary PGCE seminars are:

- relevance and accuracy;

- evidence of understanding of the issues;

- structure and organisation of the presentation, for example, providing students with a variety of discussion points and other activities;

- reference to school experience. Trainees are expected to illustrate the topic with reference to their own experience and to provide a forum for debate in which the other students can compare and debate the policies and practices they have observed at their school;

- standard of oral presentation;

- ability to set suitable, supervised, focused tasks prior to and during the presentation which involve the whole group in critical reflection and discussion.

(iv) *students' writing:* This can often give an idea of the ways in which they reflect, theorise and make sense of practice. Examples are:

(1) SCHOOL EXPERIENCE FILES, together with self-evaluations and reflections on practice;

(2) REFLECTIVE ASSIGNMENTS BASED UPON AUTOBIOGRAPHY: A popular assignment is to ask students to reflect upon their own education and produce a short autobiography. Key elements are:

- the activities which helped them learn;

- teachers who inspired them;

- positive and negative experiences.

Reference can be made to such factors as teachers' attitude, the ethos of the school, relationships between school staff and pupils, the behaviour of adolescents, lesson content, methodology, home background, parental attitudes, social class, gender and ethnicity. Conclusions can then be drawn about the nature of learning and teaching. This is especially helpful in the early stages of an ITET course in which mentors are helping students develop their ideas.

(3) PERSONAL WRITING DURING A SCHOOL PLACEMENT: Personal writing can be undertaken at various points within school experience and build upon the autobiographies completed in the early stages of the ITET course. Questions which may be set include:

- Look at yourself, your past and the assumptions you made when you began to teach. Have these assumptions changed in the light of your school experiences this year?

- If so, in what way have they changed?

- What has caused you to change your thinking about learning and teaching?

(4) SELF-PORTRAITS: Richards (1998) offers a reflective model incorporating the creation and analysis of a 'self-portrait'. The model has four steps:

- The student monitors an aspect of teaching which he/she wishes to explore, for example, communications with the class.

- The results of this monitoring are analysed and any problems are highlighted. For example, it may be discovered that the pupils failed to understand some concept taught by the student.

- Any such discoveries emanating from the analysis are incorporated into a 'self-portrait'. This, says Richards, could involve disclosing "parts of myself that I may prefer remain hidden" (p. 35), for instance, that in addressing a class I speak too quickly and for too long a period.

- The self-portrait is used to make decisions about change and future policy. The student may put the questions: "Am I ready to alter this situation? How might I do things differently?"

Richards concludes that "creating self-portraits provides opportunities for teachers to identify classroom behaviours such as too much 'teacher talk' that are not congruent with their students' growth. Self-portraits also call attention to teachers' decisions and actions that are particularly exemplary and beneficial" (p. 38).

(5) VISUAL IMAGES: Johnson (2001a and 20001b), developing the ideas of Kennedy (1982), Kennedy, Green and Veraeke (1993) and Garner (1997), describes a system whereby fourth year students on a BEd course compile, on average, ten pages of A4 drawings and text to describe aspects of their school experience. Pictures often involve metaphors of the role of the pre-service teacher, for example, a bird learning to fly, a chrysalis, a noise controller, a juggler of theory and practice and a promoter of critical thining. In review sessions with their mentors they are asked to discuss the key themes in their picture books, those themes they think may persist for all students at any time and in any place, and any specific aspects of their visual work and written language which they have used to convey their meaning. Typical questions which arise in dialogue with mentors are:

- What do the practices evidenced in my picture book say about my assumptions, values and beliefs about teaching (e.g. gender roles, social customs, social class or cultural identities)?

● Where did these ideas originate?

● What alternative cultural and ideological assumptions have been left out in my representation of classroom activities and in my talk about teaching?

● Are the cultural and ideological assumptions upon which my teaching is based consistent throughout my pictorial narratives or are there traces of conflicting thinking?

● What causes me to maintain my theories about teaching?

● What interests seem to be served by my practices?

● What acts to constrain my views of what is possible in teaching?

● What other ways are there to act within the institutional framework of teaching?

Johnson also refer to 'membership categorisation analysis', (Baker, 2000, Emmison and Smith, 2000) in which mentors help students to locate the content of their drawing under different categories, for example, people and places, and reflect upon the courses of social action implied.

(6) JOURNALS AND DIARIES which are kept over the whole ITET programme to help the student reflect upon experience. They are maintained on a regular day-by-day basis and contain some form of personal response. Certain writers have suggested the use of questionnaires to guide reflection (e.g. Bibik, 1997). Journals and diaries allow students to gain a fuller understanding of their actions and intentions (Goodfellow, 2000) and to reflect about their aims and purposes (Bain, Ballantyre, Packer and Mills, 1999; Bleakley, 2000).

Students monitored in the research conducted by Calderhead and Shorrock (1997) were expected to maintain a diary over their entire ITET year. They found the experience to be useful in clarifying their thinking about particular aspects of their teaching, especially in the first phase of the course. The principal disadvantage was the amount of time that was needed for this task. The researchers noted that "by the second term most students had ceased to write regularly in their diaries, and reported no longer finding it as helpful as they did in the early stages of the course" (p. 169).

(7) INVESTIGATIVE ASSIGNMENTS, for example, relating to whole-school and professional issues. Typical topics are: whole-school policy on assessment; strategies for combating bullying; the prevention of truancy; equal opportunities and the curriculum; the role of the school governors; target setting; performance management; school inspection; and parents' rights.

At UWIC, secondary PGCE students submit a written assignment which further develops their ideas on the topic they offered for their seminar presentation. They are expected to discuss this topic with the ITET co-ordinator, to make full reference to school policy and to take into account perspectives gained from reading and discussion with other students in seminar classes. The assessment criteria are:

- critical reflection upon the topic, which must be whole-school and not solely subject related. Judgements should be based upon personal and observed experiences in school and associated reading;

- attention to the wider context of the educational system, showing a critical engagement and an appreciation that issues in education are developmental and often controversial;

- an acceptable standard of spelling, punctuation, syntax and general presentation.

(8) SUBJECT-SPECIFIC ASSIGNMENTS RELATING TO CLASSROOM TEACHING. In a secondary ITET course students preparing to teach design and technology may be asked to design a brief for their pupils which will emphasise the key stages of the design process, develop respective competences in the classroom, involve a critical evaluation of the end products produced by the children and reveal evidence of appropriate reading. Another example would be for them to select a topic with which they are familiar from their school experience and to investigate ways in which teaching resources can be differentiated to meet the needs of a mixed ability class.

On UWIC's primary PGCE course students have been expected to set work to groups of pupils which requires them either to create a document or graphic or to search for information using a computer. The task should involve learning intentions which relate to other work the pupils are doing and require more than mere computer capability. The students are to monitor the work by close, non-participant observation. After the activity, they comment on:

- the pupils' progress towards achieving the learning intentions;

- the appropriateness of using the computer for the purpose;

- the level of independence shown;

- the efficiency with which the children used the facilities of the programme involved, including consideration of opportunities which were missed;

- the viability of the size of the groups and the nature of the interactions between them;

- any points of general significance for their teaching which arose from the experience.

Where assignments of this type are set, there are opportunities for mentors to participate in their assessment.

(9) PORTFOLIOS OR COLLECTIONS OF EVIDENCE RELATING TO THE STUDENT'S PROFESSIONAL DEVELOPMENT. Portfolios may include:

- a week-by-week response to their school experience, for example, classes at the HEI, lessons given at the various schools they have attended, and any seminars they have delivered;

- a professional development log with records of observations, details of planning and resourcing and pupil case studies;

- feedback forms from mentors and tutors which record progress in teaching and other aspects of the course.

Portfolios are seen by Loughran and Russell (1997) as a valuable means of bringing about reflection on the part of the learner and of allowing him/her to articulate understanding. One student in their research study stated that the teaching portfolio helped her "look at things done in science teaching … and pick out various incidents and put them … under some sort of title and say what I have learned from it … and how it will improve on my teaching in the future" (p. 171). Similarly, Werner, Avila, Resta, Vanglar and Cuttin (1995) feel that, if the ideals of the reflective practitioner are to be achieved, mentors need some trigger questions to help students structure their thinking. Logs and portfolios, they believe, can be a valuable source for this

On the other hand, there is the same problem which has been noted in the discussion of diaries and journals, that the time taken to compile the portfolio may be better used in lesson planning and contemplating alternative teaching techniques. In a study by Jones (2000), students commented that "the portfolio is extremely tedious and consumes vast amounts of time. It is possible to reflect without compiling a report the size of Yellow Pages" (pp. 68-69).

(v) *discussion* where the mentor encourages the student to theorise about and reflect upon experience. Specific techniques could be questioning students to probe their thinking, analysis of critical incidents, and the 'strands of reflection' approach which was described in the last chapter.

(vi) *profiles* which have been defined by the Council for National Academic Awards (1992) as documents which record "student developments and/or achievements gained either within the academic setting or workplace ... which provide the framework for teaching, learning and the assessment process by means of explicit learning objectives".

Some of the points raised by writers on profiles in ITET are:

- Comments in profiles can be drawn from evidence in a portfolio, journal, diary. teaching practice file, educational studies assignment and student-led seminar as well as from classroom performance. Reference can then be made to many of the elements in the 'professional artistry' model, for example, students' educational and professional knowledge, their judgement in the classroom, their ability to work within a team with others, and their personal qualities. In this respect a profile can reflect the personal and professional progress of the student.

- When profiles are drawn up which are based upon competence-based assessment, it is necessary to consider carefully what counts as evidence of competence. Generalisation from a *single* context should be avoided. Hence, when the outcomes of assessment are recorded, reference should be made to all the contexts in which the student was working.

- Negative inferences should not invariably be drawn from negative situations. For example, failure to respond appropriately may be the result of self-doubt and insecurity rather than lack of competence. Hence, it is important to check students' interpretations and understanding of the context.

- Profiles should make clear to employers that mastery of the standards prescribed in

DFES and National Assembly for Wales circulars is deemed to be merely part of the assessment process.

(c) **Style of Assessment:** Opinions differ concerning the merits of grading systems within ITET courses. Some mentors favour the establishment of scales (for example, a 1-5 scale) together with a clear explanation of the criteria relevant to each position on the scale.

Shaw (1995) gives an example of a scheme of assessment in ITET with five levels:

Level 1 = not yet evident.
Level 2 = basic awareness.
Level 3 = growing competence.
Level 4 = basic proficiency.
Level 5 = extended proficiency.

Where a system of this type is used, the exact meaning of the scales should be clear to all users: mentors; student; tutors; and employers.

Other writers, like Fish (1995b), advocate a simple overall PASS/FAIL for each of the areas listed in the professional artistry model discussed above.

Assessment should be based on evidence of development throughout the course and the student should be responsible for presenting much of this material. Fish suggests that at least three of the modes of assessment listed above should be included and at least three professionals should be involved in reaching a judgement. The establishment of a group of people to conduct assessment has also been welcomed by both English and German students in the research published by Jones (2000). Trainees in the two countries were concerned that the views of their mentors should be brought to bear upon the final verdict.

Where students are failing, feedback should be offered to enable them to work on the issues identified as areas of weakness. This should be provided in good time to permit them to remedy the deficiencies to which their attention has been drawn.

(d) **Moderation:** Moderation is the system whereby external agents check that assessment is being carried out in a reliable and consistent manner and that standards in one school correlate with those in others. Moderation arrangements may vary in different partnerships, but important aspects of it are:

(i) the role of the *ITET coordinator* in checking that mentors are consistent in their standards of assessing students in the classroom;

(ii) the role of *college tutors* in moderating assessment arrangements in the schools with which they have entered into partnership;

(iii) the role of *external examiners* appointed by the HEI to review the performance of selected students. External examiners usually have experience of a number of partnerships and are able to compare their standards.

› Issues for consideration

1. Read section I (*modes of assessment*). Define the following terms and give examples of ways in which mentors would use them with students pursuing a course of ITET:

(a) *formative assessment;*

(b) *ipsative assessment;*

(c) *summative assessment.*

2. On the basis of your experience state what you consider to be the main advantages and limitations of assessment of ITET students by means of the QTS standards.

3. Read section II (*current requirements for assessment in courses of ITET*), and state any significant changes you would make to your response to question 2 above.

4. Many writers on ITET have made reference to the concept of professional artistry, which, in their view, should be the focus of assessment. Explain briefly the meaning of 'professional artistry' as it is used in this context, showing how it supplements the competence-based approach inherent in the use of the standards.

5. What types of evidence might be collected to assess a student in terms of the following aspects of professional artistry?

(a) *ability to 'read' a situation, to respond to it and to improvise;*

(b) *capacity for professional collegiality;*

(c) *ability regularly to reflect upon practice and to learn from this reflection;*

(d) *ability to theorise in practice and to recognise theories underlying one's own actions;*

(e) *the student's 'personal repertoire' including qualities of character and disposition, general knowledge base, self-knowledge and the ability to develop this repertoire.*

6. Read section III (*forms of assessment in ITET*).

(a) Does the ITET documentation at your school contain a clear statement of aims on assessment?

(b) List any changes you would make to the policy statement on aims in the light of your reading.

(c) With reference to policy at your school describe the arrangements made for lesson observation. Refer to:

- *the scope of assessment;*

- *the range of situations in which the student is observed;*

- *the number of assessors involved;*

- the methods of assessment used.

7. Describe the involvement of mentors at your school in the following modes of assessment.

(a) *students' performance in the light of the standards (What procedures do mentors follow to achieve consistency in their judgement about the extent to which students are meeting the standards?);*

(a) *student-led seminars;*

(b) *students' school experience file and lesson evaluations;*

(c) *reflective assignments undertaken by students;*

(d) *personal writing, self-portraits and/or visual images;*

(e) *journals or diaries;*

(f) *subject or age-related assignments;*

(g) *portfolios of evidence of professional development.*

8. Set out your own recommendations for assessment policy. Make reference to the items listed below.

(a) *the key components for assessment (e.g. standards, aspects of the professional artistry model);*

(b) *the number of lessons to be assessed and the people who should assess them;*

(c) *the use of the QTS standards in such a way as to avoid the problems outlined in the text;*

(d) *aspects of students' work to be assessed other than classroom performance and the people who should assess them;*

(e) *the use of grading systems;*

(f) *the form of moderation which should be adopted.*

9. In the light of your reading and the recommendations you have made in response to the questions above, list any suggestions you may have for improving your school's assessment policy in relation to ITET.

Profiling in initial teacher education and training

11

I: Profiling: requirements of ITET providers

Staff involved with school-HEI partnerships or schemes of school-centred ITET are required to maintain profiles of their students and to complete the career entry profile (CEP) towards the end of the course of initial teacher education (DFES-TTA, 2002, p. 15). In England the requirement has been in force since the school year 1998-1999 and in Wales from 1999-2000. The career entry profile was originally developed by the Teacher Training Agency (TTA) for use in England, while the Welsh Office had responsibility for producing a similar version for the Principality. It is to be completed by the student and the providers of the ITET course and passed to the employer. The government envisages that it will then serve as the basis of systematic profiling which will chart a teacher's progress throughout the induction year, details of which are set out in DFES guidance document 582/2001 (DFES, 2001b)

II: Developments in profiling in ITET

The development of profiling in ITET can be traced to a number of factors:

(a) **The Development of Profiling in Schools:** In the 1980s there was a growth of interest in the issue of profiles and records of achievement in schools. They were regularly used in pre-vocational schemes of that time, notably the Technical and Vocational Education Initiative (TVEI), and several examination boards developed schemes of profile reporting, for example, the Oxford Certificate of Educational Achievement (OCEA).

In November 1983 the then Education Secretary, Sir Keith Joseph, discussed with interested parties proposals for a framework for the development of schemes of records of achievement in all secondary schools. The idea was well received, since teachers felt that by focusing upon personal qualities and interests profiles would give a fuller and more accurate picture of a pupil's capabilities than traditional academic reports. It was also believed that they would be of greater value to employers and would motivate pupils by giving them recognition for endeavour and involving them in the process of assessment.

Hence, in 1985 the White Paper *Better Schools* (Department of Education and Science, [DES], 1985) proposed that arrangements should be made "under which all pupils leaving school will be provided with a record of achievement" (p.36). To avoid the problem of subjectivity in assessment, it was argued that schools should base assessments "on concrete examples of what a pupil has achieved and experienced, from which personal qualities and skills may be inferred" (p.37).

To enable schools to operate a system of profiles the then Department of Education and Science subsequently provided, through education support grants, funds for nine pilot schemes, the progress of which was reviewed by a Records of Achievement National Steering Committee (RANSC). The RANSC submitted its final report in January 1989 (RANSC, 1989). Although there is currently no legal requirement for all schools to operate any one system of profiling (provided that they supply parents with the information on their child's progress which is required by the DFES and National Assembly for Wales), many schools do operate schemes of profiling, and all school leavers receive a Progress File/Achievement Planner, which is a form of profile.

With the development of profiling in schools, it was argued that a similar system should be created in ITET.

(b) **The Development of Competence-Based Assessment:** The growth of competence-based assessment in the UK, where students are assessed on their ability to carry out practical tasks against pre-determined criteria, has been described in previous chapters. In the 1990s it was urged by government that similar systems of assessment should be implemented in ITET. Thus, the then Education Secretary, Kenneth Clarke, at the 1992 North of England Education Conference stated that:

> *The government considers that more emphasis [should be placed] on the achievement of professional competence and the achievement of defined levels of professional competence. ... The required competences should be realistic in terms of what can be expected of newly qualified as distinct from experienced teachers* (paragraph 25).

Profiling was seen as a suitable method for recording a person's progress in mastering the knowledge, understanding and skills which formed part of the performance criteria underlying this system of assessment. A document could be devised which would list the competences to be acquired, and the student's achievements could be recorded in relation to each item within that list.

(c) **The Use of Quality Control Indicators in Education:** One of the issues frequently raised by central government from 1983 onwards (DES, 1983) has been quality control, and the appraisal of teachers against pre-determined criteria has been seen as a mechanism for ensuring that the teaching profession is staffed only by those who are capable of fulfilling their role. Ridding the teaching profession of the incompetent is a theme which has been developed by politicians and others throughout the last two decades.

Thus, in January 1984 the then Secretary of State for Education, Sir Keith Joseph, speaking at the annual North of England Education Conference in Sheffield, argued that "those teachers whose performance cannot be raised to an acceptable standard" should be removed "from a profession where they can do so much harm". Some years later the question of incompetent teachers was given further publicity by the former Chief Inspector for Schools (England), Chris Woodhead, who in 1996-97 made frequent reference to the figure of 15,000 incompetent teaching staff (revised to 13,000 in the 1997 annual report from OFSTED). On taking office in May 1997, the Labour government stressed the need to remove such people as quickly as possible from the classroom, and discussion ensued on the optimum means of achieving this. In November of that year new rules were announced whereby the incompetent could be dismissed within six months, or, in extreme cases, one month.

Such arguments rest on the assumption that elements of effective practice can be isolated and defined. By establishing specific competences for QTS, the government hopes that students who are unable to perform satisfactorily when judged against these standards will be refused entry to the profession. Hence, *Qualifying to Teach: Professional Standards for QTS and Requirements for Initial Teacher Training* (DFES-TTA, 2002) states categorically that in order to be awarded QTS students must demonstrate proficiency in *all* the standards listed under the headings 'professional values and practice', 'knowledge and understanding' and 'teaching'. The use of a profile in which progress can be judged in the light of agreed criteria is one strategy for identifying students who have no place in the teaching profession.

(d) **Teachers' Career Structure:** The Labour Party which came to power in 1997 published the White Papers *Excellence in Schools* (DFEE, 1997b) and *Building Excellent Schools Together* (Welsh Office, 1997) which promised to modernise the career structure for teachers by introducing more rigorous appraisal based on targets. Fuller details were announced in the Green Papers *Teachers: Meeting the Challenge of Change* (DFEE, 1998a) and *The BEST for Teaching and Learning* (Welsh Office, 1999), and standards have been devised to define the roles of the subject leader, the special educational needs co-ordinator, the advanced skills teacher and the headteacher (TTA, 1998). The ideas of monitoring teachers' performance, conducting appraisal and setting targets have all been built into the format of the CEP, and it is intended that this document will serve as the first stage of a profile for a teacher which can be built up over her/his entire career and be used in making decisions about in-service needs.

(e) **Involving Students in their Own Assessment:** The idea of employing profiles in schools to allow pupils to undertake assessment of their own work has had an impact upon ITET, and it has been claimed that schemes of this type, which allow students the opportunity to be involved in evaluation of their own progress and development, can enhance motivation and commitment.

(f) **Early Developments in Profiling in ITET:** Many ITET institutions experimented with types of profile towards the end of the 1980s and during the early 1990s for a number of reasons:

(i) Goldsmiths College introduced a system of profiling in 1988 with the following intentions:

- to make explicit to students tutors' assumptions and criteria for good practice;

- to facilitate the involvement of students in monitoring their own progress and make it easier for them to engage in debate about good practice in teaching;

- to enable students to experience for themselves the kinds of records of achievement which were contemporaneously being employed in schools;

- to begin to develop exit profiles for employers (Hutchinson, 1994; Mahoney and Harris,1996).

The profile, which was developed for primary BEd and primary and secondary PGCE courses at Goldsmiths College, covered:

- knowledge of curricular areas and the learning context;

- planning for pupils' learning;

- the management of pupils' learning in the classroom;

- assessment and evaluation of pupils' learning;

- evaluation of the students' own teaching;

- professional relationship and qualities.

(ii) Peter Limm in 1991 outlined three distinct competence domains in teaching history:

- the *ideological* domain, concerned with beliefs and values which underlie practice;

- the *knowledge* domain, relating to subject content and pedagogy, together with an understanding of the ways in which children learn and of wider educational issues;

- the *action* domain, concerned with planning, teaching and evaluating performance.

These domains, he argued, could form the basis for a student's profile.

(iii) In the context of helping newly qualified teachers (NQTs) during their induction year the Surrey LEA adopted a 'New Teacher Competency Profile' consisting of:

- 'menu cards' to be used when selecting a focus;

- peel off sticky labels with the competences written on them, ready to be attached to the appropriate column;

- a competence 'tracker' which was used to record coverage of the competences across the three terms (Gifford, 1995).

Other early profiling systems were devised at Bath College of Higher Education (Ward and Ritchie, 1994), Worcester College of Higher Education (Vaughan, 1992) and the University of York (Davies, 1993).

III: Techniques of profiling in ITET

The following four styles are commonly used (Broadfoot, 1987; Hitchcock, 1990; Gipps, 1994):

(a) **Grid Style Profiling:**

(i) *Forms:* There are two main forms of grid:

(1) a series of hierarchical statements is provided, and the assessor selects the statement which is most applicable to the student, for example,

No evidence of ability to create and maintain a purposeful learning environment. Basic awareness of strategies conducive to creating and maintaining a purposeful

learning environment.

Growing competence in the skills needed to create and maintain a purposeful learning environment.

Generally proficient in creating and maintaining a purposeful learning environment.

Highly proficient in creating and maintaining a purposeful learning environment.

(2) a grading system is utilised with an explanatory statement for each grade, for example,

A   indicates outstanding performance;
B   indicates an above average performance;
C   indicates achievement of an acceptable standard;
D   indicates a performance which gives rise for concern;
E   indicates a totally unsatisfactory performance.

This grading system is then applied to a range of statements and/or competences, for example, (*see opposite*)

(ii) *Advantages of the Grid:*

1. It is easy to complete.

2. It can cover a wide range of skills, attitudes and qualities.

3. It can be informative for users, and the information is presented in a compact and uniform manner which is simple to understand.

4. It can help to motivate students by encouraging them to reach the next level.

5. The approach is familiar to both teachers and employers from the use of profiles in schools.

(iii) *Disadvantages of Grid-style Profiles:*

1. Although they appear to provide precise categories, in practice some of the statements used in this type of profile can be rather vague, especially where terminology includes such phrases as 'a range of situations or 'a variety of contexts'. The adverbs 'often' and 'frequently' are also open to subjective interpretation, while grades relating to terms such as 'satisfactory', 'average' or 'above average' invite value-judgements which may vary considerably with different assessors.

2. Where hierarchical statement are employed, care must be taken to ensure that the steps between the different levels in the hierarchy are even.

3. The practice of ticking boxes or ringing numbers increases the danger that students will be labelled and categorised. The allocation of the lower grades in the early stages may harm students' confidence and perhaps result in the creation of self-fulfilling prophecies.

KNOWLEDGE AND UNDERSTANDING   (Please ring the appropriate grade)

1.1 mastery of knowledge and concepts
     relevant to the lesson   A B C D E

1.2 mastery of practical skills   A B C D E

1.3 understanding of the NC PoS and ATs   A B C D E

1.4 understanding of syllabuses outside the NC   A B C D E

PLANNING, EXPECTATIONS AND TARGETS

2.1 selects appropriate aims for sequences
     of lessons   A B C D E

2.2 selects appropriate objectives for
     lessons suited to the age, ability and level
     of attainment of the pupils   A B C D E

2.3 can ensure continuity and progression
     within and between classes   A B C D E

2.4 can select and prepare resources and
     plan for their safe and effective organisation A B C D E

TEACHING AND CLASS MANAGEMENT

3.1 makes learning objectives clear to pupils   A B C D E

3.2 promotes active and independent learning
     which enables pupils to think for themselves and
     to plan and manage their own learning   A B C D E

3.3 can differentiate their teaching to meet the
     needs of pupils, including the more able and those
     with special educational needs   A B C D E

3.4 sets high expectations for pupils' behaviour A B C D E

3.5 uses ICT effectively in teaching lessons   A B C D E

etc.

4. There is the danger that users will consider only the top grades attainable and overlook any lower levels of achievement, especially where grades A-E are used.

(b) **Comment Banks:** In this approach the assessor selects a comment appropriate to the student's attainment in each area of the course.

(i) *Types:* Two approaches can be used:

(1) **closed banks**, where a statement is selected from a list appropriate to some element of the course. Examples with respect to monitoring and assessment are:

Always selects and uses appropriate methods for regular and systematic monitoring and assessment strategies to evaluate pupils' progress towards planned objectives.

Usually judges accurately from pupils' classwork and homework how well teaching objectives have been achieved and uses this information to improve planning and teaching.

Has been able to use records as a basis for reporting on pupils' attainment and progress orally and in writing with help from the class teacher.

(2) an **open** bank where the teacher is free to write an independent comment if none in the list is thought to be suitable.

Comment banks can cover more than just academic knowledge and skills; they are frequently used to include personal characteristics. In many schemes they are presented in continuous prose rather than a list of accomplishments. It is usually accepted that reference should be made only to positive qualities and achievements.

(ii) *Advantages of Comment Banks:*

1. A wider and more accurate range of expression, terminology and vocabulary is made available than that usually found in the grid system.

2. Students are presented with a series of positive statements in clear English at all stages.

3. There is no suggestion of grading in the summative statement. Comments relate solely to the student's positive achievements and accomplishments.

4. The labelling of students by means of grades is avoided during the course.

5. Norm-referencing where students are compared with other students in the same year cohort is avoided.

(ii) *Disadvantages of Comments Banks:*

1. Reliability among assessors depends upon consensus about procedures and the use of very precise comments.

2. It is sometimes difficult to determine the statement which 'best fits' the student's level of capability, especially where comments in the bank contain adverbs such as 'consistently' or 'effectively'.

3. There may be little indication of what the student is not capable of achieving, which may be a disadvantage in the eyes of some employers.

4. Assessors may become so familiar with the list of statements that the profiles become stereotyped.

5. The use of open banks can be very time-consuming.

(c) **Criterion Checklist:**

(i) *Definition and Examples:* This is a form of criterion referencing. A list of criteria is presented and the mentor indicates the items of knowledge, skills and understanding which have been achieved.

A criterion-referenced profile could appear as follows. The mentor would enter a tick in the right hand column to indicate that a standard had been attained:

• sets challenging objectives relevant to pupils in the class	☐
• uses learning objectives to plan lessons	☐
• promotes active and independent learning that enables pupils to think for themselves	☐
• sets tasks which are differentiated to meet the needs of pupils	☐
• organises and manages the physical teaching space safely and effectively	☐
• organises and manages teaching and learning time effectively	☐
• establishes a clear framework for classroom discipline to anticipate and manage pupils' behaviour	☐
• plans opportunities to contribute to pupils' spiritual, moral, social and cultural development	☐
• ensures coverage of the National Curriculum programmes of studies or relevant examination specifications	☐

(ii) *Advantages of Criterion Checklists:*

1. A readily assimilated list of competences is available in an easily understood format.

2. Biased and subjective assessments are avoided in profiling schemes where it is stipulated that evidence must be available to show that a particular skill or item of knowledge has been mastered.

3. Profiles of this type allow students to demonstrate mastery of a specific skill without reference to others on the course.

(ii) *Disadvantages of Criterion Checklists:*

1. If the list of statements is too long there is the danger that the profile will become unwieldy.

2. Formative assessment is not always given as high a priority in the infrastructure of this model as it is in other forms of profiling.

(d) Student Recording

(i) *The Process:* The student records the outcome of the assessment. The assessor may countersign it, but he/she would not necessarily make any further comment on the student's progress. This is essentially a system of self-evaluation. It is very much part of formative and ipsative assessment.

An example of one approach is given:

With reference to the standards of *professional values and practice, knowledge and understanding,* and *teaching (planning, expectations and targets, monitoring and assessment and teaching and class management),* use the spaces provided below briefly to identify the following:

Progress and Achievement Since the Last Self-Evaluation	Action Plan for Areas which Require Improvement

Mentor Comment: ....

Tutor Comment: ....

(ii) *Advantages of Student Recording:*

1. This approach ensures that students are fully involved in their own assessment. By diagnosing strengths and weaknesses and determining their own action plans they will be better aware of the ways in which they can improve their performance.

2. Formative and ipsative assessment are given a high priority.

3. Students' attention is focused throughout upon the QTS standards.

4. The profile offers scope for discussion with the mentor and the application of many of the strategies of reflective practice outlined in earlier chapters.

5. This approach can be used within target setting along the lines discussed in chapter eight.

(iii) *Disadvantages of Student Recording:*

1. Student recording can be time-consuming if undertaken on a regular basis.

2. This approach, unless supplemented with other forms of profiling, does not always lend itself very well to summative assessment.

3. There may be difficulties in accepting as objective some of the student's comments.

IV: Formative profiling in ITET: Tracking students' progress

The career entry profile (CEP) is essentially summative. It is, however, expected that mentors and tutors will regularly maintain a formative profile, the contents of which will permit them to help the student complete the CEP towards the end of the course. Thus, OHMCI (1998c) states that mentors should maintain "an effective and manageable profiling system which is used to identify and record trainees' progress in relation to teaching competences" (p. 4).

Various guidelines have been suggested:

(a) **Criteria for a Profile in ITET: Good Practice:** Pendry and McIntyre (1996) argue that a system of profiling in ITET should meet the following criteria:

- It should be easy to use.

- It should be valuable to *all* its users: the student; the mentor; the tutor; potential employers, etc.

- It should reflect continuity by charting the student's progress from the time that he/she embarks upon the ITET course right up to her/his entry into the profession as a newly qualified teacher.

- It should be based upon a coherent philosophy of the standards required of people entering the teaching profession and the ways in which these may be acquired.

- It should promote and support the kinds of learning which the partnership schools and HEI wish to foster.

(b) **Professional Development Profiles:** Brooks and Sikes (1997) offer examples of profiles employed in schools. Although a variety of formats has been adopted, the content in most cases consists of:

- the student's *curriculum vitae* which he/she compiles at the commencement of the course;

- a statement of the student's personal philosophy of education;

- the student's written reflection on the personal and professional skills and qualities needed to succeed in teaching and the means of developing them;

- the student's attendance register for the course;

- examples of lesson plans and associated evaluations by subject mentors, ITET co-ordinators and tutors;

- examples of pupils' work assessed by the student;

- the student's self-evaluation forms, for example, in academic counselling at the HEI;

- copies of all assignment feedback forms, for example, for student-led seminars and written assignments;

- copies of weekly record forms in which the student notes the main points arising from meetings with mentors, ITET co-ordinators and tutors together with targets agreed in the light of debriefings. This process allows students to record strengths as well as areas which need to be addressed in order to make satisfactory progress and helps them at a later stage to complete the second section of the CEP;

- copies of the final summative report and standards report forms for each period of school experience.

It is useful if one copy of the profile is retained by the student, a second by the mentor, a third by the ITET co-ordinator and a fourth by the HEI. Professional development profiles of this type can incorporate more than one mode of profiling, for example, open comment banks, criterion checklists and student recording.

(c) **Student Profile of Competence in the Standards:** Staff at Trinity and All Saints University College, Leeds, have developed a system for charting students' progress in which a profile is used with a list of the QTS standards, each identified by a number. Thus, the first standard concerning students' professional values and practice is 1.1. For each standard the student is graded on the following scale:

Q = meets the requirement for QTS.
E = meets requirements for QTS at an exceptional level.
X = does not meet the requirements for QTS.
? = inconsistent or contradictory assessment.
N = not assessed or information not recorded or included.

These gradings in relation to the standards can be used on student's lesson evaluation forms and transferred to a separate profile document over the duration of the course. The argument in favour of this practice is that it enables mentors and tutors to track progress *in relation to all the standards.* Where reference is made to Q at some stage in the year, for example, in a lesson which has been observed by a mentor, there is evidence that the student has achieved the requisite standard. Not all the standards relate to classroom lessons; some of them (for example, those listed under the heading of 'professional values and practice') require evidence of understanding rather than specific teaching competence (for example, being aware of the statutory frameworks relating to teachers' responsibilities). In order to achieve a Q or E in these areas, the student would have to show evidence that he/she met the standard, perhaps by means of a written assignment or seminar presentation. Such a system incorporates aspects of the grid and criterion referencing.

(d) **The University College Worcester Profile:** This profile is described by Ghaye and Ghaye (1998) in *Teaching and Learning Through Critical Reflective Practice*. The key headings are:

DATE	FOCUS	EVIDENCE	FEEDBACK/TARGETS

The focus column relates to the standards and the evidence is provided by the student, who is expected to answer the fundamental questions: "What did I do?" and "What did I learn?" The mentor completes the feedback/targets column. An example is given of a student's profile with reference to standards grouped under the heading "Teaching and Class Management".

DATE	FOCUS	EVIDENCE	FEEDBACK/TARGETS
20 May 2002	3.3.2 3.3.3 3.3.7 3.3.9	In today's science lesson the children were arranged for work in groups. I sat with each group to make sure all were on-task and using their time productively. I made the rules clear at the start of the lesson, for example, they needed to share, and I stopped them on occasion to reinforce things. I used careful questioning.	A well-thought-out lesson, planned and thoroughly researched. A confident presentation and excellent questioning technique. When working with one group, keep your eye on the others.

Use is also made of a series of comment banks and a grid describing the performance of students who are:

- highly proficient in meeting the standards;
- competent;
- satisfactory;
- requiring a high degree of support.

These profiles are used in compiling the summative assessment of the student's school experience.

(e) **The 'QED' Profile:** The 'QED' profile was devised by the author and a mentor at a school in South Wales (Geen and Hutt, 2000). An initial draft was piloted during the school year 1998-99 to take account of the standards of Welsh Office Circular 13/98. It was modified after consultation with mentors at local schools.

(i) *Aims:* The aims of the profile are to:

- evaluate students' progress regularly over the entire course;

- pinpoint, as far as possible, the stage at which mentors consider that each standard has been achieved;

- ensure that mentors provide evidence to justify their judgements;

- afford students the maximum opportunity to reflect critically upon their teaching;

- provide a system which is easy to operate and which does not overwhelm users with paperwork;

- feed easily into the CEP.

(ii) *Format:* In total, the profile involves five documents:

(1) A FEEDBACK FORM in which mentors offer an analysis of a lesson in the manner they feel to be most appropriate. Thus, they can use a chronological approach or set out a commentary which follows the order of the standards, a summary of which is printed on the back of the sheet.

However, they are expected to enter evidence for the conclusions reached. To assist them, each standard is identified by its paragraph number in Circular 13/98 and mentors are requested to enter these numbers in a column adjacent to their written lesson evaluation to show which of them have in their judgement been met. The reasons for making this judgement must also be explicit in their commentary. Hence, if it is claimed that a student had attained the standard of *'providing opportunities to develop pupils' understanding by relating their learning to real and work-related examples'* (Welsh Office 1998, p.13), some aspect of the lesson has to be mentioned in order to substantiate this statement, for example, by showing how the student explained the application of a process to the catering industry.

Moreover, where a number is entered in the 'standards met' column, it must be qualified by the addition of one of three letters:

- Q indicates that the standard has been mastered.

- E highlights performance at an exceptional level.

- D draws attention to areas in which further development is desirable.

Designation of the appropriate grade is dependent upon the judgement of the mentor in the light of the evidence available.

Printed at the bottom of this form is a section entitled 'key points for consideration' in which mentors are asked to list the principal questions they wish to put to students to stimulate critical reflection during a debriefing session. Discussion based upon these points culminates in the setting of targets together with appropriate success criteria.

(2) A SUMMARY FORM which lists students' strengths and learning needs. Mentors are expected to discuss their progress with them at the end of each week, taking into account the extent to which lesson targets have been achieved, and to maintain a record of the conversation. Three columns are set out in relation to each of the targets examined:

- No change in reaching the targets set;

- Has partly achieved the targets set;

- Has fully achieved the targets set.

(3) A RECORD OF STUDENTS' REFLECTIONS: This is an optional sheet used to record the outcomes of students' reflection upon a series of lessons or wider educational issues emanating from school experience. This encourages mentors to put into practice such strategies as the strands of reflection approach described in chapter nine and discursive dialogue. In this way, opportunities are available for trainees to review practice in the light of formal theory derived from reading and to contemplate ethical issues pertinent to their classroom experience. To ensure that the standards of Circular 13/98 are not neglected, this form is subdivided into five boxes headed: *subject knowledge and understanding, planning, teaching and class management, monitoring, assessment, recording, reporting and accountability* and *other professional requirements.* The 'standards met' and 'QED' columns are again included together with a space for entering any priorities for development.

(4) STUDENTS' SELF-EVALUATIONS: This is an obligatory self-evaluation form on which students record their analysis of at least one lesson every day. To help them in this task they are expected to refer to the questions contained in the general evaluation criteria and the more precise focused evaluation criteria which were outlined in chapter eight. At the end of each week they are asked to refer to the standards and to assess themselves on the 'QED' rating scale. Mentors or tutors then confirm this judgement by appending their signature.

(5) SUMMARY SHEET: This consists of a checklist to facilitate the transfer of information from the previous forms to a single source, which serves as the definitive document for tracking progress over the course. It can be viewed by the ITET co-ordinator and HEI tutor as well as the mentor. The full set of standards is listed on this sheet together with the

columns 'D' 'E' and 'Q', into which mentors insert a date to show when they feel that sufficient evidence has been accumulated to merit the designation of one of these grades for each standard. In this way, development over a period of time can be constantly monitored, and assistance and guidance provided where necessary. This checklist helps the student make decisions about the content of the CEP. Thus, standards which are graded as an 'E' or a 'D' can be used as the basis for negotiation with that student about her/his areas of strength and priorities for further support during the induction year.

V: Sumative profiling in ITET: The career entry profile

A provisional draft of a profile for the CEP was piloted by the TTA during the 1995-96 academic year, based mainly on the principle of comment banks (closed and open). Its progress was evaluated by a team from the Scottish Council for Research in Education and the University of Northumbria led by Janet Powney. Following consultation, it was substantially revised, and in England all newly qualified teachers (NQTs) have been required to take a completed CEP to their first post from September 1998. In Wales the first version of the CEP was drawn up by the Welsh Office, and subsequent drafts have been the responsibility of the National Assembly. The current profile utilised by students successfully completing ITET courses seeks to:

- provide information, in relation to the standards for the award of QTS, about new teachers' strengths and priorities for further professional development; and

- require new teachers to set objectives for professional development and develop an action plan for their first year of teaching.

It endeavours to support schools and NQTs working together to:

- make the best use of the skills and abilities the NQTs bring with them;

- use the QTS standards to build on their achievements;

- devise a focused and individualised programme of professional development to improve the NQT's practice in areas identified for development during the first year of teaching;

- recognise the importance of effective professional development from the earliest stage in the NQT's career, and consider the new teacher's longer term professional development;

- make sustained and significant improvements in the quality of the NQT's teaching in relation to her/his objectives, the school's development plan, and local and national priorities.

The profile has three sections:

SECTION A: a summary of initial teacher education, for example, the training provider, the title of the course, its length, whether the student was full or part-time, the date of her/his completion of the course, the age range on which the course focused, the subject specialism and any other relevant information, for example, distinctive features of training, additional qualifications, previous employment in related fields, extra curricular activities, taster courses and physical education safety training.

SECTION B: a statement of up to four areas of strength in relation to the standards for the award of QTS and up to four areas in which, although the standards have been met, the trainee teacher's professional development would particularly benefit from support during the first year of teaching.

Examples given for STRENGTHS in the notes of guidance for the CEPs for England and Wales are:

- good knowledge and understanding of mathematics in KS2, and an ability to recognise and use connections across the subject in teaching;

- very good understanding of the needs of more able pupils, reflected in both planning and teaching;

- skilful use of questioning, in both plenary sessions and small groups, to elicit pupils' understanding and further their learning;

- good feedback provided to pupils through discussion and marking, enabling pupils to understand what they have done well and how to improve further, and supporting the setting of clear targets;

- excellent use made of assessment information in establishing challenging expectations for pupils' learning and for translating these into specific learning targets.

Examples of PRIORITIES FOR FURTHER PROFESSIONAL DEVELOPMENT are:

- develop subject and pedagogic knowledge in primary music beyond that covered on ITET taster course;

- develop confidence and skill in setting well-defined targets for the improvement of pupils' achievement and in monitoring and recording progress towards their attainment;

- improve management and structure of lessons to ensure that plenary activities are productive, that sound use is made of summaries and that checks of learning are made against identified objectives;

- use personal ICT experience and competence to develop new approaches to medium and long term planning;

- better use of homework to make a direct contribution to learning objectives;

- make better ongoing use of assessment information as part of teaching.

These two sections are completed by the ITET provider and trainee in May or June of the final term of the course. Both parties sign section B. Once QTS is formally recommended in June or July, the provider reviews the sections, signs the profile again, keeps a copy and sends the original to the NQT. During the period June to August the NQT considers priorities for objective setting and action planning in preparation for developing her/his action plan for the induction year.

In September the NQT and the member of the school staff with responsibility for the NQT (the induction tutor) complete:

SECTION C: an action plan, including objectives, for the induction period. It consists of:

- a list of *objectives* to which NQTs can work on a day-to-day basis as part of their normal teaching role. Objectives should be achievable and realistic. They should relate to the areas of strength and areas for further professional development identified in Section B of the CEP, to the induction standards outlined in DFES Guidance Document 582/2001 (DFES, 2001b) and to the demands of the first teaching post. Some may involve the support of other school staff or expertise from outside the school, for example, HEIs, LEAs, subject associations.

- the *action to be taken* to achieve these objectives and the people who must take this action;

- the *success criteria* which will enable judgements to be made about the extent to which each objective has been met;

- the *resources*, if any, which will be needed;

- *target dates* for the achievement of these objectives;

- *dates* when progress will next be reviewed

Both the NQT and the induction tutor sign the action plan whenever section C is used to set or revise objectives. Both keep a copy of the document.

The following are examples of entries to section C. They are taken from the notes of guidance to accompany the CEPs for England and for Wales: (*see opposite page*)

VI: Advantages and limitations of profiling ITET students

(a) Profiling in ITET provides a clear-cut system for structuring students' experience and ensuring that negotiation, problem-solving and target setting are on-going processes.

(b) It has the advantage that students are aware of their progress at all stages of the ITET course. The 'QED' profile was welcomed by students for this reason.

(c) Schemes such as the profile devised at Trinity and All Saints University College and the 'QED' profile allow mentors to chart students' progress in mastery of the standards and to have evidence for the judgements reached.

(d) Research undertaken in 1996 by P. Earley suggests that competence-based profiles have been useful in promoting reflection and have led to sharply focused and effective action planning. Similarly, Ghaye and Ghaye (1998) show how the profile used at University College, Worcester has helped student teachers reflect on their practice and identify areas where improvements may be made (p. 70).

(e) A study by Anne Williams of King Alfred's College, Winchester, and Stephanie Prestage

OBJECTIVE	ACTION TO BE TAKEN AND BY WHOM	SUCCESS CRITERIA	RESOURCES	TARGET DATE FOR ACHIEVEMENT	DATE FOR REVIEW
To secure effective management of pupil behaviour in class 9C	To secure effective management of pupil behaviour in class 9C Detailed briefing by Ms Jones on school policy and procedures for behaviour. NQT to observe 9C in an art and science lesson. NQT to establish clear expectations and develop agreed rules for classroom behaviour with 9C.	More effective pupil-teacher relationship. Lessons start smoothly and pupils are swiftly focused on the work. Fewer pupils detained.	0.5 day for lesson observation by NQT. 0.25 day for briefing on behaviour policy, observation of NQT's lesson by Ms Jones and debriefing	End of autumn term	12 December
To familiarise self with ICT equipment available and plan the use of ICT	ICT co-ordinator to induct and work together with NQT. Incorporate ICT work in planning.	Working knowledge of available hardware and software. Planning shows appropriate learning objectives for pupils' ICT and for the use of ICT to support learning in the subject.	ICT equipment already in school. 0.25 day for ICT co-ordinator and NQT to work together	End of October	12 December
To provide clear information to parents that will enable them to be more fully involved in the support of children's learning	NQT to discuss own preparation for next parents' evening with deputy head. NQT to review use of 'home-school contact books' with induction tutor and to develop strategies to improve their use.	Improved use of 'home-school contact books'. Effective communication at parents' evening.	0.2 day release for deputy head to support preparation for discussion with parents. 0.2 day release for induction tutor to review 'home-school contact books'.	End of spring term	4 April

of the University of Birmingham, funded by the Association of Teachers and Lecturers, concluded that the CEP was "a valuable starting point for induction and as a focus of discussion" (Williams and Prestage, 2000, p. 38).

(f) Research undertaken by staff working for *The Times Educational Supplement* (Revell, 1998) has shown that most inservice training co-ordinators welcomed the CEP as it offered them a way to target support.

(g) Kevan Bleach (1999) in a chapter on the Career Entry Profile in *The Induction and Mentoring of NQTs: A New Deal for Teachers* feels that requiring the student to record up to four areas of strength is an excellent means of developing motivation and confidence.

(h) Profiles in themselves do not correct inconsistencies in the quality of the assessment process on the part of mentors and tutors.

(i) It is sometimes difficult to say with certainty that a specific standard has been reached. In a lesson seen by a mentor, a student may have shown evidence of excellence in the standard of *selecting and preparing resources and planning for their safe and effective organisation, taking account of pupils' interests and their language and cultural backgrounds.* However, this excellence may not be evident on another occasion or with another class. Schemes which require mentors and tutors to enter 'Q' for attainment of a standard and 'E' for attainment at an exceptional level present difficulties for this reason. Where a student has been awarded an 'E' grade at one point in the course and, then, at a later stage, perhaps at a second placement school, a mentor feels that a much lower grade is applicable, that teacher may be reluctant to adjust the original designation. Moreover, trainees may well be aggrieved if such an alteration were to be made. To help mitigate this problem, course literature has to stress that the award of a grade is intended to help a student gauge her or his progress, is not irrevocable and will not be transferred to the CEP unless there is evidence of consistency in performance.

(j) Assessment of certain of the standards grouped under the heading 'professional values and practice' can be problematic for mentors, since achievement in these areas cannot always easily be measured on the three-point scale in an evaluation of a lesson. Whereas pedagogic and disciplinary issues feature prominently during debriefing, it is rare for reference to be made to students' understanding of the contribution which support staff and other professionals make to teaching and learning, the need to communicate sensitively with parents or carers or the legal frameworks relevant to the responsibilities of teachers. The best solution is for ITET co-ordinators to play a substantial role in compiling the profile, using their knowledge of students' contribution to seminars concerned with whole-school issues. Alternatively, HEI tutors could enter comments where they have assessed written work in the field of educational and professional studies.

(k) It is not always possible to profile students against all the standards, since opportunities are not available for them to present the requisite evidence. For example, under the heading of 'monitoring and assessment' trainees are to "use records as a basis for reporting on pupils' attainment and progress orally and in writing, concisely, informatively and accurately for parents, carers, other professionals and pupils" (DFES-TTA, 2002, p. 10). In schools, especially secondary schools, reports for parents are usually issued during the latter part of the summer term when students have completed their course.

(l) In the research conducted by Williams and Prestage (2000), some NQTs argued that setting targets based on their ITET course was not always helpful because the demands of their role during their first year of employment were very different from the expectations made of them as students.

(m) Ghaye and Ghaye (1998) comment that "the expectation by providers of initial teacher training that student teachers will manage the profiling process themselves and be responsible for the gathering of evidence regarding their professional development … takes a certain degree of skill, motivation and confidence, and an ability to recognise where professional development has indeed taken place" (p. 77). This degree of skill, motivation and confidence, they feel. is not always present.

(n) Where students receive a 'Q' or 'E' in a profile, they may consider that they have achieved the respective standard and relax their efforts in future lessons.

(o) Some students find it difficult to take part in the free and frank exchange which is required in self-assessment with a person whose role is assessor as well as counsellor. As Brooks and Sikes (1997) write, there can be an uneasy relationship between student self-assessment and summative assessment (p. 137).

(p) Husbands (1993) fears that summative profiles devised by the government will result in tighter management and assessment of entrants to the teaching profession. Schools, it is argued, already make considerable demands of students, and the introduction of further controls in future years will only serve to exacerbate this situation.

(q) Busher and Saran (1995) are concerned that not all schools will have the resources necessary to employ the profile in such a way that it will ultimately provide adequate professional support for NQTs.

(r) Arthur, Davison and Moss (1997) note that many HEI-school partnerships have developed their own profiles which relate to competences which they see as being especially relevant to the students they train and educate. This was certainly true of the specialist courses in design and technology offered at University College Cardiff during the 1990s. Under the CEP system, however, reference has to be made to standards which have been determined solely by the DFES and National Assembly for Wales.

(s) Similarly, Tomlinson (1995) argues that different subjects have different competences; the CEP is generic and does not take these differences into account.

Issues for consideration

1. Read sections I and II (*profiling: requirements of ITET providers* and *developments in profiling in ITET*). Give five reasons why profiling has been adopted in recent years in ITET.

2. Read section III (*techniques of profiling in ITET*) and define the following types of educational profile:

(a) *grid style profiling;*

(b) *comment banks;*

(c) *criterion checklist;*

(d) *student recording.*

3. State with reasons the approach you favour for the formative assessment of ITET students.

4. Read section IV (*formative profiling in ITET: tracking students' progress*). Explain the role of mentors at your school in the profiling of students. What steps are taken to meet the following criteria?

(a) *a system which is manageable for students and mentors;*

(b) *a system which is valuable to all its users;*

(c) *the tracking of progress throughout the entire ITET course;*

(d) *emphasis upon the standards;*

(e) *the use of evidence to substantiate judgements;*

(f) *ways of mitigating the problem of subjectivity in judgement;*

(g) *ways of feeding into the Career Entry Profile.*

5. Suggest any steps which could be taken to improve the quality of profiling ITET students at your school.

6. Summarise the key sections which comprise the Career Entry Profile.

7. Tomlinson (1995) argues that different subjects have different competences and that profiling should take these into account. With reference to your subject specialism, list any special considerations which you feel should be taken into account in devising a profile for charting students' progress.

8. Students who are experiencing difficulties on an ITET course will need additional support. Consider the role which a system of profiling may play in helping students of this type, for example:

(a) *the type of profiling you would employ;*

(b) *the ways in which specific problems would be pinpointed;*

(c) *the frequency with which the mentor would meet the student;*

(d) *the type of feedback which would be provided;*

(e) *the ways in which the student would be involved in her/his own assessment;*

(f) *the ways in which subsequent action would be monitored.*

9. If you were the induction mentor for a group of NQTs who had entered the following targets in their CEPs, what action plan, success criteria and resources would you negotiate to help them?

- *To improve management of pupil behaviour;*

- *To acquire further knowledge and skills in a subject area for which only a 'taster' course was available during ITET;*

- *To ensure the effective use of learning support assistants in improving pupils' learning;*

- *To gain greater understanding of subject-specific industry applications and how to teach these effectively;*

- *To acquire a deeper knowledge and understanding of examination specifications in relation to my subject.*

10. Consider carefully the merits and limitations in systems of profiling outlined in the chapter. What courses of action would you recommend to help overcome the limitations which have been identified?

Quality control and mentoring

I: Requirements of ITET providers

Since the system of partnership was instituted, the DFES and National Assembly for Wales have been concerned with issues of quality and quality assurance in the conduct and delivery of ITET courses. Thus, the final section of *Qualifying to Teach: Professional Standards for Qualified Teacher Status and Requirements for Initial Teacher Training* (DFES-TTA, 2002, p. 17) is devoted to quality assurance requirements. In this chapter, it is proposed, first, to examine the meaning of concepts concerned with 'quality', and, then, to discuss their implications for initial teacher education and training.

II: Quality related concepts

(a) **Quality:** This has been defined by the British Standards Institute (1990) as "the totality of features and characteristics of a service that bear on its ability to satisfy a given need". In other words, quality denotes fitness for purpose and satisfaction on the part of customers with a service.

(b) **Quality Control** is an operational function applied at all levels of an organisation and is concerned to:

- prevent quality problems;

- ensure that products reaching the customer are of the desired quality;

- ensure the evaluation of the organisation's products in the light of its objectives, which may be set out in a formal 'mission statement'.

(c) **Quality Assurance** has been defined as "a management system designed to control activities at all stages ... to prevent quality problems and ensure only conforming products reach the customer" (Munro-Faure and Munro-Faure, 1992, p. 6).

(d) **Quality audit** is the actual monitoring of those structures and mechanisms by which staff in institutions ask themselves how they make sure that their standards are adequate.

(e) **Total Quality Management** (TQM) is a philosophy built upon the assumption that the fulfilment of clients' expectations is the first priority in any enterprise. It is to a large extent derived from the work of the American statistician W. Edwards Deming (1982), whose early ideas on management were enthusiastically adopted by Japanese industrialists in the 1950s, and the writings of Joseph Juran (1989) and Philip B. Crosby (1985).
TQM embraces a number of principles, of which the following are the most important:

(i) Quality is defined by the customer, not the supplier. Hence, in many organisations the views of the client on the quality of the services offered are ascertained, for example, by means of questionnaires and rating scales.

(ii) Quality consists of meeting stated needs, requirements and standards. As C.P. Loder (1995) writes, "quality assurance mechanisms must be explicit rather than implicit ... Institutions should be able to demonstrate their commitment to maintaining and raising the quality of their work in a manner consistent with their recognised objectives" (p. 5).

Hence, in many organisations there are clearly documented policies for the quantification of standards which are communicated to the public, for example, in hotels where the services available are made clear to customers. Citizens' Charters and other forms of charters (for example, Fair Trading Charters) serve as an instance of this aspect of TQM.

(iii) Quality is achieved through continuous improvement in the light of evaluation of the end product or services provided. Hence, there is an internal or external process of assessment designed to provide feedback on the total impact and value of a project or activity. Thus, Deming sees part of the role of management to be seeking continuously to improve the standards of the organisation. The 'Deming wheel' plan for management consists of the following stages:

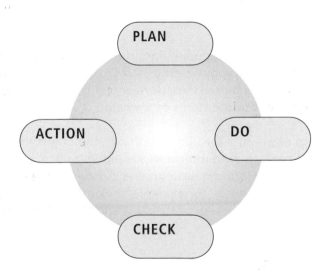

In this process of evaluation he stresses the importance of *zero defects*. Managers try to be proactive rather than reactive in anticipating customers' future needs, and in this way they seek to eliminate at the outset any goods or services which are likely to be of an unsatisfactory character. Stress is placed on the prevention rather than the detection of faults. TQM is concerned to optimise outcomes at the start rather than to remedy defects and problems at a later stage. The Japanese use the term *kaizen* to refer to this process of continuous improvement.

(iv) Where standards fall below a level deemed by customers to be satisfactory, they are encouraged to register a formal complaint. A complaint is defined in legislation governing the role of the Ombudsman as "any expression of dissatisfaction, however made, about the standard of service, actions or lack of action".

In the past a complaint was seen as one of the hazards of the job, and was dealt with as quickly as possible, usually in isolation from the rest of the services offered. With the advent of TQM and the quest for zero defects, complaints are seen in a constructive light as a means of improving the products and services on offer. To be able to benefit from a customer complaint it is necessary to:

- be aware of what constitutes a complaint;

- have set procedures in place for the complaint to be dealt with efficiently;

- have trained staff who know both how to deal with a complaint and how to document the complaint after the event;

- have some mechanism for utilising the complaint to improve services.

(v) Quality is achieved only if there is total commitment on the part of all employees to the maintenance of standards. Thus, TQM is essentially a question of organisational ethos and the development of attitudes, the continuous application of processes which seek to highlight problems and identify solutions, the encouragement of customers to use procedures to register any dissatisfaction and the realisation that complaints received from this source offer an opportunity for improving services rather than apportioning blame.

Hence, quality has to pervade human relationships in the work place; there must be shared goal setting and acceptance of common purposes.

(vi) Staff development, education and training are important in equipping the workforce to perform this role. In most organisations committed to TQM, company members at all levels are expected to draw attention to any barriers which they feel hinder their job performance and to undertake appropriate forms of training.

(vii) Managers operating TQM establish a mission statement - the objectives to which the organisation is working - with performance indicators for judging the standard of the service their company offers. In completing questionnaires customers are expected to focus on these performance indicators. In a hotel, for example, they may be asked to complete a 1-5 rating scale with reference to the courtesy of the staff and the reliability of the main services.

Examples of performance indicators and standards of current importance are:

(1) ISO09000: These are standards established by the Geneva-based International Standards Organisation which are recognised as symbols of quality. Some 20,000 companies in the UK are ISO09000 registered. Most are concerned with manufacturing, but recently service industries and professional bodies such as solicitors, architects and management consultants have also gained registration.

The ISO09000 series was first published in the UK in 1979, when it was known as BS (British Standard) 5750. It lists stringent standards for organisations. One example is demonstrating capability of meeting customer requirements through:

- clear procedures and working methods;

- systems of communication;

- set responsibilities;

- documentation and control of systems;

- training.

(2) THE INVESTORS IN PEOPLE INITIATIVE. To achieve the status of 'Investors in People' organisations are expected to:

- set out their goals and targets;

- identify the human investment, for example, in terms of skills, needed to achieve these goals;

- identify any gap that exists between what is needed and what is available;

- define a training plan to close the gap;

- evaluate whether the gap has been effectively closed;

- review regularly the training and development needs of all employees on recruitment and throughout their employment in accordance with the organisation's goals.

(viii) Organisations practising TQM can seek accreditation on the part of nationally recognised bodies which define objective standards. Usually, representatives of one of these bodies inspect an organisation and, if they feel that it does adhere to the agreed standard, it will be accredited and can advertise this fact in promotional literature.

Examples of accrediting bodies are:

(1) BRITISH STANDARDS INSTITUTION QUALITY ASSURANCE, LLOYDS REGISTER QUALITY ASSURANCE AND YARDLEY QUALITY ASSURANCE. These are registered with the appropriate government department and undertake the accreditation of organisations under the aegis of the National Accreditation Council for Certification Bodies. They scrutinise institutions, which, if they meet the ISO9000 specification, are registered and allowed to use a quality systems logo in their marketing. The standard is usually awarded for three years only, after which the organisation has to seek re-accreditation.

During the period between the formal external audits for accreditation, the organisation is expected to undertake its own internal audits. If it cannot maintain its quality control systems and procedures to the level of the standard, registration can be withdrawn.

(2) INVESTORS IN PEOPLE UK: This is the body which is responsible for the accreditation of institutions as *Investors in People*. Its auditors visit organisations seeking accreditation, interview staff, examine documentary evidence and judge the extent to which the standards laid down by Investors in People UK are being met. Use is made of assessment criteria, for example:

- There is a written but flexible plan which sets out the organisation's goals.

- Training and development needs are regularly reviewed against the organisation's goals.

- Managers are competent to carry out their responsibilities for developing staff.

- The organisation evaluates the extent to which its goals are being achieved.

- Top management understands the broad costs and benefits of developing staff.

(ix) The performance of organisations is assessed against objective criteria, and the results of this assessment are made available to clients and the public. In some contexts, their performance is set out in league tables, in which the best and worst performing companies can be identified by any interested parties. It is then assumed that the organisations offering the top quality services will continue to prosper and expand, while the weakest will have to improve in order to gain clients, or else they will be shunned by the public and eventually go out of business.

III: Implications for courses of Initial Teacher Education and Training

(a) **Standards and Criteria for ITET Courses:** Before 1983, the overall provision for ITET was very much the responsibility of HEIs. Courses were validated by universities and other bodies, but there was no national system of accreditation. Since that time, a series of initiatives has been launched by both Conservative and Labour governments with the aim of establishing standards and criteria for such courses and ensuring that all programmes of ITET are rigorously inspected and accredited. The main developments are traced below.

(i) *The 1983 White Paper and DES Circular 3/84 (Welsh Office Circular 21/84)*: The first official document to announce that specific national standards would be established for all courses of ITET was the 1983 White Paper *Teaching Quality* (DES, 1983). Subsequently, DES circular 3/84 (Welsh Office circular 21/84) (DES, 1984), issued by the Education Secretary, Sir Keith Joseph, set out a list of seventeen criteria to which all courses had to adhere. Examples are:

- the establishment of close links between schools and HEIs, for example, teachers sharing responsibility for the selection of students for ITET courses and the planning, supervision and assessment of students' school experience;

- the need for staff concerned with pedagogy to have recent and relevant school experience;

- a maximum of twenty weeks' teaching practice for students on a four year BEd course;

- the need for courses to pay attention to aspects of the teacher's work outside subject teaching, for example, pastoral and administrative responsibilities and relationships with parents;

- the award of qualified teacher status to be granted only to those students whose classroom performance was judged to be satisfactory.

(ii) *DES Circular 24/89 and DFE Circulars 9/92 and 14/93 (Welsh Office Circulars 59/89, 35/92 and 62/93)* (DES, 1989a, DFE 1992, DFE, 1993b): The criteria established in 1983-84 were then revised by the next Secretary of State for Education, Kenneth Baker, in 1989 in DES Circular 24/89 (Welsh Office Circular 59/89) (*Initial Teacher Training: Approval of Courses*) and again by the Education Secretary, John Patten, in DFE Circular 9/92 (Welsh Office Circular 35/92)

(*Initial Teacher Training [Secondary Phase]*) and DFE Circular 14/93 (Welsh Office Circular 62/93) (*The Initial Training of Primary School Teachers: New Criteria for Courses*).

DFE Circular 9/92 (Welsh Office Circular 35/92) stressed that "all newly qualified teachers entering maintained schools should have achieved the levels of knowledge and standards of professional competence necessary to maintain and improve standards in schools" (p. 7), while the 1993 paper *The Government's Proposals for the Reform of Initial Teacher Training* insisted that "regular and rigorous quality control is the responsibility of all providers of higher education. Qualified teacher status is given automatically to all successful students on an approved course. Providers of training therefore have an important responsibility to ensure that course standards are maintained and improved, and only students demonstrating the necessary competence are allowed to qualify" (DFE, 1993a, p. 10).

DFE circular 9/92 was the first document issued by central government to establish competences which students were to acquire in order to achieve QTS.

(iii) *DFEE Circulars 10/97 and 4/98 and Welsh Office Circular 13/98:* (DFEE, 1997c, DFEE, 1998b, Welsh Office, 1998): In 1997 and 1998 revised requirements for courses of ITET were published. These included:

- a list of the standards which *all* students had to meet before they could be awarded QTS;

- subject-specific standards for students teaching the core areas of the National Curriculum;

- revised selection procedures for entrees to ITET courses, for example, ability to communicate clearly and grammatically in written and spoken English/Welsh, possession of at least a grade C in the GCSE in English and in mathematics and, for students born on or after 1st September 1979, in science;

- the length of courses (for example, thirty-six weeks for a full-time PGCE);

- partnership requirements. For example, schools were to be involved in the planning and delivery of ITET as well as the selection and final assessment of trainees. Effective selection criteria for partnership schools were to be established, which took account of such indicators as inspection reports, test and examination results and exclusion rates;

- course requirements. It was stated that trainees should be given opportunities to observe good teachers at work and to work alongside them. Only those schools and teachers who could offer appropriate training and support were to be used to provide ITET. The content and structure of courses had to be designed to develop trainees' knowledge and understanding and to ensure that the standards for the award of QTS were met.

(b) **Clear Definition of Roles and Responsibilities and the Documentation of Procedures:**
Literature on TQM requires institutions to maintain clearly defined roles and procedures so that everyone is aware of the steps to be taken where difficulties are encountered. This allows for the correction of problems associated with quality.

The current requirements for courses of ITET state that all providers must set up partnership agreements which make clear to everyone involved each partner's roles and responsibilities (DFES-TTA, 2002, p. 16). It is therefore essential that the duties of ITET co-ordinators, mentors and college tutors be carefully documented. This is usually achieved by means of a partnership handbook, which may also set out procedures for such areas as moderation and assessment.

Specific details of internal procedures in relation to ITET have to be decided by schools on an individual basis. An excellent example is the system operated at St Cenydd School in Caerphilly, South Wales, (Smallwood, 1997) where the following procedures have been adopted:

(i) Quality assurance of ITET is seen primarily as a joint responsibility of the ITET co-ordinator and the link tutor from the HEI.

(ii) It is also closely linked with the school's overall monitoring procedures, and therefore the headteacher assists in the process.

(iii) The headteacher monitors lessons across the curriculum areas with all mentors and students to ensure quality assurance - one lesson per student each term.

(iv) All students receive verbal feedback in relation to at least one lesson each week in accordance with specific criteria/ standards.

(v) All students have written feedback on at least six lesson evaluations in accordance with these criteria/ standards.

(vi) Copies of all formal lesson evaluation forms completed by mentors are submitted to the ITET co-ordinator.

(vii) All subject and professional studies mentors meet with the ITET co-ordinator and headteacher four times a year:

- September (to discuss arrangements for the forthcoming year);

- December (to review the functioning of ITET arrangements during term 1);

- March (to review the functioning of ITET arrangements during term 2);

- July (to review the functioning of ITET arrangements during term 3).

(viii) All mentors attend staff development courses in this field, internal and external, wherever appropriate.

(ix) All mentors discuss quality assurance issues with tutors from the HEIs, wherever possible.

(x) Curriculum tutors from the HEIs discuss quality assurance issues with the appropriate mentor and the ITET co-ordinator, wherever possible, when they visit the school.

(xi) The ITET co-ordinator, or another appropriate member of staff, attends cross-institutional meetings and reports the proceedings to all other mentors.

(xii) Any identified concerns are referred to the ITET co-ordinator and the HEI as soon as possible.

(xiii) Action plans for the provision of ITET are regularly drawn up.

(c) **Moderation of Standards:** The current requirements for ITET state that all providers must "ensure that rigorous, internal, and independent external, moderation procedures are in place to assure the reliability and accuracy of assessments" of student teachers (DFES-TTA, 2002, p. 17).

In most partnerships this is achieved by means of the following procedures:

(i) Students' progress is monitored by mentors.

(ii) The assessment of mentors is moderated by the ITET co-ordinator.

(iii) The assessment of school staff in moderated by HEI tutors;

(iv) The assessment of school and HEI staff is moderated by external examiners.

A further possibility is the idea of *cross-moderation*, whereby staff from one school moderate ITET provision and the quality of students' teaching in another.

One problem which has been identified is the moderation of standards in school-centred schemes. In a report published by the Office for Standards in Education (OFSTED, 2002) of seventy-two trainees involved in the Graduate Teacher Programme from late 2000 to early 2001, it was noted that quality assurance was poor in a third of schools operating the scheme and weak in another third. Moderation procedures for the approval of applications were seen essentially as a paper exercise that took too much on trust, and school-based trainers were not always adequately prepared to fulfil their role. Inconsistent practices were noted in reviewing the progress of students, and assessment was sometimes based upon inadequate evidence. The difficulties were especially acute in the primary sector. The fear has been expressed that schools with no experience of partnership arrangements take on graduate teachers in the hope of solving recruitment problems and do not always have clear systems in place for moderating standards (Foster, 2001, Thornton, 2001, 2002a and 2002b, Thornton and Barnard, 2001).

(d) **Continuous Review:** The DFES and TTA regulations state that the providers of ITET must ensure that the systems operated by them are kept under continuous review to ensure that they comply with the requirements of central government and that the quality of these systems is improved. They should especially:

- identify targets for improvement;

- review provision against these targets;

- specify the action to be taken to secure improvements;

- ensure that the specified action is taken and that it leads to improvement (DFES-TTA, 2002, p.17).

Consequently, any quality issues raised through internal and external moderation should be investigated, and the outcomes of these investigations used to establish appropriate priorities for improving courses. Plans for course development should be acted upon, monitored, evaluated and reviewed against criteria for success.

Review can be undertaken by:

(i) *staff in schools:* For example, in the St Cenydd model mentioned above, ITET provision is reviewed each term at a meeting of subject mentors, professional studies mentors, the ITET co-ordinator and the headteacher. Action planning is also used to ensure that key aspects of the school's provision are regularly subjected to scrutiny.

(ii) *HEI staff and mentors in partner schools:* Regular meetings can be organised involving ITET staff in the schools and at the HEI to evaluate current provision, identify any problems and decide upon appropriate action plans to remedy deficiencies.

(iii) *students on courses of ITET:* One approach to quality control, to which reference was made in an earlier chapter, is to ask students in questionnaires to indicate their views on the quality of the provision made for them both in school and in the HEI and to offer suggestions for the alleviation of any problems which they can identify. It is also possible for college tutors to contact former students at the end of their first year of teaching to ascertain their views on the ITET course in the light of their experience.

(iv) *employers:* These may be regarded as 'customers' in the sense that they utilise a product (newly qualified teachers) emanating from a school-HEI partnership. Hence, DFEE Circular 4/98 and Welsh Office Circular 13/98 required that "information about the effectiveness of newly qualified teachers in their first year of teaching is collected and used to improve training courses" (DFEE, 1998b; Welsh Office, 1998, p. 84).

(v) *development planning:* It is important that, when reviews are carried out, action plans are devised to remedy any defects which come to light. An effective development plan includes:

(1) REVIEW where the feedback is acquired from staff at the school and the HEI, from present and past students and from employers. The current DFES and TTA regulations also require ITET providers to benchmark their performance over time and against other, similar providers.

(2) EVALUATION in which questions are asked about the quality of the various elements and experiences, for example, the extent to which previously agreed targets have been achieved, what has been satisfactory and what needs improvement.

(3) ESTABLISHING AN ACTION PLAN incorporating:

- future targets;

- procedures for achieving these targets;

- the establishment of criteria for success;

(4) IMPLEMENTATION AND MONITORING OF THE ACTION PLAN;

(5) EVALUATION OF THE OUTCOME: The degree of success in attaining the targets is gauged with reference to the criteria for success established at stage 3. In the light of this evaluation future goals are set. The process of evaluation is constantly undertaken.

In many HEIs the comments of all interested parties – students, mentors, tutors and employers - are incorporated into an annual course report, which identifies constraints and difficulties and sets out suitable action plans and dates by which innovations should be introduced to remedy the deficiencies indicated. Effective course reports also identify the people with responsibility for taking this action, which ensures a high degree of personal accountability.

Where it can be shown that mentors at a school do not fulfil their role adequately, the HEI is expected to take action. DFEE Circular 4/98 and Welsh Office Circular 13/98 made it clear that schools which did not respond to guidance should be de-selected.

(e) **Implementing Programmes of Staff Development:** The regulations state that those involved in training ITET students should be properly prepared. They should have the appropriate knowledge, understanding and skills to discharge their roles and responsibilities competently.

Writing in the *Cambridge Journal of Education*, Margaret Wilkin (1992) argues that quality is ultimately dependent upon the people who operate the programme of ITET. Mentors in schools, she writes, need to demonstrate that they are fit persons to undertake student training, that they have planned their operations systematically and with an understanding of student needs and that they keep adequate records of student performance (p. 89).

Similarly, Sir William Taylor, formerly chairman of the Council for the Accreditation for Teacher Education, feels that quality is achieved only if the right people are chosen to educate and induct teachers. Hence, the key to quality control in his view is systematic staff development (Taylor, 1994).

This points to the need for facilities for continuous staff development for mentors and HEI tutors. Examples could be:

- external courses, for example, a structure of postgraduate qualifications in this field - certificates, diplomas and degrees;

- one day conferences, for example, annual conferences for mentors organised by HEIs;

- school-based forms of staff development. Many different approaches are possible, some of which have been discussed in earlier chapters. Examples are:

- strategies to help mentors reflect critically about their role: Holly (1989) suggests that, as a starting point, mentors keep professional journals in which they write down experiences derived from specific lessons or other mentoring events which they then analyse in the light of their reading of relevant empirical and theoretical literature. This process can lead them to plan changes to the existing system of ITET.

- action research: Some innovation in the provision of ITET is developed in a school and put into practice. Its success is then assessed in the light of its objectives (McNiff, 2002).

- developing the notion of the 'professional development' school: Mentors plan and undertake research in ITET, either independently or in collaboration with HEI tutors. Eighty-six per per cent of respondents who participated in the UWIC survey concerned with mentor training (Geen, 2001c) expressed enthusiasm for the concept of the 'professional development' school pioneered in the United States of America, in which school-HEI partnerships are established not only to train student teachers but also to conduct research (Grossman, 1992; Fullan, 1993; Edwards and Collison, 1996). A parallel system in the UK would encourage mentors to explore innovative strategies and disseminate their findings. In this way, school staff who are directly involved in the training and education of students could enhance the quality of ITET through the publication of reports which highlight practices they have successfully pioneered.

(f) **Validation and Accreditation:** Courses of ITET are:

(i) *validated* by their awarding body. In most HEIs this involves gaining the formal approval of such academic authorities as course committees, academic boards, faculty boards and senates. It is the role of a validating body to judge the academic merit of a course and to determine whether a student successfully completing it should be awarded a first degree or other qualification (Bines and Welton, 1995).

Moreover, in recent years, many quality assurance mechanisms have been devised in HEIs in accordance with directives issued by the Quality Assurance Agency (QAA), a body which was established by the Committee of Vice-Chancellors and Principals.

(ii) *accredited:* Accreditation involves the review of a course by some national body to ensure that it meets the required standards, and, in the case of ITET, that it is suitable for the professional preparation of teachers.

The 1983 White Paper *Teaching Quality* established the principle that all courses of ITET were to be accredited by the Council for the Accreditation of Teacher Education (CATE), a quango, the members of which were appointed by the Secretary of State for Education and Science. In the first instance, courses were to be approved by a local professional committee, consisting primarily of course leaders and teachers. These committees were centred upon individual HEIs. Only when courses had the approval of the local professional committee could they be submitted to CATE for formal accreditation. Approval by this body was dependent upon conformity with the seventeen criteria of DES Circular 3/84. CATE then advised the Secretary of State whether or not formally to approve the course. Its remit extended to both England and Wales.

Under the revised policy of DES circular 24/89, the system of local committees was reorganised so that one committee monitored the provision of all HEIs within an area and examined their applications for accreditation before these were submitted to CATE. The circular stated that membership of local committees should be confirmed by CATE and that each committee would "scrutinise approved courses at ... institutions to ascertain whether they continue to satisfy the criteria". It would then "propose to the Council for the Accreditation of Teacher Education whether or not such courses should be approved" (DES, 1989a, p. 24).

DFE Circular 9/92 (Welsh Office Circular 35/92) introduced further changes. Previously, approval had been given by CATE to specific courses. Thus, any HEI offering separate BEd and PGCE courses had to have each course scrutinised individually. Circular 9/92 introduced the system of institutional accreditation, whereby HEIs, rather than individual courses, were accredited.

Under the 1994 Education Act CATE was disbanded and a new quango established: the Teacher Training Agency (TTA), the members of which are appointed by the Secretary of State for Education and Skills. The TTA was set up on 21st September 1994 by the then Education Secretary, Mrs Gillian Shephard. Under section 14 of the 1994 Act and sections 177 and 294 of the consolidating 1996 Education Act students can be awarded qualified teacher status in England only if they successfully complete an ITET course at an institution *accredited by the TTA*. Moreover, the Secretary of State made it clear in her letter of remit to the TTA that "if any institution is found to be failing to satisfy the criteria I shall want the Agency to take quick action, leading if necessary to the withdrawal of accreditation. If accreditation were withdrawn, no courses run by the institution concerned would lead to qualified teacher status".

Furthermore, sections 1-15 of the Labour government's Teaching and Higher Education Act of 1998 have established a General Teaching Council (GTC) for England and another for Wales. These are respectively to advise the Secretary of State for Education and Skills in England and the National Assembly in Wales on a number of matters including teaching standards, standards for the conduct of teachers, recruitment and fitness to teach. They are to maintain registers of all those who are qualified to teach. At the present time, however, they have no power to accredit ITET courses.

(g) **Inspection:** The 1983 White Paper and DES Circular 3/84 stated that all ITET courses would have to be inspected by Her Majesty's Inspectorate (HMI) before CATE would consider accreditation. Evidence from this source would be carefully considered by CATE in deciding whether accreditation would be granted. Thus the Circular stated that "HM Inspectors will visit teacher training institutions in the public sector and, by invitation, university departments of education. The findings of these visits will be reported to the Secretaries of State, who will make them available to the Council (CATE). ... The Secretaries of State will also expect the Council, in offering its advice, to draw on all relevant information, including submissions made by individual institutions, evidence based on any visits made by members of the Council or any working parties it might establish for the purpose, and in all cases the findings of HMI visits" (DES, 1984, pp. 2-3).

The arrangements for inspection continued with the establishment of the TTA, and section 20 of the Teaching and Higher Education Act of 1998 clarifies the right of the Chief Inspectors of Schools for England and for Wales to scrutinise teacher training provision. The inspectorate must be given access to the premises of ITET institutions at all reasonable times and has the right to inspect any documents which the Chief Inspectors feel to be relevant.

In England the framework for the inspection of ITET institutions is set out by OFSTED and the TTA in the *Framework for the Assessment of Quality and Standards in Initial Teacher Training* (TTA and OFSTED, 1998). The principal areas for inspection are:

(i) the quality of trainees' teaching against national standards for the award of QTS;

(ii) the quality of the training;

(iii) the accuracy and consistency of the assessment of trainees against the standards for QTS;

(iv) the effectiveness of the management and quality assurance of the training;

(v) selection procedures and the quality of the trainee intake, including the appropriateness of the admission policy and the selection process and the qualifications and suitability of the students for ITET.

The outcomes of an inspection are normally reported in terms of a grade for each 'cell' inspected, compiled in accordance with the scale: 1 = very good; 2 = good; 3 = adequate; and 4 = poor quality. The first three grades indicate that the ITET provision complies with the current criteria established by the Secretary of State. A grade 4 is given to provision which fails to meet these criteria.

In Wales inspection is conducted in accordance with the Welsh Inspectorate's *Framework for the Assessment of Quality and Standards in Initial Teacher Training* (OHMCI, 1998a) which focuses upon

(i) the standards of trainees' teaching competence, assessed in accordance with the requirements of the current regulations;

(ii) the quality of the teaching and assessment of students. This covers the overall design and content of the ITET programme, the training process, students' response to the course and their progress towards achieving the standards for the award of QTS. The assessment of trainees is also inspected;

(iii) selection and the quality of the trainee intake;

(iv) the quality of staffing, learning resources and accommodation, for example, admission policy and selection procedures, trainees' qualifications and their suitability for ITET;

(v) management and quality assurance, for example, the management of partnership and the internal monitoring of quality and standards.

Grades are given on a five point scale, and there is an overall course grade. The grades are defined:

1. Very good: many good features, some of them outstanding;
2. Good: good features and no major shortcomings;
3. Satisfactory: good features outweigh shortcomings;
4. Unsatisfactory: some satisfactory features, but shortcomings in important areas;
5. Poor: many shortcomings.

(h) **Performance Indicators and League Tables:** In November 1996 the TTA announced plans for the publication of 'league tables' of ITET courses in England. These would be based upon information derived from OFSTED inspectors and would be produced with the aim of allowing students (as 'consumers') to choose those courses which topped the league. Subsequently, the TTA has annually published *Initial Teacher Training Performance Profiles*, a summary of which is available in the educational press, for example, *The Times Educational Supplement*. This information is also available on the TTA website (http://www.canteach.gov.uk).

In Wales, the Higher Education Funding Council (HEFCW) uses performance indicators which include:

- grades for the five performance indicators used in inspection;

- the number and percentage of students starting a course who successfully complete it;

- the number and percentage of undergraduate students who gain the various degree classifications.

(i) **Quality through Funding:** As well as accrediting the providers of ITET, the TTA allocates student numbers and funds initial teacher education and training in England. Government ministers see powers of this type as major instruments of quality control.

In making its funding decisions under section 5(4) of the 1994 Act, the TTA is required to have regard to evidence from HMI about the quality of training provided in institutions. It is to work closely with OFSTED to identify areas where it requires evidence relating to the quality of provision to inform its allocations of funding and student numbers. The Teaching and Higher Education Act of 1998 also states that the Chief Inspectors of Schools should advise the appropriate funding agency in the light of the findings of inspection.

In Wales the funding of courses and the allocation of numbers have been functions of the HEFCW. Under the 1994 Education Act it must have regard to evidence from the Welsh Inspectorate, Estyn. If provision is judged by Estyn to be failing to meet the statutory requirements, it must inform HEFCW within two weeks of the completion of a report. The Secretary of State's remit to HEFCW states that the quality of ITET provision should be maintained and enhanced through linking funding to inspection evidence.

The Green Paper of 2001, *Schools: Building on Success*, makes clear the Labour government's intention that programmes of ITET which are judged to be successful in terms of the inspection criteria will be permitted to expand, while those which fail to respond adequately to weaknesses pinpointed by HMI will have accreditation withdrawn (DFEE, 2001b, p. 66).

If an ITET provider scores grade 4 for any aspect of its training, its course numbers are cut by half. This step was taken with respect to primary places at Exeter University in 2001. If the provider fails re-inspection, accreditation is withdrawn. The closure of La Sainte Union College in Hampshire and the Douay Martyrs School-Centred Initial Teacher Training scheme in Middlesex illustrates this aspect of government policy (Gardiner and Barnard, 1997; Barnard, 1998).

(j) **Utilisation of the Findings of Research:** One of the aims of the TTA is to promote high quality teaching and teacher education through the investigation and dissemination of key features of effective classroom and training practice. In this way it hopes to make available to HEIs and their partner schools strategies for improving the quality of ITET (TTA, 1995, pp. 18-19).

(k) **Quality through Selection of Students:** In 1997 the TTA launched a campaign to recruit more able graduates to teaching and set a target by which ninety-five per cent of postgraduate entrants to ITET courses by 2002 would possess at least a second class honours degree (Passmore and Lepkowska, 1997).

IV: Observations on Quality Assurance and ITET

(a) Sir William Taylor (1994) argues that the application of quality related concepts drawn from industry and commerce to ITET is not always straightforward. He writes that "students are not just 'consumers' or 'customers'. The teacher-student relationship is much more than a one-way provision of goods and services. Education should not simply satisfy the expectations of employers, parents and pupils; it should help *redefine* their expectations. Research in universities and colleges is not a production-line activity ... Much of what teachers do is subject to influence by social and personal factors outside their control" (p. 162).

(b) Geoffrey Whitty (1992) feels that systems of quality assurance in ITET in the UK would be improved if there were a clearer sense of partnership between the various stakeholders, for example, HEIs, schools and LEAs. Government quangos, he feels, are confrontational bodies whose role can seem to be threatening. He writes that "an effective quality assurance mechanism requires commitment from those whose quality it seeks to assure. ... The ideal is an approach that generates internal commitment and external confidence and one in which the external elements of quality assurance stimulate a real concern with quality control within institutions" (p. 47). Similar comments were made in the Sutherland report of 1997 on the future of ITET in England and Wales (National Commission of Inquiry into Higher Education, 1997).

Accordingly, Whitty strongly supports the creation of a General Teaching Council (GTC) incorporating staff from HEIs, schools and LEAs, and hopes that it will ultimately perform the functions currently allocated to the TTA. As has been noted, the Labour government elected in 1997 did establish a GTCs for England and another for Wales, but in 1998 David Blunkett, the then Secretary of State for Education and Employment, made clear his intention of retaining the TTA (Rafferty, 1998; Barnard, 1999).

(c) Newby (1999b) rightly stresses the importance of quality assurance in higher education. However, many commentators feel that there are already enough controls without the need for the systems imposed by the TTA. HEIs are subject to quality assurance procedures operated by the Higher Educational Funding Councils (for England and for Wales), reviews by the Quality Assurance Agency and schemes of staff appraisal. The addition of further controls, it has been argued, is unnecessary and will add to the workload of teachers and lecturers (West-Burnham, 1994; Fish, 1995a; Sallis, 1996; Underwood, 2001).

(d) Management writers have in recent years criticised the concept of TQM, for example, Hammer and Champy (1993), Lawler (1993) and Hammer and Stanton (1995), Many of their objections have been accepted by writers in the field of education, for example, Brent Davies and John West-Burnham (1997). TQM, it is alleged, concentrates too much on improving existing standards rather than taking a wider perspective and considering radically new ideas. Lawler, for example, reports that the Florida Power and Light Company won the prestigious Deming award for total quality, but two years after this it abandoned TQM. The principal reason was that it made managers focus too much on minor change relating to quality issues, and this reduced their ability to respond quickly to other, more important, management needs.

Again, Hammer and Champy argue that the three 'C's of 'change', 'competition' and 'customer expectations' are altering so quickly that minor quality improvements are unlikely to prove to be adequate responses in the early twenty-first century. Hence, they recommend what they call 're-engineering': "Business re-engineering means starting all over, starting from scratch. ... At the heart of business re-engineering lies the notion of discontinuous thinking - identifying and abandoning the outdated rules and fundamental assumptions that underlie current business operations" (pp. 2-3). Brent Davies (1994) feels that these criticisms are as true of the educational setting as the industrial.

V: Research into Quality Assurance in school-based ITET

(a) **Research Findings:** Research published by Geen, Bassett and Douglas (1999a) into the extent to which quality control mechanisms were being utilised in a sample of sixty-seven schools committed to ITET during the school year 1997-98 found that

(i) sixty per cent of schools had documentation defining the roles of staff who acted as mentors;

(ii) eighty-two per cent of such staff had attended appropriate training courses to equip them to fulfil their role;

(iii) ninety-one per cent claimed to have systems in place for checking that procedures were being followed and that, where problems were identified, they could be remedied. For example, the ITET co-ordinator would check that subject mentors were fulfilling the terms of their role in the partnership agreement.

However, questionnaire responses from 160 students suggested that quality defects did arise, of which their mentors were not always aware. For example, fourteen per cent of students failed to obtain a copy of the whole-school policy for discipline and forty-two per cent received no information on assessment procedures, although provision of this documentation was required under the partnership agreement.

(iv) Regular evaluation of the quality of mentoring was undertaken at forty-one per cent of schools, usually by means of annual audits. At only twenty-two per cent were students involved in this assessment. In nearly every case this took the form of response to questionnaires. In some smaller schools it was claimed that 'informal review' by word of mouth was sufficient.

(v) Ninety-one per cent of ITET co-ordinators stated that they moderated students' teaching and eighty-one per cent regularly met with subject mentors and class teachers to review trainees' progress.

(vi) The role of HEI tutors as moderators was welcomed by all but twelve respondents who did not comment because of lack of experience. Ninety-seven per cent saw little merit in school-centred initial teacher training (SCITT) because of the lack of quality control on the part of a HEI or other body.

(vii) The concept of quality control by teachers from other schools through cross-moderation was well received by only forty-one per cent of mentors. Problems were thought to be the time, costs and additional workload involved. Eleven per cent noted that additional training would have to be provided. Fears were expressed that, where different approaches were utilised, some mentors might view unfavourably techniques which differed from their own.

(viii) Whereas seventy-two per cent of respondents saw some merit in systems of 'league tables' in ITET, only thirty-two per cent favoured the government's current regime. Too many extraneous factors were thought to exist for any reliable judgement to be made of the quality of a course, notably, commitment, motivation and enthusiasm on the part of the students. Opinion was divided over the issue of allocating funding on the basis of inspection reports. Twenty-seven per cent of mentors stressed the need for some measure of 'value added' in ranking ITET courses and noted that HEIs which were penalised in terms of resources were unlikely to improve.

(ix) Seventy-seven per cent favoured the idea of the dissemination of research focusing on good practice, though there was less agreement whether the TTA was the best body to undertake this role.

(x) Fifty-six per cent felt that obtaining the views of headteachers and LEAs on the quality of NQTs was valuable, but twenty-six per cent noted that the progress made by NQTs depended on factors other than the quality of their ITET course. A key issue was deemed to be the standard of the induction arrangements provided by schools.

(xi) Two-thirds of mentors did not consider that the idea of setting targets along the lines advocated by the TTA for recruiting a higher proportion of PGCE students with an upper second class honours degree was possible or even desirable. It was noted that there was no clear correlation between high academic performance and the ability to teach, for which personality played a key role as well as subject knowledge. As one respondent noted:

> *Whereas I can understand that the profession does not want graduates who cannot find a job elsewhere, it does not follow that a person with a first class honours will be a good teacher.*

Again Hayes (1999) in a survey of the views of primary school mentors on the qualities they expected of student teachers found that personal attributes such as willingness to act upon advice and readiness to listen and learn were the most important factors in determining satisfactory progress.

(xii) Over half the respondents, while conceding the need for quality control mechanisms, agreed with the comments of William Taylor, John West-Burnham and Brent Davies. The view which emerged was that, whereas many of the recent developments in quality control in ITET were beneficial, they all added to the teacher's workload. The warning was received that: "You have to be careful how much extra you expect schools to do. Some schools may decide not to take students."

(xiii) Whitty's comments were applauded by ninety per cent of respondents who felt that government would gain more from mentors if it adopted a less confrontation stance.

(b) **Recommendations:** The chief recommendations emanating from the study were:

(i) *Quality assurance within schools:* Schools need to ensure that quality assurance mechanisms are in place and are being operated. Examples of good practice which were noted in the research were:

(1) THE USE OF BOOKLETS WHICH SET OUT THE BASIC 'STUDENT ENTITLEMENT' and provide a tick list so that trainees can indicate on a weekly basis when the school's obligations under the partnership agreement have been met. ITET co-ordinators and tutors check the tick lists at regular intervals to ensure that the school is undertaking all the activities to which students are entitled. Where problems are noted and the ITET co-ordinator is unable to resolve them, staff at the HEI must become involved and provide the appropriate guidance. Schools which fail to respond are then de-selected.

(2) CROSS-MODERATION OF THE WORK OF MENTORS BY THEIR COUNTERPARTS. In secondary schools cross-moderation can be taken by mentors from other departments. In the primary sector class teachers of the same age range may assume this responsibility.

(3) WEEKLY MEETINGS OF MENTORS WITH THE ITET CO-ORDINATOR: In this way co-ordinators can check that all systems are operating and that there is consistency in the organisation of ITET throughout the school.

(4) A REVIEW OF ITET PROVISION AT THE END OF EACH SCHOOL YEAR, culminating in the setting of targets for the following session with a timescale and the names of the staff members responsible for carrying out policy relating to these targets.

(ii) *The need for greater consistency in the expectations of HEIs:* One reason why some ITET co-ordinators are unable to meet all the requirements of the partnership agreements set out by their HEIs is that these vary considerably and that periods of school experience rarely coincide. This problem has been identified in research cited in earlier chapters. Consequently, it is very difficult for co-ordinators to find time to see all students at their school and to meet all the different expectations of these HEIs. Eighty-three per cent of mentors in the survey felt that the introduction of some common pattern of school experience and student entitlement would be highly desirable. The bodies best suited to make decisions on these matters were thought to be the General Teaching Councils for England and Wales.

(iii) *The need for legislation:* Mentors felt that two pieces of legislation could be beneficial:

(1) to ensure that the funding provided by HEIs to schools for ITET is used solely for that purpose. In many schools funding is transferred to other budget headings. Such resources, it was argued by respondents, could be used to offer some free time to ITET co-ordinators to enable them to liaise with colleagues and HEI tutors, to appraise current methods of working, to identify any shortcomings relating to quality control, to set appropriate targets and to review the progress made in achieving them.

(2) to require the governors of schools which accommodate students to ensure that any common 'student entitlement' defined by the GTCs is met at their school.

(iv) *The funding of professional development for mentors:* Government needs to provide more funding to allow a *continuous* cycle of professional development to be offered to mentors. There was support for the proposal mentioned in an earlier chapter that a national professional qualification for mentors be established on a par with the national standards for subject leaders and other grades of teacher.

⟩ Issues for consideration

1. Read sections I and II (*requirements of ITET providers* and *quality-related concepts*) and define:

(a) *quality control;*

(b) *quality assurance;*

(c) *quality audit.*

2. Summarise the key aspects of total quality management.

3. Read section III (*implications for courses of initial teacher education and training*) and explain the key implications of total quality management for courses of ITET.

4. Describe the documentation available at your school to define the roles and responsibilities of staff involved in mentoring and the procedures which are used in the provision of ITET.

5. State the extent to which the following quality assurance mechanisms are followed at your school in the context of ITET:

(a) *having a co-ordinator to check that students receive the necessary documentation on whole-school policies;*

(b) *having a co-odinator to check that students receive the necessary documentation on departmental or class policies;*

(c) *having a co-ordinator to check that students receive the range of experience outlined in the HEI partnership handbook (e.g. shadowing a form tutor);*

(d) *having a co-ordinator to check that students receive constructive written feedback on observed teaching at least once a week from mentors;*

(e) *having a co-ordinator to observe at least one lesson given by each student for the purposes of moderation;*

(f) *having a co-ordinator to scrutinise mentors' formal lesson evaluations;*

(g) *having a co-ordinator to meet regularly with mentors to discuss students' progress;*

(h) *having a co-ordinator to liaise with mentors and college tutors in cases where students experience difficulties;*

(i) *having a co-ordinator to examine students' professional development profile towards the end of their school experience;*

(j) *having systems of cross-moderation.*

6. Briefly describe any mechanisms in operation at the school for the moderation of standards with respect to ITET.

7. Describe any procedures employed at your school for reviewing the provision made for ITET with reference to the following:

(a) *opportunities for staff to submit comments on the provision made;*

(b) *opportunities for students to comment on the provision made;*

(c) *opportunities for employers to comment on the quality of students;*

(d) *holding regular reviews of the provision made;*

(e) *establishing targets with criteria for success in the planning process;*

(f) *arranging for mentors to attend staff development events with respect to quality control in ITET.*

8. Explain the difference between *VALIDATION* and *ACCREDITATION* in the context of ITET.

9. State any advantages and limitations you can identify in the current system of inspection, the identification of performance indicators and the publication of leagues tables of ITET courses.

10. Read section IV (*observations on quality assurance and ITET*). Summarise and state with reasons your views on the comments made in the text by the following people concerning quality assurance and ITET:

(a) *Sir William Taylor;*

(b) *Geoffrey Whitty;*

(c) *John West-Burnham, et al.;*

(d) *Michael Hammer and James Champy, et al.*

11. Read section V (*research into quality assurance in school-based ITET*). In the light of your reading suggest any ways in which the quality assurance mechanisms at your school may be improved.

12. Design suitable questionnaires concerned with quality control which could be distributed to:

(a) *students on a course of ITET training;*

(b) *newly qualified teachers at the end of their first year of teaching;*

(c) *employers.*

13. TQM is essentially concerned with continuous, incremental change. Re-engineering is a more radical concept. Consider the merits and problems of these two managerial philosophies with reference to ITET.

Bibliography

ABELL S., DILLON D., HOPKIN C., McINERNEY W. & O'BRIEN D. (1995) Somebody to Count On: Mentor/Intern Relationships in a Beginning Teacher Internship Programme, *Teaching and Teacher Education*, 11,2.

ACTON R., KIRKHAM G. & SMITH P. (1992) *Mentoring: A Core Skills Pack*, Crewe and Alsager College of Higher Education.

ADAIR J. (1983) *Effective Time Management*, Penguin.

ADEY K. (1997) First Impressions Do Count: Mentoring Student Teachers, *Teacher Development 1*, 1.

ALEXANDER R. (1990) Partnership in Initial Teacher Education: Confronting the Issues, in: BOOTH M., FURLONG J. & WILKIN M. *Partnership in Initial Teacher Training*, Cassell.

ALLEN D. & RYAN K. (1969) *Micro-Teaching*, Addison-Wesley.

ALLISON G. (1971) *Essence of Decision*, Little, Brown.

ALLSOP T. (1994) The Language of Partnership, in: WILKIN M. & SANKEY D. *Collaboration and Transition in Initial Teacher Training*, Kogan Page.

ANDERSON E. & SHANNON A. (1988) Towards a Conceptualisation of Mentoring, *Journal of Teacher Education*, 39, 1.

ANDERSON E. & SHANNON A. (1995) A Conceptualisation of Mentoring, in: KERRY T. & SHELTON MAYES A. *Issues in Mentoring*, Routledge & Open University Press.

ANDREWS P. (1997) Learning to Teach: Some Perceptions of Trainee Teachers of Mathematics on Working Collaboratively in the Classroom, *Mentoring and Tutoring*, 5, 2.

ARGYRIS C. (1972) *The Applicability of Organisational Sociology*, Cambridge University Press.

ARTHUR J., DAVISON J. & MOSS J. (1997) *Subject Mentoring in the Secondary School*, Routledge.

BACK D. & BOOTH M. (1992) Commitment to Mentoring, in: WILKIN M. *Mentoring in Schools*, Kogan Page.

BAIN J., BALLANTYRE R., PACKER J. & MILLS C. (1999) Using Journal Writing to Enhance Student Teachers' Reflectivity during Field Experience Placement, *Teachers and Teaching: Theory and Practice*, 5, 1.

BAKER C. (2000) Locating Culture in Action: Membership Categorisation in Texts and Talk, in: LEE A. & POYNTON C. *Culture and Text: Discourse and Methodology in Social Research and Cultural Studies*, Allen and Unwin.

BARBER M. (1995) Reconstructing the Teaching Profession, in: BINES H. & WELTON J. *Managing Partnership in Teacher Training and Development*, Routledge

BARKER S., BROOKS V., MARCH K. & SWATTON P. (1994) *Initial Teacher Education in Secondary Schools*, Institute of Education of the University of Warwick.

BARNARD N. (1998) Training Stakes Raised, *The Times Educational Supplement*, 22 May.

BARNARD N. (1999) Teacher Training Agency Survives … *The Times Educational Supplement*, 21 May.

BARTLETT S., BURTON D. & PEIM N. (2001) *An Introduction to Educational Studies*, Paul Chapman.

BELASCO J. & ALUTTO J. (1975) Decisional Participation and Teacher Satisfaction, in: HOUGHTON V., McHUGH R. & MORGAN C. *Management in Education*, Ward Lock Educational in Association with the Open University Press.

BELL A. (1981) Structure, Knowledge and Relationships in Teacher Education, *British Journal of Sociology of Education*, 2, 1.

BIBIK J. (1997) Metaphors for Teaching: How Health and Physical Education Teachers Describe their Roles, ERIC Document Reproduction Service, No. ED412 198.

BINES H. & WELTON J. (1995) Developing and Managing Partnership, in: BINES H. & WELTON J. *Managing Partnership in Teacher Training and Development*, Routledge.

BLACK P. & WILIAM D. (1998) *Inside the Black Box: Raising Standards through Classroom Assessment*, King's College London School of Education.

BLANFORD S. (1998) *Managing Discipline in Schools*, Routledge.

BLANK M. (1998) Mentoring and the Process of Becoming a Teacher, unpublished doctoral dissertation, University of Tennessee, Knoxville.

BLEACH K. (1999) *The Induction and Mentoring of Newly Qualified Teachers: A New Deal for Teachers*, David Fulton.

BLEAKLEY A. (2000) Writing with Invisible Ink: Narrative, Confessionalism and Reflective Practice, *Reflective Practice 1*, 1.

BOLTON G. (2001) *Reflective Practice: Writing and Professional Development*, Paul Chapman.

BOOTH M. (1995) The Effectiveness and Role of the Mentor in School: The Students' View, in: KERRY T. & SHELTON MAYES A. *Issues in Mentoring*, Routledge.

BOOTH M. (2001) Partners in Experience: Developing School Liaison within Initial Teacher Training, *Education Today, 51, 3*.

BOTTERY M. & WRIGHT N. (2000) *Teachers and the State: Towards A Divided Profession*, Routledge.

BOVA B. & PHILLIPS R. (1984) Mentoring as a Learning Experience, *Journal of Higher Education*, 35.

BRAYBROOKE D. & LINDBLOM C. (1970) *A Strategy of Decision,* Free Press.

BRIDGES D., ELLIOTT J. & McKEE A. (1995) *Competence Based Higher Education and the Standards Methodology: Final Report*, University of East Anglia.

BRITISH STANDARDS INSTITUTE (1990) *British Standards Institute Handbook: Quality Assurance*, British Standards Institution.

BROADFOOT P. (1987) *Profiling: A Practical Manual*, Macmillan.

BROOKS V. & LITTLE V. (1995) *'I'm Still Using GRASP®...' Independent Evaluation of the Dudley/Comino GRASP® Project*, University of Warwick.

BROOKS V. & SIKES P. (1997) *The Good Mentor Guide: Initial Teacher Education in Secondary Schools*, Open University Press.

BROWN G. (1975) *Micro-teaching:A Programme of Teaching Skills*, Methuen.

BROWN R. (1970) *The Administrative Process in Britain*, Methuen.

BRYCE J. (1834) cited in: DENT H. (1975) *The Training of Teachers in England and Wales*, Hodder and Stoughton.

BULLOUGH R. & GITLIN A. (1994) Challenging Teacher Education as Training: Four Propositions, *Journal of Education for Teaching*, 20, 1.

BURGESS H. & BUTCHER J. (1999) To Challenge or Not to Challenge: the Mentor's Dilemma, *Mentoring and Tutoring*, 6, 3.

BURN K. (1992) Collaborative Teaching, in: WILKIN M. *Mentoring in Schools*, Kogan Page.

BURN K., HAGGER H., MUTTON T. & EVERTON T. (2000) Beyond Concerns with Self: The Sophisticated Thinking of Beginning Student Teachers, *Journal of Education for Teaching*, 26, 3.

BURT M. (1985) *Pair Teaching in the Training of Teachers*, School of Education, University College of North Wales.

BUSH A. & WEST-BURNHAM J. (1994) *The Principles of Educational Management*, Longman.

BUSHER H. & SARAN R. (1995) *Managing Teachers as Professionals in Schools*, Kogan Page.

CALDERHEAD J. & GATES P. (1993) *Conceptualising Reflection in Teacher Development*, Falmer Press.

CALDERHEAD J. & SHORROCK S. (1997) *Understanding Teacher Education*, Falmer Press.

CANTER L. & CANTER M. (1977) *Assertive Discipline: Positive Behaviour Management for Today's Schools*, Lee Canter Associates.

CAPEL S., LEASK M. & TURNER A. (1999) *Learning to Teach in the Secondary School*, Routledge

CARMIN C. (1988) Issues in Research in Mentoring: Definitional and Methodological, *International Journal of Mentoring*, 2, 2.

CARNER S. & HAGGER H. (1996) Working with Beginning Teachers: The Impact on Schools, in: McINTYRE D. & HAGGER H. *Mentors in Schools: Developing the Profession of Teaching*, David Fulton.

CARR W. (1992) Four Dimensions of Educational Professionalism, *Westminster Studies in Education*, 15, 1.

CARR W. & HARTNETT A. (1996) *Education and the Struggle for Democracy: Politics of Educational Ideas,* Open University Press.

CARR W. & KEMMIS S. (1986) *Becoming Critical: Education, Knowledge and Action Research*, Falmer Press.

CATT R. & SWEENEY T. (1995) Student Voices: 'A Lot of Theory Jammed into their Brain?' in FISH D. *Quality Learning for Student Teachers: University Teachers' Educational Practices*, David Fulton.

CHAPLAIN R. (1998) *Developing Effective Discipline: A Practical Guide for Schools*, Pearson.

CHARLTON A. & DAVID K. (1989) *Managing Misbehaviour in Schools*, Macmillan.

CHOWN A. & LAST J. (1993) Can the NVQ Model Be Used for Teacher Training? *Journal of Further and Higher Education*, 17,2.

CLIFTON R., MADZUK D. & ROBERTS L. (1994) The Alienation of Undergraduate Students: A Case Study of a Canadian University, *Journal of Education for Teaching*, 20, 2.

COMMITTEE ON HIGHER EDUCATION (1963) *Higher Education: The Report of the Committee Appointed by the Prime Minister under the Chairmanship of Lord Robbins* 1961-63, HMSO.

CONNERY A. (2001) A Teacher's Response to 'Reflection-in-Action', in: SOLER J., CRAFT A. & BURGESS H. *Teacher Development: Exploring*

Our Own Practice, Paul Chapman and Open University Press.

CORBETT P. & WRIGHT D. (1994) Issues in the Selection and Training of Mentors for School-Based Primary Initial Teacher Training, in: McINTYRE D., HAGGER H. & WILKIN M. *Mentoring Perspectives on School-Based Teacher Education*, Kogan Page.

COUNCIL FOR NATIONAL ACADEMIC AWARDS (CNAA) (1992) *Profiling in Higher Education: Guidelines for the Development and Use of Profiling Schemes*, CNAA.

COWLEY S. (1999) *Starting Teaching: How to Succeed and Survive*, Cassell.

COWLEY S. (2001) *Getting the Buggers to Behave*, Continuum.

CROSBY P. (1985) *Quality Without Tears: The Art of Hassle-Free Management*, New American Library.

CROSS R. (1995) The Role of the Mentor in Utilising the Support System for the Newly Qualified Teacher, *School Organisation*, 15.

CROSS R. (1999) What Time Constraints Face the Junior School Teacher Taking on the Role of Student Mentor? *Mentoring and Tutoring*, 7, 1.

DAFT R. (2001) *Organisation Theory and Design*, South Western College Publishing.

DART L. & DRAKE P. (1996) Subject Perspective in Mentoring, in: McINTYRE D. & HAGGER H. *Mentors in Schools: Developing the Profession of Teaching*, David Fulton.

DAVIES B. (1994) TQM: A Theory Whose Time Has Come and Gone, *Management in Education*, 8, 1.

DAVIES B. & WEST-BURNHAM J. (1997) *Re-engineering and Total Quality in Schools: How to Reform and Restructure*, Pitman.

DAVIES I. (1993) Using Profiling in Initial Teacher Education, *Journal of Further and Higher Education*, 17, 2.

DAVIES R. & FERGUSON J. (1997) Teachers' Views of the Role of Initial Teacher Education in Developing their Professionalism, *Journal of Education for Teaching*, 23, 1.

DEAN J. (1996) *Beginning Teaching in the Secondary School*, Open University Press.

DEMAINE J. (1999) *Education Policy and Contemporary Politics*, Macmillan.

DEMING W. (1982) *Out of the Crisis: Quality, Productivity and Competitive Position*, Cambridge University Press.

DEPARTMENT FOR EDUCATION (DFE) (1992) *Initial Teacher Training (Secondary Phase)*, Circular 9/92, DFE.

DFE (1993a) *The Government's Proposals for the Reform of Initial Teacher Training*, DFE.

DFE (1993b) *The Initial Training of Primary School Teachers: New Criteria for Courses*, Circular 14/93, DFE.

DEPARTMENT FOR EDUCATION AND EMPLOYMENT (DFEE) (1997a) *Excellence for All Children: Meeting SEN*, DFEE.

DFEE (1997b) *Excellence in Schools*, DFEE.

DFEE (1997c) *Teaching: High Status, High Standards: Requirements for Courses of Initial Teacher Training*, DFEE.

DFEE (1998a) *Teachers: Meeting the Challenge of Change*, DFEE.

DFEE (1998b) *Teaching: High Status, High Standards: Requirements for Courses of Initial Teacher Training*, Circular 4/98, DFEE, 1998.

DFEE (2000a) *Expanding Employment-Based Routes into Teaching: A Consultative Document*, (DFEE).

DFEE (2000b) *Professional Development: Support for Teaching and Learning*, DFEE.

DFEE (2001a) *Learning and Teaching: A Strategy for Professional Development*, DFEE.

DFEE (2001b) *Schools Building on Success*, The Stationery Office.

DEPARTMENT FOR EDUCATION AND SKILLS (DFES) (2001a) *Schools Achieving Success*, The Stationery Office.

DFES (2001b) *The Induction Period for Newly Qualified Teachers*, Guidance Document 582/2001, DFEE.

DFES & TEACHER TRAINING AGENCY (TTA) (2002) *Qualifying to Teach: Professional Standards for Qualified Teacher Status and Requirements for Initial Teacher Training*, DFES-TTA.

DEPARTMENT OF EDUCATION AND SCIENCE (DES) (1972) *Teacher Education and Training: A Report by a Committee of Inquiry Appointed by the Secretary of State for Education and Science, under the Chairmanship of Lord James of Rusholme*, HMSO.

DES (1983) *Teaching Quality*, HMSO.

DES (1984) *Initial Teacher Training: Approval of Courses*, Circular 3/84, DES.

DES (1985) *Better Schools*, HMSO.

DES (1989a) *Initial Teacher Training: Approval of Course*, Circular 24/98, DES

DES (1989b) *The Education (Teachers) Regulations*, HMSO.

DEVLIN L. (1995) The Mentor, in: GLOVER, D. and MARDLE G. *The Management of Mentoring: Policy Issues*, Kogan Page.

DOCKING J. (1987) *Control and Discipline in Schools: Perspectives and Approaches*, Paul Chapman.

DODGSON J. (1986) Do Women in Education Need Mentors? *Education Canada*, Spring.

DOWNIE R. (1990) Professions and Professionalism, *Journal of Philosophy of Education*, 24, 2.

DREVER E. & COPE P. (1999) Students' Use of Theory in an Initial Teacher Education Programme, *Journal of Education for Teaching*, 25, 2.

DRUCKER P. (1964) *Managing for Results*, Harper and Row.

DRUCKER P. (1966) *The Effective Executive*, Harper and Row.

EARLEY P. (1996) Competence Frameworks and Profiles for NQTs, in: HUSTLER D. & McINTYRE D. *Developing Competent Teachers*, David Fulton.

EBEL R. & FRISBIE D. (1991) *Essentials of Educational Measurement*, Prentice Hall.

EDWARDS A. & COLLISON J. (1996) *Mentoring and Developing Practice in Primary Schools*, Open University Press.

ELLIOTT B. & CALDERHEAD J. (1995) Mentoring for Teacher Development: Possibilities and Caveats, in: KERRY T. & SHELTON MAYES A. *Issues in Mentoring*, Routledge.

ELLIOTT J. (1991) A Model of Professionalism and Its Implications for Teacher Education, *British Educational Research Journal*, 17, 4.

EMMISON M. & SMITH P. (2000) *Researching the Visual*, Sage.

ERAUT M. (1989) Initial Teacher Training and the NCVQ Model, in: BURKE J. *Competency-Based Education and Training*, Falmer Press.

ERAUT M. (1994) The Acquisition and Use of Educational Theory by Beginning Teachers, in: HARVARD G. & HODKINSON P. *Action and Reflection in Teacher Education*, Ablex.

EVANS L. & ABBOTT I. (1997) Developing as Mentors in School-Based Teacher Training, *Teacher Development*, 1, 1.

FAGAN M. & WALTERS G. (1982) Mentoring Among Teachers, *Journal of Educational Research*, 76, 2.

FEIMAN-NEMSER, S. & BUCHMANN, M. (1985) Pitfalls of Experience in Teacher Preparation, *Teachers College Record*, 81.

FIDLER B. & LOCK N. (1994) Mentorship and Whole-School Development, in: McCULLOGH M. & FIDLER B. *Improving Initial Teacher Training?* Longman.

FIELD B. (1994a) New Role of Teaching – Mentoring, in: FIELD B. & FIELD T. *Teachers as Mentors: A Practical Guide*, Falmer Press.

FIELD B. (1994b) The Past Role of the Teacher – Supervision as Socialisation, in: FIELD B. & FIELD T. *Teachers as Mentors: A Practical Guide*, Falmer Press.

FISH D. (1995a) *Quality Learning for Student Teachers: University Tutors' Educational Practices*, David Fulton.

FISH D. (1995b) *Quality Mentoring for Student Teachers: A Principled Approach to Practice*, David Fulton.

FISH D., TWINN S. & PURR B. (1991) *Promoting Reflection: Improving the Supervision of Practice in Health Visiting and Initial Teacher Training*, West London Institute.

FITZ J., DAVIES B. & EVANS J. (2001) *Educational Policy and Social Reproduction*, Routledge Falmer Press.

FOLLETT M. (1941) Constructive Conflict, in: METCALF H. & URWICK L. *Dynamic Administration*, Pitman.

FOSTER R. (2001) *The Graduate Teacher Route to QTS: Motorway, By-Way or By-Pass?* Paper delivered at the British Educational Research Association Conference.

FRANCIS D. (1990) *Effective Problem Solving: A Strategic Approach*, Routledge.

FRANCIS P. (2001) *The Best Policy? Honesty in Education 1997-2001*, Liberty Books.

FREEMAN R. & LEWIS R. (1998) *Planning and Implementing Assessment*, Open University Press.

FREIRE P. (1972) *Pedagogy of the Oppressed*, Penguin.

FROMM E. (1955) *The Sane Society*, Rinehart.

FULLAN M. (1993) *Change Forces: Probing the Depths of Educational Reform*, Falmer Press.

FURLONG J. (1990) School-Based Training: the Students' Views, in: BOOTH M., FURLONG J. & WILKIN M. *Partnership in Initial Teacher Training*, Croom Helm.

FURLONG J. (1995) The Limits of Competence: A Cautionary Note on Circular 9/92, in: KERRY T. & SHELTON MAYES A. *Issues in Mentoring*, Routledge/Open University.

FURLONG J., BARTON L., MILES S., WHITING C. & WHITTY G. (2000) *Teacher Education in Transition: Reforming Professionalism?* Open University Press.

FURLONG V.J., HIRST P., POCKLINGTON K. & MILES S. (1988) *Initial Teacher Training and the Role of the School*, Open University Press.

FURLONG J. & MAYNARD T. (1995) *Mentoring Student Teachers: The Growth of Professional Development*, Routledge.

GARDINER J. & BARNARD N. (1997) Agency Shuts Training College, *The Times Educational Supplement*, 2 May.

GARLAND P. (1994) Using Competence-Based Assessment Positively on Certificate in Education Programmes, J*ournal of Further and Higher Education*, 18, 4-5.

GARNER P. (1997) In-Service Teachers' Use of Graphical Accounts to Illustrate Aspects of their Teaching in Special Needs Education, *Teacher Development*, 1.

GAY B. & STEPHENSON J. (1998) The Mentoring Dilemma: Guidance and/or Direction? *Mentoring and Tutoring*, 6, 12.

GEEN A. (1985) Team Teaching in the Secondary Schools of England and Wales, *Educational Review*, 37, 1.

GEEN A. (2001a) Debriefing Students: Improving Current Practice, *Teacher Development*,. 5, 1.

GEEN A. (2001b) *Effective Teaching for the Twenty-First Century: Priorities in Secondary Education*, UWIC Press.

GEEN A. (2001c) The Selection and Training of Secondary School Mentors, *Education Today*, 51, 3.

GEEN A., BASSETT P., DAVIES J. & DOUGLAS L. (1998) The Concept of Partnership in Initial Teacher Education: Perceptions of UWIC Students, *Concord*, 8, 1.

GEEN A., BASSETT P. & DOUGLAS L. (1998) Developing Partnership in Initial Teacher Education: The Role of the Senior Mentor, *The Welsh Journal of Education*, 7/1.

GEEN A., BASSETT P. & DOUGLAS L. (1999a) Quality Assurance in School-Based Initial Teacher Education, *Education Today*, 49, 2.

GEEN A., BASSETT P. & DOUGLAS L. (1999b) The Role of the Secondary School Subject Mentor: An Evaluation of the UWIC Experience, *Mentoring and Tutoring*, 7, 1.

GEEN A., BASSETT P. & DOUGLAS L. (2000) Benefits and Costs: The Impact of Partnership in Initial Teacher Education upon Secondary Schools in South-East Wales, *The Welsh Journal of Education*, 9, 2.

GEEN A., BASSETT P. & DOUGLAS L. (2001) Preparing Student-Teachers to Assess Pupils' Achievements, *Westminster Studies in Education*, 24, 1.

GEEN A. & HARRIS C. (2002) Collaborative Teaching, *UWIC Education Papers: The Research Journal of the Cardiff School of Education*, 1.

GEEN A. & HUTT R. (2000) 'QED': Assessing and Profiling Food and Textiles Students in Initial Teacher Education, *The Data Journal*, 5, 3.

GHAYE A. & GHAYE K. (1998) *Teaching and Learning Through Critical Reflective Practice*, David Fulton.

GIFFORD S. (1995) Surrey New Teacher Competency Project, in: KERRY T. & SHELTON MAYES A. *Issues in Mentoring*, Routledge/Open University.

GILROY P. (1993) Reflection on Schon: Epistemological Critique and a Practical Alternative, in: GILROY P. & SMITH M. *International Analyses of Teacher Education*, Carfax.

GIPPS C. (1994) *Beyond Testing: Towards a Theory of Educational Assessment*, Kogan Page.

GLASS G. (1978) Standards and Criteria , *Journal of Educational Measurement* 15, 4.

GLENNY G. & HICKLING E. (1995) A Developmental Model of Partnership, in: BINES H. & WELTON J. *Managing Partnership in Teacher Training and Development*, Routledge.

GLOVER C. (1996a) Paired Teaching Practice: Maximising or Inhihibiting Learning Opportunities? *Westminster Studies in Education*, 19.

GLOVER C. (1996b) The Development of Peer Support by a 'Buddy System' in PGCE Technology Teaching, *Westminster Studies in Education*, 19.

GLOVER D. & MARDLE G. (1995) *The Management of Mentoring: Policy Issues*, Kogan Page.

GLOVER D. & MARDLE G. (1996) Issues in the Management of Mentoring, in: McINTYRE D. & HAGGER H. *Mentors in Schools: Developing the Profession of Teaching*, David Fulton.

GOODFELLOW J. (2000) Knowing from the Inside: Reflective Conversations with and through the Narratives of One Co-operating Teacher, *Reflective Practice*, 1, 1.

GORE C., MURRAY K. & RICHARDSON W. (1992) *Strategic Decision Making*, Cassell.

GORE J. (1987) Reflecting on Reflective Teaching, *Journal of Teacher Education*, 37, 3.

GOULD S. (1991) *Bully for Brontosaurus: Reflection in Natural History*, Norton.

GRAY J. & RICHER J. (1988) *Classroom Responses to Disruptive Behaviour*, Macmillan.

GRIFFITHS V. & OWEN P. (1995) *Schools in Partnership*, Paul Chapman.

GROSSMAN P. (1992) In Pursuit of a Dual Agenda: Creating a Middle Level Professional

Development School, in: DARLING-HAMMOND L. *Professional Development Schools: Schools for Developing a Profession*, Teachers College Press.

HAGGER H., BURN K. & McINTYRE D. (1993) *The School Mentor Handbook*, Kogan Page.

HALLIDAY J. (1996) *Back to Good Teaching: Diversity Within Tradition*, Cassell.

HAMILTON M.L. (1998) *Reconceptualizing Teaching Practice: Self-Study in Teacher Education*, Falmer Press.

HAMMER M. & CHAMPY J. (1993) *Re-engineering the Corporation*, Harper Collins.

HAMMER M. & STANTON S. (1995) *The Re-engineering Revolution: the Handbook*, Harper Collins.

HARGREAVES D. (1990) Another Radical Approach to the Reform of Initial Teacher Training, *Westminster Studies in Education*, 13.

HARRIS A. (1999) *Teaching and Learning in the Effective School*, Ashgate.

HARRIS A. (1975) Decisions, Decisions ..., in: DOBSON L., GEAR A. & WESTOBY A. *Management in Education*, Ward Lock in association with the Open University.

HAY McBER (2000) *Research into Teacher Effectiveness: A Model of Teacher Effectiveness*, DFEE.

HAYES D. (1999) A Matter of Being Willing? Mentors' Expectations of Student Primary Teachers, *Mentoring and Tutoring*, 7, 1.

HAYES D. (2001) The Impact of Mentoring and Tutoring on Student Primary Teachers' Achievements: A Case Study, *Mentoring and Tutoring*, 9, 1.

HEALEY C. & WELCHERT A. (1990) Mentoring Relations: A Definition to Advance Research and Practice, *Educational Researcher*, 19.

HELSBY G. (1996) Defining and Developing Professionalism in English Secondary Schools, *Journal of Education for Teaching*, 22, 2.

HER MAJESTY'S INSPECTORATE (HMI) (1979) *Developments in BEd Degree Courses: A Study Based on Fifteen Institutions*, HMSO.

HMI (1987) *The New Teacher at School: A Survey of HM Inspectors in England and Wales*, HMSO.

HMI (1993) *The New Teacher at School: A Survey in England and Wales*, HMSO.

HERZBERG F. (1966) *Work and the Nature of Man*, World Publishing Company.

HEXTALL I., LAWN M., MENTER I., SIDGWICK S. & WALKER S. (1991) *Imaginative Projects: Arguments for a New Teacher Education*,

Goldsmiths' College.

HIGHER EDUCATION FUNDING COUNCIL FOR WALES (HEFCW) (2000) *Initial Teacher Training Partnership Initiatives 1998- 1999 Abstracts*, HEFCW.

HILLGATE GROUP (1989) *Learning to Teach*, Claridge Press in association with the Educational Research Centre.

HIRST P. (1996) The Demands of a Professional Practice and Preparation for Teaching, in: FURLONG J., & SMITH R. *The Role of Higher Education in Initial Teacher Training*, Kogan Page.

HITCHCOCK G. (1990) *Profiles and Profiling: A Practical Introduction*, Longman.

HOLLY M. (1989) *Writing to Grow: Keeping a Personal-Professional Journal*, Heinemann.

HOPKINS D. & REID K. (1985) *Rethinking Teacher Education*, Croom Helm.

HUSBANDS C. (1993) Profiling of Student Teachers: Context, Ownership and the Beginnings of Professional Learning, in: BRIDGES D. & KERRY T. (1993) *Developing Teachers Professionally*, Routledge.

HUSTLER D. & McINTYRE D. (1996) *Developing Competent Teachers*, David Fulton.

HUTCHINSON D. (1994) Competence-Based Profiles for Initial Teacher Training and Induction: The Place of Reflection, *British Journal of Inservice Education*, 20, 3.

HYATT D. & BEIGY A. (1999) Making the Most of the Unknown Language Experience: Pathways for Reflective Teacher Development, *Journal of Education for Teaching*, 25, 1.

HYLAND T. (1993) Training, Competence and Expertise in Teacher Education, *Journal of Teacher Development*, 2.

JACQUES K. (1992) Mentoring in Initial Teacher Education, *Cambridge Journal of Education*, 22, 3.

JEFFREYS D. (1975) How Psychology Fails the Teacher, *British Journal of Teacher Education*, 1.

JOHNSON G. (2001a) Accounting for Pre-Service Teachers' Use of Visual Metaphor in Narratives, *Teacher Development*, 5, 1.

JOHNSON G. (2001b) Teacher Reflection Narrative: A Post-Structural Approach, *Journal of Education for Teaching*, 27, 2.

JONES L., REID D. & BEVINS S. (1997) Teachers' Perceptions of Mentoring in a Collaborative Model of Initial Teacher Training, *Journal of Education for Teaching*, 23, 3.

JONES M. (2000) Trainee Teachers' Perceptions of

School-Based Training in England and Germany with Regard to their Preparation for Teaching, Mentor Support and Assessment, *Mentoring and Tutoring*, 8, 1.

JONES M. (2001) Mentors' Perceptions of their Roles in School-Based Teacher Training in England and Germany, *Journal of Education for Teaching*, 27, 1.

JURAN J. (1989) *Juran on Leadership for Quality*, Collier Macmillan.

KAST F. & ROSENZWEIG J. (1985) *Organisation and Management: A Systems and Contingency Approach*, McGraw-Hill.

KENNEDY J. (1982) Metaphors in Pictures, *Perceptions*, 11.

KENNEDY J., GREEN C. & VERAEKE J. (1993) Metaphoric Thought and Devices in Pictures, *Metaphor and Symbolic Activity*, 8.

KERRY T. & SHELTON MAYES A. (1995) *Issues in Mentoring*, Routledge/Open University.

KORNHAUSER A., DUBIN R. & ROSS A. (1954) *Industrial Conflict*, McGraw-Hill.

KORTHAGEN F. (1993) The Role of Reflection in Teachers' Professional Development, in: KREMER-HAYON L., VONK H. & FESSLER R. *Teachers' Professional Development: A Multiple Perspective Approach*, Swets and Zeitlinger.

KYDD L. & WEIR D. (1993) Initial Teacher Training: The Professional Route to Technician Status, *British Journal of Educational Studies*, 41, 3.

LABOSKEY V. (1993) A Conceptual Framework for Reflection in Pre-service Teacher Education, in: J. CALDERHEAD & P. GATES *Conceptualising Reflection in Teacher Development*, Falmer Press.

LAVE J. & WENGER E. (1991) *Situated Learning: Legitimate Peripheral Participation*, Cambridge University Press.

LAWLER E. (1993) *The Ultimate Advantage: Creating the High Involvement Organisation*, Jossey-Bass.

LAWLOR S. (1990) *Teachers Mistaught: Training in Theories or Education in Subjects*, Centre for Policy Studies.

LAZARUS E. (2000) The Role of Intuition in Mentoring and Supporting Beginning Teachers, in: ATKINSON T. & CLAXTON G. *The Intuitive Practitioner*, Open University Press.

LEAT D. (1995) The Cost of Reflection, *Cambridge Journal of Education*, 25, 2.

LEWIN K. (1935) *A Dynamic Theory of Personality*, McGraw-Hill.

LIMM P. (1991) The Professional Craft Knowledge of the History Teacher, *History Teaching*, June.

LINDBLOM C. (1968) *The Policy-Making Process*, Prentice-Hall.

LOCAL EDUCATION AUTHORITIES IN ASSOCIATION WITH HIGHER EDUCATION INSTITUTIONS (1993a) *Developing Teaching Skills: Primary*, LEAP Consortium.

LOCAL EDUCATION AUTHORITIES IN ASSOCIATION WITH HIGHER EDUCATION INSTITUTIONS (1993b) *Developing Teaching Skills: Secondary*, LEAP Consortium.

LOCKE E. & LATHAM G. (1990) Work Motivation: The High Performance Cycle, in: KLEINBECK U., QUAST H. & HACKER H. *Work Motivation*, Lawrence Erlbaum.

LODER C. (1995) Turmoil in Success, *Quality Assurance and Accountability in Higher Education*, 1. 1.

LOUGHRAN J. (1996) *Developing Reflective Practice: Learning about Teaching and Learning Through Modelling*, Falmer Press.

LOUGHRAN J. & NORTHFIELD J. (1998) A Framework for the Development of Self-study Practice, in: M. HAMILTON *Reconceptualising Teaching Practice: Self-study in Teacher Education*, Falmer Press.

LOUGHRAN J. & RUSSELL T. (1997) Meeting Student Teachers on Their Own Terms: Experience Precedes Understanding, in: RICHARDSON V. *Constructivist Teacher Education: Building New Understandings*, Falmer Press.

LOWE T. & POLLARD I. (1989) Negotiation Skills, in: RICHES C. & MORGAN C. *Human Resource Management*, Open University Press.

LUND R. (1996) *A Whole School Behaviour Policy*, Kogan Page.

LUTHANS F. (1989) *Organisational Behaviour*, McGraw-Hill.

McCULLOGH M. (1994) Teacher Competences and their Assessment, in: McCULLOGH M. & FIDLER B. *Improving Teacher Training?* Longman.

McDIAMID (1993) Changes in Beliefs about Learners among Participants in Eleven Teacher Education Programmes, in: CALDERHEAD J. & GATES P. *Conceptualising Reflection in Teacher Development*, Falmer Press.

MacGRATH M. (1998) *The Art of Teaching Peacefully*, David Fulton.

McGUINESS J. (1993) *Teachers, Pupils and Behaviour: A Managerial Approach*, Cassell.

MacGUIRE M., DILLON J. & QUINTRELL M. (1998) *Finding Virtue, Not Finding Fault: Stealing the*

Wind of Destructive Reforms, Association of Teachers and Lecturers.

McINTYRE D. (1988) Designing a Teacher Education Curriculum, in: CALDERHEAD J. *Teachers' Professional Learning*, Falmer Press.

McINTYRE D. (1989) Criterion-Referenced Assessment of Teaching, in: SIMONS H. & ELLIOTT J. *Rethinking Appraisal and Assessment*, Open University Press.

McINTYRE D. (1994) Classrooms as Learning Environments for Beginning Teachers, in: WILKIN M. & SANKEY D. *Collaboration and Transition in Initial Teacher Training*, Kogan Page.

McINTYRE D. & HAGGER H. (1996) *Mentors in Schools: Developing the Profession of Teaching*, David Fulton.

McINTYRE D., HAGGER H. & BURN K. (1994) *The Management of Student Teachers' Learning: A Guide for Professional Tutors in Secondary School*, Kogan Page.

McINTYRE D., HAGGER H. & WILKIN M. (1993) *Mentoring: Perspectives on School-Based Teacher Education*, Kogan Page.

McLAUGHLIN T. (1994) Mentoring and the Demands of Reflection, In: WILKIN M. & SANKEY D. *Collaboration and Transition in Initial Teacher Education*, Kogan Page.

McNIFF J. (2002) *Action Research: Principles and Practice*, Routledge-Falmer.

McPHILLIMY W. (1996) *Controlling Your Class: A Teacher's Guide to Managing Classroom Behaviour*, Wiley.

MAHONEY P. & HARRIS V. (1996) Profiling in Practice: The Goldsmiths' Experience, in: HUSTLER D. & McINTYRE D. *Developing Competent Teachers*, David Fulton.

MARCH J. & SIMON H. (1958) *Organisations*, Wiley.

MARTIN S. (1994) The Mentoring Process in Pre-Service Teacher Education, *School Organisation*, 14.

MASLOW A. (1954) *Motivation and Personality*, Harper.

MAYNARD T. (2000) Learning to Teach or Learning to Manage Mentors? Experiences of School-Based Teacher Training, *Mentoring and Tutoring*, 8, 1.

MAYNARD T. & FURLONG J. (1995) Learning to Teach and Models of Mentoring, in: KERRY T. & SHELTON MAYES A. *Issues in Mentoring*, Routledge and Open University Press.

MEHRABIAN A. (1971) *Silent Messages*, Wadsworth.

MERCER D. & ABBOTT T. (1989) Democratic Learning in Teacher Education: Partnership Supervision in the Teaching Practice, *Journal of Education for Teaching*, 15, 2.

MESSICK S. (1984) The Psychology of Educational Measurement, *The Journal of Educational Measurement*, 21.

MINISTRY OF EDUCATION (1951) *Education 1900 – 1950*, HMSO

MONDY R., SHARLIN A. & FLIPPO E. (1988) *Management Concepts and Practices*, Allyn and Bacon.

MOYLES J., SUSCHITZKY W. & CHAPMAN L. (1998) *Teaching Fledglings to Fly…? Mentoring and Support Systems in Primary Schools*, Association of Teachers and Lecturers.

MULHOLLAND J. (1991) *The Language of Negotiation: A Handbook of Practical Strategies for Improving Communication*, Cassell.

MULLAN C. & LICK D. (1999) *New Directions in Mentoring*, Falmer Press.

MUNRO-FAURE L. & MUNRO-FAURE M. (1992) *Implementing Total Quality Management*, Pitman.

MURRAY M. with OWEN M. (1991) *Beyond the Myth and Magic of Mentoring*, Jossey-Bass.

NATIONAL ASSEMBLY FOR WALES (NAW) (2001) *The Learning Country: A Comprehensive Education and Lifelong Learning Programme to 2010 in Wales*, NAW.

NATIONAL COMMISSION OF INQUIRY INTO HIGHER EDUCATION (1997) *Higher Education in the Learning Society*, Report No. 10 *Teacher Education and Training*, HMSO.

NELSON-JONES R. (1993) *Practical Counselling and Helping Skills*, Cassell.

NEWBY M. (1999a) Never Mind Ticks, Go for Quality, *The Times Educational Supplement*, 10 December.

NEWBY M. (1999b) *New Investment in Higher Education is Vital for the Knowledge Economy*, Keynote Address at CVCP Annual Residential Meeting.

NEWMAN S. (1996) Reflection and Teacher Education, *Journal of Education for Teaching*, 22, 3.

NICHOLLS G. (1999) *Learning to Teach: A Handbook for Primary and Secondary School Teachers*, Kogan Page.

NORRIS N. (1991) The Trouble with Competence, *Cambridge Journal of Education*, 21, 3.

OFFICE FOR STANDARDS IN EDUCATION (OFSTED) (2002) *The Graduate Teacher Programme*, OFSTED.

OFFICE OF HER MAJESTY'S CHIEF INSPECTOR (OHMCI)

(1997) *Assessment, Recording and Reporting in Key Stage 3 and Key Stage 4*, OHMCI.

OHMCI (1998a) *Framework for the Assessment of Quality and Standards in Initial Teacher Training*, OMHCI.

OHMCI (1998b) *Improving Standards and Quality in Secondary Schools*, OHMCI.

OHMCI (1998c) *Mentoring in Initial Teacher Training: Secondary Phase: A Good Practice Document*, OHMCI.

O'HEAR A. (1988) *Who Teaches the Teachers?* Social Affairs Unit, Research Report 10.

O'HOLLIGAN C. (1997) Theory in Initial Teacher Education: Students' Perceptions on its Utility – A Case Study, *British Educational Research Journal*, 23, 4.

OLIVERO J. (1970) *Micro-teaching: Medium for Improving Instruction*, C.E. Merrill.

OLSEN J. & COOPER P. (2001) *Dealing With Disruptive Students*, Kogan Page.

O'NEILL J. (2000) *Primary Curriculum Project: Art and Design, Science in Action, Schools of Education*, University of Wales Institute, Cardiff.

PASSMORE B. & LEPKOWSKA, D. (1997) No-one Forgets a Good Teacher, *The Times Educational Supplement*, 17 October.

PATRICK H., BERNBAUM G. & REID K. (1982) *The Structure and Process of Initial Teacher Education within Universities in England and Wales*, Leicester School of Education.

PEASE A. (1991) *Body Language*, Camel Publishing.

PENDRY A. & McINTYRE D. (1996) Trying to Make Profiling Useful for Teacher Education: The Oxford Experience, in: HUSTLER D. & McINTYRE D. *Developing Competent Teachers*, David Fulton.

PENNINGTON R. & GOODERHAM D. (1987) *Negotiation in Schools*, Department of Management Studies, Flatts Lane Centre

PETTY G. (1995) *Teaching Today*, Stanley Thornes.

PORTER L. (2000) *Behaviour in Schools: Theory and Practice for Teachers*, Open University Press.

POWNEY J., EDWARDS S., HOLROYD C. & MARTIN S. (1993) *Monitoring the Pilots: Moray House Institute PGCE (Secondary)*, Scottish Council for Research in Education.

PRICE C. (1994) A New *Vice Anglaise, The Times Educational Supplement*, 14 January.

PRING R. (1984) *Personal and Social Education in the Curriculum: Concepts and Content*, Hodder and Stoughton.

PULTORAK E. (1993) Facilitating Reflective Thought

in Novice Teachers, *Journal of Teacher Education*, 44.

RAFFERTY F. (1998) Sharp Talk Ahead of Third Lords Defeat, *The Times Educational Supplement*, 13 March.

RECORDS OF ACHIEVEMENT NATIONAL STEERING COMMITTEE (1989) *Records of Achievement*, DES and Welsh Office.

REVELL P. (1998) Take A Close Look, *The Times Educational Supplement*, 1 May.

RICHARDS C. (1999) Ethical Primary Policy, *The Times Educational Supplement*, 26 November.

RICHARDS J. (1998) Turning to the Artistic: Developing an Enlightened Eye by Creating Teaching Self-portraits, in: M. HAMILTON *Reconceptualising Teaching Practice: Self-study in Teacher Education*, Falmer Press.

RICHARDS J. & LOCKHART C. (1994) *Reflective Teaching in Second Language Classrooms*, Cambridge University Press.

ROBBINS S. (2001) *Management*, Prentice Hall.

ROBERTSON J. (1989) *Effective Classroom Control*, Hodder and Stoughton.

ROBINSON C. (1994) *An Evaluation of the University of Nottingham PGCE Partnership Scheme: Its First Year of Operation*, 1993-94, University of Nottingham School of Education.

ROGERS C. & ROETHLISBERGER F. (1952) Barriers and Gateways to Communication, *Harvard Business Review*, 30.

ROGERS E. (1997) *History of Communication Study*, Free Press.

ROGERS W. (2000) *Behaviour Management: A Whole School Approach*, Paul Chapman.

ROSAEN C. & SCHRAM P. (1998) Becoming a Member of the Teaching Profession: Learning a Language of Possibility, *Teaching and Teacher Education*, 14.

ROSS E. (1992) Teacher Personal Theorising and Reflective Practice in Teacher Education, in: ROSS E., CORNETT J. & McCUTCHEON G. *Teacher Personal Theorising*, State University of New York.

ROTH R. (1999) *The Role of the University in the Preparation of Teachers*, Falmer Press.

RUSSELL T. (1989) Documenting Reflection-in-Action in the Classroom: Searching for Appropriate Methods, *Qualitative Studies in Education*, 2, 4.

SALLIS J. (1996) *Total Quality Management in Education*, Kogan Page.

SALMONS Y. (1997) The Classroom Aide Paired

Placement in Initial Teacher Education, *Mentoring and Tutoring*, 5, 2.

SAMMONS P., HILLMAN J. & MORTIMORE P. (1995) *Key Characteristics of Effective Schools: A Review of School Effectiveness*, OFSTED.

SCHERMERHORN J., HUNT J. & OSBORN J. (1991) *Managing Organisational Behaviour*, Wiley.

SCHMIDT J. & WOLFE J. (1980) The Mentor Partnership: Discovery of Professionalism, *National Association of Secondary School Principals' Journal*, 17.

SCHMUCK R. (1985) *The Handbook of Organisation Development in Schools*, Mayfield.

SCHON, D. (1983) *The Reflective Practitioner*, Basic Books

SCHON, D. (1987) *Educating the Reflective Practitioner: Towards A New Design for Teaching and Learning in the Professions*, Jossey-Bass.

SCOTT W. (1967) *Organisation Theory*, Irwin.

SERGIOVANNI T. (1969) Factors which Affect Satisfaction and Dissatisfaction of Teachers, in: CARVER F. & SERGIOVANNI T. *Organisations and Human Behaviour: Focus on Schools*, McGraw Hill.

SHAW R. (1995) *Teacher Training in Secondary Schools*, Kogan Page.

SIMON H. (1947) *Administrative Behaviour*, Macmillan.

SIXSMITH C. & SIMCO N. (1997) The Role of Formal and Informal Theory in the Training of Student Teachers, *Mentoring and Tutoring*, 5/1.

SKRTIC T. & WARE L. (1992) Reflective Teaching and the Problem of School Organisation, in: ROSS E., CORNETT J. & McCUTCHEON G. *Teacher Personal Theorising*, State University of New York.

SMALLWOOD R. (1997) *Initial Teacher Training Handbook: St Cenydd School Partnership with University of Wales, Swansea, University of Wales Institute, Cardiff, University of Wales College, Newport and the Open University.*

SMITH C. & LASLETT R. (1993) *Effective Classroom Management: A Teacher's Guide*, Routledge.

SMITH R. (1992) Theory: An Entitlement to Understanding, *Cambridge Journal of Education*, 22.

SNYDER R. & PAIGE G. (1958) The United States' Decision to Resist Aggression in Korea: The Application of an Analytic Scheme, *Administrative Quarterly*, 3.

STENGELHOFEN J. (1993) *Teaching Students in Clinical Settings*, Chapman and Hall.

STEPHENS P. (1996) *Essential Mentoring Skills: A Practical Handbook for School-Based Teacher Educators*, Stanley Thornes.

STERNBERG R. & HOVARTH J. (1995) A Prototype View of Expert Teaching, *Educational Researcher*, 24, 6.

STIDDER G. & HAYES S. (1998) Mentoring: Rhetoric and Reality, *Mentoring and Tutoring*, 5, 3.

STIERER B. (2000) School Teachers' Writing At University: What Kind of Knowledge is at Stake? *Teacher Development*, 4, 2.

TANN S. (1994) Supporting the Student Teacher in the Classroom, in: WILKIN M. & SANKEY D. *Collaboration and Transition in Initial Teacher Training*, Kogan Page.

TAYLOR W. (1994) Quality Assurance, in: WILKIN M. & SANKEY D. *Collaboration and Transition in Initial Teacher Training*, Kogan Page.

TEACHER TRAINING AGENCY (TTA) (1995) *Corporate Plan*, TTA.

TTA (1998) *National Standards for Qualified Teacher Status, Subject Leaders, Special Educational Needs Co-ordinators and Headteachers*, TTA.

TTA (2001) *Routes into Teaching*, TTA.

TTA & OFSTED (1998) *Framework for the Assessment of Quality and Standards in Initial Teacher Training*, TTA and OFSTED.

THOMPSON H. (1965) Management Decisions in Perspective, in: SCHLENDER W., SCOTT W. & FILLEY A. *Management in Perspective*, Houghton Mifflin.

THORNTON K. (2001) Initial Training Much Criticised, *The Times Educational Supplement*, 2 November.

THORNTON K. (2002a) Inservice Training 'Highly Variable', *The Times Educational Supplement*, 11 January.

THORNTON K. (2002b) 'Weak' Training Criticised by Inspectors, *The Times Educational Supplement*, 2 February.

THORNTON K. & BARNARD N. (2001) Inspectors Crack Down on Training, *The Times Educational Supplement*, 7 December.

TIBBLE J. (1966) *The Study of Education*, Routledge and Kegan Paul.

TOMLINSON P. (1995) *Understanding Mentoring: Reflective Strategies for School-Based Teacher Preparation*, Open University Press.

TRETHOWAN D. (1983) *Target Setting*, Industrial Society.

TURNER M. & BASH L. (1999) *Sharing Expertise in Teacher Education*, Cassell.

UNDERWOOD D. (2001) Assessing the Quality of Quality Assessment: The Inspection of Teaching and Learning in British Universities, *Journal of Education for Teaching*, 26, 1.

VAN MANEN M. (1990) Beyond Assumptions: Shifting the Limits of Action Research, *Theory into Practice*, 30.

VAUGHAN G. (1992) Profiling: A Mechanism for the Professional Development of Students, *Cambridge Journal of Education*, 22, 2.

VICKERS G. (1967) *Towards a Sociology of Management*, Chapman.

VISSER J. (2000) *Managing Behaviour in Classrooms*, David Fulton.

WALL M. & SMITH M. (1993) Mentoring and Newly Qualified Teachers , in: SMITH P. & WEST-BURNHAM J. *Mentoring in the Effective School*, Longman.

WARD D. & RITCHIE R. (1994) Profiling in Initial Teacher Education to Support Professional Development in Primary Science, *Teacher Development*, 3, 2.

WATKINS C. (1992) An Experiment in Mentor Training, in: WILKIN M. *Mentoring in Schools*, Kogan Page.

WATKINS C. & WHALLEY C. (1993) *Mentoring Resources for School-Based Development*, Longman.

WATT D. (1995) The Role of the Mentor and Link Tutor in Primary School Mentor Training, *Mentoring and Tutoring*, 3.

WELSH OFFICE (1992) I*nitial Teacher Training (Secondary Phase)*, Circular 35/92, DFE and Welsh Office.

WELSH OFFICE (1993) *The Initial Training of Primary School Teachers: New Criteria for Courses*, Circular 62/93, Welsh Office.

WELSH OFFICE (1997) *Building Excellent Schools Together*, Welsh Office.

WELSH OFFICE (1998) *Requirements for Courses of Initial Teacher Training*, Circular 13/98, Welsh Office.

WELSH OFFICE (1999) *The BEST for Teaching and Learning*, Welsh Office.

WERNER P., AVILA L., RESTA V., VANGLAR V. & CUTTIN P. (1995) Feedback Measure in Field Experience Programmes, in: SLICK G. *The Field Experience: Creating Successful Programmes for New Teachers*, Corwin Press.

WEST-BURNHAM J. (1994) Inspection, Evaluation and Quality Assurance, in: BUSH A. & WEST-BURNHAM J. *The Principles of Educational Management*, Longman.

WHITTY G. (1992) Quality Control in Teacher Education, *British Journal of Educational Studies*, 40, 1.

WHITTY G. & WILLMOTT E. (1991) Competence-Based Teacher Education: Approaches and Issues, *Cambridge Journal of Education*, 21.

WHITTY G. & WILLMOT E. (1995) Competence-Based Teacher Education Approaches and Issues, in: KERRY T. & SHELTON MAYES A. *Issues in Mentoring*, Routledge/Open University Press.

WILKIN M. (1994) Initial Training as a Case of Postmodern Development: Some Implications for Mentoring, in: McINTYRE D., HAGGER H. & WILKIN M. *Mentoring Perspectives on School-Based Teacher Education*, Kogan Page.

WILKIN M. (1990) The Development of Partnership in Initial Teacher Training, in: BOOTH M, FURLONG J. & WILKIN M. *Partnership in Initial Teacher Training*, Cassell.

WILKIN M.. (1992) On the Cusp: From Supervision to Mentoring in Initial Teacher Training, *Cambridge Journal of Education*, 22, 1,

WILKIN M. & SANKEY D. (1994) *Collaboration and Transition in Initial Teacher Training*, Kogan Page.

WILLIAMS A. & PRESTAGE S. (2000) *Still in at the Deep End? Developing Strategies for the Induction of New Teachers*, Association of Teachers and Lecturers.

WILLIAMS A. & SOARES A. (2000) The Role of Higher Education in the Initial Training of Secondary School Teachers: The Views of the Key Participants, *Journal of Education for Teaching*, 26, 3.

WINTER R. (1989) Teacher Appraisal and the Development of Professional Knowledge, in: CARR W. *Quality Teaching: Arguments for a Reflective Profession*, Falmer Press.

WRAGG E. (1993) *Class Management*, Routledge.

WRAGG E. (1999) *An Introduction to Classroom Observation*, Routledge.

WRIGHT D. (2001) *Managing Behaviour in the Classroom*, Heinemann.

WRIGHT N. & BOTTERY M. (1997) Perceptions of Professionalism by the Mentors of Student Teachers, *Journal of Education for Teaching*, 23, 3.

YEANY R. (1976) *The Effects of Micro-teaching with Videotaping on the Teaching Strategies of Pre-Service Secondary Science Teachers*, ERIC.

YOUENS B., HALL C. & BISHOP P. (2000) *Pupils as Mentors in Initial Teacher Training*, Paper delivered at the British Educational Research Association Annual Conference.

ZEICHNER K. & LISTON D. (1987) Teaching Student Teachers to Reflect, *Harvard Educational Review*, 57.

ZEICHNER K. & TABACHNICK B. (2001) Reflections and Reflective Teaching, in: SOLER J., CRAFT A. & BURGESS H. *Teacher Development: Exploring Our Own Practice*, Paul Chapman and Open University Press.

ZEY M. (1984) *The Mentor Connection*, Dow Jones-Irving.